T

Checkered Sunshine

Mrs. Frank Stranahan in 1900, the year of her marriage

Checkered Sunshine

THE STORY
OF
FORT LAUDERDALE
1793 - 1955

by

PHILIP J. WEIDLING

and

AUGUST BURGHARD

University of Florida Press - Gainesville - 1966

A University of Florida Press Book

Published under the sponsorship of the
FORT LAUDERDALE HISTORICAL SOCIETY, INC.

Copyright © 1966 by the Board of Commissioners
of State Institutions of Florida

Library of Congress Catalog Card No. 66–23068

Manufactured by Rose Printing Company, Inc.
Tallahassee, Florida

Looking north across New River at Tarpon Bend

History is supposed to be dry, except when moistened by human tears; and old-time residents of Fort Lauderdale have shed their full share. It is supposed to be dull, except when it echoes the laughter and triumph of human hearts; and Fort Lauderdalians of the past have danced their share. It is supposed to be solemn, except for the glitter of accomplishments that created for us the glories that exist today. The struggle against what seems a cruel fate is what makes life worth living and a history worth writing. We think this is a worthy one.

Many of our newer residents may actually believe that this city as it now exists was always here as it is, except for the people. That it was a dismal swampland, generally considered unfit for human habitation, only seventy-five years ago, seems inconceivable to them.

v

Preface

How did all the changes take place so rapidly? Where and why were the tears shed? We shall try to tell the history of Fort Lauderdale as it really was, without blame or glorification, and without personalities. There are no villains and no heroes, other than those of circumstance or of nature itself. It is the story of a group of people, struggling against adversities that often seemed insurmountable; sometimes faltering in their wisdom and judgment, but always pressing on until the course of events turned their community into a "dream world" in which everything prospered unbelievably.

The authors have striven to tell exactly what happened, without attempting to tell why or to analyze. Needless to say, much has been left out. Space limitations preclude the relation of many worthy accomplishments. Such highly worthwhile cultural achievements as the development of the Opera Guild, the Symphony Society, the Community Concert Association, the Museum of the Arts, and all the other arts could not be detailed. The full story of the multitude of civic benefits wrought by the luncheon clubs, churches, and other organizations would fill many volumes; but our canvas is too small to depict all of these, or even to attempt it.

It is indeed easy, at this time, in noting the phenomenal growth, the lovely beaches, the landscaped waterways, and the brilliant sunshine, to reflect that this is a place that "has every advantage." The authors hope, in this book, to bring home the fact that it was not always so. The clouds that hung over the city on many occasions in the past were heavy. Even though the sunshine was bright, it was checkered with troubles and threats to the very existence of the town that made the dark squares on the checkerboard very black indeed.

Courage, hard work, and unwavering faith in the destiny of the city were the hallmarks of the pioneer leaders. Their story is told simply, exactly, and with neither praise nor condemnation. This, then, is the story of our town—of Fort Lauderdale.

Acknowledgments

THE AUTHORS gratefully acknowledge the assistance of Mrs. Florence C. Hardy, Mrs. Betty Campbell, and Mr. N. B. Cheaney, whose untiring help in researching long-buried facts and records has made this book possible. Warm appreciation is also extended to the many pioneer residents who have given us not only patient consideration in interviews but also many old photographs and documents of various kinds.

Preface

The government agencies which cooperated fully include all city and county offices, The United States Department of Archives, The Department of Justice (Kefauver Report), and the War Department. Especial thanks are due Circuit Judge Lamar Warren for procuring for us legal records that would otherwise have been unavailable.

We are indebted to Wesley W. Stout for both material and advice; the *Fort Lauderdale News* for permitting us the free perusal of its files; Dr. Ben F. Rogers, Dean of Humanities of Florida Atlantic University; Dr. R. W. Patrick, Head of the Department of History of the University of Florida; and Dr. and Mrs. Lewis F. Haines of the University of Florida Press and the Press staff, who were most helpful in developing the book. To all of these and to the scores of persons whose help and well-wishes have given us both material and encouragement: our earnest thanks!

So much for the writing of the book; but there could have been no point in all of this if arrangements had not been made for publication and financing. For this all-important factor we owe our gratitude to George W. English, who led the Historical Society into being and guided our financing at every step; to the late J. B. Fraser, whose generosity and enthusiasm actually got it "off the ground"; and to James S. Hunt, Sr., who was never too busy to reach into his pocket when an urgent need arose. These are the men who made it possible, and we hope that the result will leave them well rewarded for their faith.

For illustrations we have relied heavily upon the collection of old photographs so assiduously collected by the late J. B. Vail, use of which was granted by Mrs. Vail. We have also benefited from the generosity of Mrs. Eugene Kelcy, who has made available the fine collection compiled by her late husband during his many years in the city. The authors have also contributed from their own collections.

PHILIP WEIDLING
AUGUST BURGHARD

(KELCY PHOTO)
Seminole Indians in dugout canoe on New River at Tarpon Bend

Contents

ix

Contents

D.A.R. marker at site of Cooley massacre, Tarpon Bend

The Early Colony

In 1793 George Washington was serving his second term as the first President of the United States; the original thirteen states had increased to fifteen with the admission of Vermont and Kentucky; Florida was under Spanish rule.

Chapter 1
1793–1857

On Florida's coast, at the place where Fort Lauderdale was to have its permanent beginnings a hundred years later, lived Charles Lewis, his wife Frankee, and their children. It was a peaceful, if lonely, land. There were no Indians; the Tequestas had been killed, enslaved, or driven away by the Spaniards, and the Seminoles were yet to be driven to hide-outs in the Everglades by the Creek and First Seminole wars.

Probably from the Bahamas, Lewis had taken residence on New River and had planted the land well before 1793. A report on an investigation of Lewis by the Spanish government states that "Mr. Lewis had lived in that house for several years, . . . had a plantation two miles to the west of this house . . . [and] had five horses. The house stands on a pine bluff south of the river—a small fowl house opposite—about 30 yards from the dwelling house up the river stands a small house which we found to be a blacksmith's shop with a forge, bellows . . . [and] a small anvil—a chest with sundry tools in it belongs to Lewis."

Whether Lewis settled in the area during the period Florida was held by the British, 1763-83, or had taken up land during the Spanish regime is a matter of conjecture. At any rate, following their investigation, the Spanish let Lewis stay. According to *Niles' National Register* of November 15, 1817, "Two or three more settlements, of little consequence are about cape Florida. All these southern settlements are chiefly from Providence, Bahamas."

By the time the United States took formal possession of Florida in 1821, Charles Lewis had died and Frankee Lewis was still on the land. Three years later she petitioned the United States government for a grant of six hundred forty acres under the Donation Act of 1824. This act provided grants to those who could prove actual habitation and cultivation of property on or prior to February 22, 1819.

Her claim was confirmed and the land became known as the "Frankee Lewis Donation." The six hundred forty acres made up what is now all of Section 11, Township 50 South, Range 42 East, bounded by 12th Street on the south, Federal Highway (U.S. 1) on the west, Broward Boulevard on the north, and by a line paralleled by Hendricks Isle, Coconut Isle, through Stranahan River to a point opposite the Lauderdale Yacht Club on the east.

Frankee Lewis' son and daughter, Jonathan and Polly, had taken up and cultivated acreage in present-day Miami, and their claims were also confirmed under the act. In 1830 Mrs. Lewis sold her grant to Richard Fitzpatrick for four hundred dollars. She then joined her son and daughter at their home on the Miami River.

Although there is no record of his ever having owned the Lewis tract, William Cooley of Maryland was occupying it by 1825. Appointed by the Secretary of War, Colonel James Gadsden visited New River in connection with a survey for a road from St. Augustine to Cape Florida. In his report to Quartermaster General Thomas S. Jesup, dated

August 20, 1825, Gadsden stated that Cooley and a Mr. Williams "reside at this place, New River, either of whom will keep a ferry" should the proposed road be constructed. Cooley was reported to be growing coontie (arrowroot), and he had a mill to make it into starch, the manufacture of which appears to have been the area's first industry. By 1835, coontie starch was bringing eight cents a pound in northern markets, and many of the settlers from Jupiter to Cape Sable were involved in its manufacture.

Subsequent records indicate that Cooley and Richard Fitzpatrick were friends, and that Cooley remained on the Lewis grant after Fitzpatrick purchased it. The United States census of 1830 listed Cooley and David Williams, with family, living on New River; and Stephen R. Mallory wrote in his reminiscences that he had spent the year 1830 on Fitzpatrick's plantation on the river, and reported that Cooley and family and "other frontier" people were settled there.

By 1836 at least two other families had joined Cooley and Williams. Mrs. Mary R. Rigby, a widow with a son and two daughters, all grown, had a place on the south bank of the river, and a Williams descendant recalled that a Howe family was also living there. These settlers appear to have had friendly relations with the Seminole Indians camped near-by.

On December 28, 1835, in defiance of the threat of removal to western lands, the Indians killed Major Francis Dade and more than one hundred of his command near the Withlacoochee River, and at Fort King they killed General Wiley Thompson, the Seminole agent in charge of emigration, and four others. Word of the massacres had not reached New River on January 6, 1836. Shortly after noon of that day, the Indians descended upon the home of William Cooley and killed Mrs. Cooley, the three Cooley children, and the children's tutor.

One of the Rigby daughters, Mary, gave this account of the events: "Sister and mother stayed at Mrs. Cooley's on the Sunday night and the morning of January 6, 1836, until after breakfast, and having no fear of the Indians, returned more than a quarter of a mile to their home on the opposite side of the river. Between twelve and one o'clock on Monday, heard the report of guns and yells of Indians and the screams of Mr. Cooley's family . . . brother ran some distance down the river where he could see the Cooley house and speedily returned and told our family to run, for Mr. Cooley's family were all murdered."

William Cooley visited the site of the massacre. The *Key West Inquirer*, January 23, 1836, had this to report:

3

When he approached the peaceful home, he found the body of Joseph Flinton of Cecil County, State of Maryland, who acted as instructor to his children. His body was mangled and he evidently had been killed with an axe.

His two eldest children were found nearby, shot through the heart, one yet holding the book in her hand she had been learning, and the book of the other lay by his side. About 100 yards distant he found the bodies of his wife and infant. She had also been shot through the heart, and the small ball is supposed to have broken the infant's arm.

The house in which he kept arrowroot and the machinery with which he manufactured it were left uninjured. The Indians carried off about 12 barrels of provisions, 30 hogs and three horses, $480 in silver, his clothing, one keg of powder, over 200 pounds of lead and $7,000 worth of dry goods.

By their tracks Mr. Cooley computes the number of Indians at 20 to 30. They also carried off a Negro man and woman and a Spanish man named Emmanuel. Our bereaved friend and neighbor caused the bodies of his loved ones to be decently interred as circumstances would permit, and returned to the Lighthouse on the 10th.

The Negro man managed to escape the Indians by boat and later joined Cooley at Cape Florida where Cooley was serving as temporary keeper of the lighthouse. The slave reported that there were about fifteen Indians in the massacre party and that "they all [were] well known in that quarter." Cooley also learned that the Indians had visited his place a second time, taking off everything they had first left behind; and that they had subsequently destroyed a neighboring plantation.

Writing for the *Charleston Courier* of South Carolina, Dr. Benjamin Strobel stated that only the tutor had been scalped, and speculated that "the recollection of former friendship" may have induced the Indians to spare Mrs. Cooley and her children this indignity.

In 1840 Cooley filed a petition to the United States government asking for the sum of twelve thousand nine hundred dollars in payment for his losses on New River. Several witnesses, including Fitzpatrick and the Rigbys, testified that Cooley had been a prosperous man; that his principal business was an arrowroot starch mill; that his house, of cypress logs, sealed and floored, was one story high, twenty by fifty-five feet, and well furnished; that he had a storehouse filled with provisions, including beef, pork, coffee, and twenty-one gallons of wine; that he had twenty acres under cultivation, growing sugar cane, arrowroot, corn, and other vegetables, as well as citrus fruits and coconuts; that his livestock included eighty heads of hogs, five sheep, three horses, and a "lot of fowl"; and that he had two Negro slaves, a man and a woman.

Cooley's request for indemnity stated that his property had been destroyed, burned, or stolen by the Indians, with the exception of the two slaves, whom he had regained. His claim was not allowed.

The Second Seminole War had begun. Pressure on the Indians in north and central Florida drove them to hide-outs deep in the Everglades from which they could make sudden forays. A succession of commands had failed to halt hostilities, and the Indians continued to elude the troops and to defy all attempts toward their forced emigration. Major General Thomas S. Jesup, given command of the Army of the South and of the Florida War in November of 1836, determined to establish posts in southeast Florida to clear out the remnants of the Indians, reported to be sixteen hundred sixty warriors.

It was to speed accomplishment of the army's purpose that Andrew Jackson, in Tennessee following his terms as President of the United States, suggested to Secretary of War Joel R. Poinsett that one of his former officers in the War of 1812 and the Creek Wars raise a group of Tennessee volunteers. That officer was Major William Lauderdale, of Sumner County, Tennessee. Jackson wrote to Poinsett: "I am assured that a brigade could be raised in Tennessee in twenty days. . . . I know of but one man that I think can raise a battalion. . . . I will send for him and if he can and will undertake it, under your letter, I will authorize him to raise four companies of one hundred each and march them to Florida and report to Genl. Jesup."

Major Lauderdale mustered in five companies of one hundred men each and formed Lauderdale's Battalion of Tennessee Mounted Infantry. Again Jackson wrote to Poinsett, expressing his great faith in his fellow Tennesseans and in Lauderdale. After an overland march, Lauderdale and his Tennesseans reached Florida in late November and reported for duty to General Jesup.

The push south began after the Indians found Jesup and a large force, including Lauderdale's, at Fort Jupiter in January of 1838. Jesup had been successful in getting many of the Indians to "come in" for emigration, but others refused and continued to escape capture by the troops.

With Lauderdale in command, the troops reached New River on the night of March 5, and on the following day they selected a site for the fort on the north bank "by the windings" of the river, one-eighth of a mile "above Cooley's patch." The detachment built there a blockhouse 30-feet square, with a double tier for firing, and later in April "com-

5

1838 War Department map showing location of New River

menced building the pickets of Fort Lauderdale—60 by 50 ft.—Pickets 7 feet long—sunk 1½ foot. . . ." On March 16, Jesup issued Army Order No. 74, from Headquarters, Fort Jupiter: "The new post lately established on New River by the Tennessee Battalion of Volunteers and Company 'D' 3d Artillery will be called *Fort Lauderdale*."

Regarding the naming of the fort, Army Surgeon Jacob Rhett Motte wrote in his journal kept during his service in the Seminole War: "We left our camp at Jupiter, and took the direction of New River, whither some of the Artillery, and the Tennesseans under Major Lauderdale had a short time previously gone, and established a fort which they called Fort Lauderdale, after the brave volunteer officer of that name."

Two major expeditions into the Everglades took place during the months the fort was active in the early stages of the war. The first was led by Lieutenant Colonel James G. Bankhead, a South Carolinian, who reported on the tedious task of the combined army and navy forces under his command. After finding the Indians encamped on Pine Island, the men waded waist-deep in the water, carrying white flags in an effort to reach a truce. The flags were fired upon, the troops deployed, and the island attacked. As in so many other fruitless efforts to fight the Indians in their native habitat, the enemy escaped, leaving its camp equipment behind as it fled. In his diary Lieutenant Robert Anderson recorded "boats, jewelry, coonti, cooked provisions—found on Island."

By April 3, 1838, the six-month enlistment of Lauderdale and his men was running out and they left New River to return to their homes in Tennessee. Marching first to Fort Jupiter, they went overland to Tampa Bay, and on April 23 General Jesup ordered them to proceed to New Orleans to be mustered out and honorably discharged from service. In an order of that day Jesup commended Lauderdale and his Tennesseans. Lauderdale was not to reach home. Headed up the Mississippi River, he died at Baton Rouge on May 10, 1838.

Lieutenant James Bennett described Lauderdale as a capable officer, temperate, and well-liked, though meticulous in the performance of duty. War Department records do not indicate the burial place. The *Nashville Whig* on May 21, 1838, said: "Lauderdale's battalion of Tennessee volunteers have reached this city, on their way to their respective homes. The troops were mustered out of service at Baton Rouge, Louisiana, where we regret to learn they lost by death, their late commander *Major Lauderdale*."

On learning of Lauderdale's death, citizens of Smith and Sumner counties, Tennessee, gathered in the Union Church at Hartsville to pass a resolution in Lauderdale's memory.

Lauderdale's birth date is unknown and there are conflicting records regarding his age. At the time he wrote his will in 1836, he owned several plantations in Tennessee and some forty slaves.

Colonel William S. Harney assumed command from Bankhead on April 2, 1838, and led the second major expedition in search of the enemy. Except for a small band of about fifteen warriors under Sam Jones (Arpeika), it was believed all had fled toward Lake Okeechobee; and on May 7 the fort was abandoned.

In his volume on the Florida War (1848), John T. Sprague observes that in a document dated July 16, 1838, Jesup reported to Poinsett of his conduct of the war in Florida. He summed up not only his feelings, but also those of the officers and men who served under him:

7

FORT LAUDERDALE

Model of Fort Lauderdale presented to Historical Society by Richard Silvano, Donald Clines, and LeRoy Scott

These results, trifling as they are compared with those of the Creek campaign and with public expectations are greatly beyond what we had any right to hope when we consider the nature and extent of the country which has been the theater of operations, and our utter ignorance of the greater part of it, even when we commenced that last campaign. If our operations have fallen short of public expectation it should be remembered that we are attempting that which no other armies of our country had ever been required to do. I and my predecessors were not only required to fight, beat and drive the enemy before us, but to go into an unexplored wilderness and catch them.

But the Indians had not left southeast Florida, and the "Punic war" Jackson had expected was not over. New forces were dispatched to re-establish Fort Lauderdale. Captain William B. Davidson, commanding "K" Company, 3d United States Artillery, reported: "Fort Lauderdale re-occupied on the 14th Febry. . . . Old Blockhouse and pickets burned by the Indians." By that fall a fort was established at the beach, and it remained active throughout the war. As reported in *Niles' National Register*, November 9, 1839, "On the 26th (September) lieut. Davis, of the navy, erected a flag-staff on the beach. . . . On the 30th

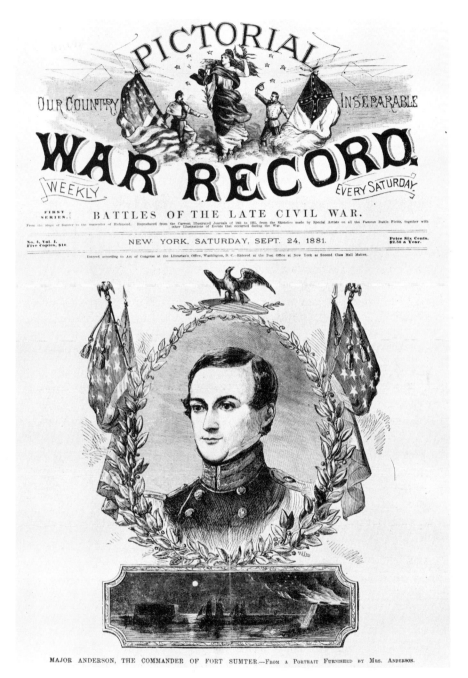

PICTORIAL

OUR COUNTRY   INSEPARABLE

WAR RECORD.

WEEKLY   EVERY SATURDAY.

FIRST
SERIES.   BATTLES OF THE LATE CIVIL WAR.

From the siege of Sumter to the surrender of Richmond. Reproduced from the Current Illustrated Journals of 1861 to 1865, from the Sketches made by Special Artists on all the Famous Battle Fields, together with other Illustrations of Events that occurred during the War.

No. 4, Vol. I,
Five Copies, $10   NEW YORK, SATURDAY, SEPT. 24, 1881.   Price Six Cents.
$2.50 a Year.

Entered according to Act of Congress at the Librarian's Office, Washington, D. C.—Entered at the Post Office at New York as Second Class Mail Matter.

MAJOR ANDERSON, THE COMMANDER OF FORT SUMTER—From a Portrait Furnished by Mrs. Anderson.

Lieutenant Robert Anderson, Major Lauderdale's executive officer. (Later, as Major Anderson, he was to surrender Fort Sumter) all hands were employed in contracting the opened piquets, so as to form a perfect rectangular enclosure with a block house at three of its angles—the three guns were placed in order to sweep the most assailable points, and all were left in a state of precaution and readiness."

In a letter to Captain Robert Anderson (the same officer who had helped establish the original fort with Major Lauderdale), Lieutenant Francis O. Wyse of the 3d United States Artillery wrote what was probably Fort Lauderdale's first tourist promotional piece:

This post pleases me much. It is situated by the seashore on a narrow strip of land separated from the mainland by New River, which at this point is not 50 yards from the sea; so by stepping a few yards out the back door, we can take a fresh water bath, or if the salt is preferred, we have but to step a few paces to the front and plunge into the surf. This is to me pleasant, for I love the roar of the ocean, and I am also delighted to be at a place where I can take the surf bath, which I am in hopes will very much improve my health.

Troops from Fort Lauderdale participated in several expeditions into the Everglades with forces from Fort Dallas, bolstered by Navy men and Marines attached to the forts. These expeditions gradually thinned the ranks of the remaining warriors.

Fort Lauderdale was again abandoned on February 15, 1842. After meeting with Chief Billy Bowlegs, the United States agreed that the some three hundred Indians left in Florida should remain within a small section in the southwest of the peninsula.

Fort Lauderdale was occupied briefly during 1856-57 at the time of further Indian uprisings, but the stated purpose of the reoccupation was the building of a road between Fort Jupiter and Fort Dallas.

By the end of this Third Seminole War four thousand Indians and Negroes had been removed to the West and fifteen hundred members of the armed forces had died in the wars. Left in the Everglades were small numbers, estimated at from ninety to one hundred and twenty, of stubborn Seminoles, ignored by the government and keeping to themselves. From these have come Florida's Seminole Indians of today.

The doughty warrior from Tennessee gave Fort Lauderdale his name in an unpromising site carved out of swampy, jungle wilderness. It was to be almost two decades after the final troops left in 1857, before any activity of significance or importance could be recorded—the building of a House of Refuge to succor shipwrecked seamen.

The beginnings of the city-to-be were far in the future.

S H Webb
Marshel Packen House
New River
1893

(GIFT, FRED NASBE)

First Permanent Settlers

With the abandonment of the fort on New River began what might be called the "dark age" of the entire area surrounding what is now Fort Lauderdale. When considered at all it was like a dank, pest-ridden swampland, unfit for habitation.

Florida became a state in 1845 and joined the Confederacy during the Civil War, but there are no known reports of activity of any kind in this area during the conflict. Instead it seems to have been mostly a hide-out, a haven for runaway slaves and deserters from both armies. A Department of the Interior map dated 1875 shows the entire area, with the exception of a narrow strip along the coast, as being "unsurveyed and unexplored." It was virtually inaccessible, except, to a limited extent, by boat. The coastal ridge was surveyed in 1870, and in all of what is now Broward County the only privately owned land was the six hundred forty acres of the old Frankee Lewis donation.

Chapter 2
1845–1900

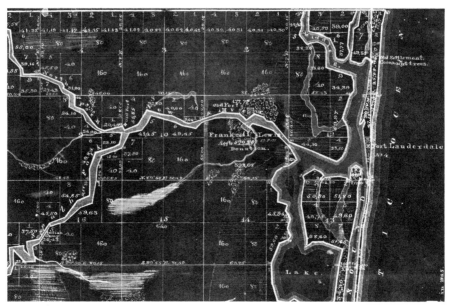

1870 map shows lake that was to become Port Everglades (GIFT, MC-LAUGHLIN ENGINEERING CO.)

Dangerous reefs extending out from shore along this coast presented then, as now, a hazard to ships seeking to sail close-in to avoid the northward current of the Gulf Stream. High onshore winds were common in some seasons of the year, adding to the peril. Shipwrecks were common; this was indeed a bad place for survivors, for there was almost no access to the mainland. Stranded sailors could obtain fresh water by digging a shallow well, but most were not aware of this. In any case, a shipwrecked mariner is not likely to have brought with him any equipment with which to dig.

In recognition of these circumstances, in 1876 the United States government built five "Houses of Refuge," spaced twenty-five miles apart along the southeast Florida coast. Fort Lauderdale was chosen as the site for "House No. Four," which was first built on a site just south of what is now Hugh Taylor Birch State Park, but which in 1891 was moved to what is now the site of Bahia Mar. It was at that time the site of the old fort, by then already rotted away. Though wooden, these houses were sturdily built with diagonal sheathing underneath clapboard, framed with Dade County pine, and well anchored. The keeper appointed to each house was charged with providing food, shelter, and other necessities to any shipwrecked travelers fortunate enough to reach shore. All were built on the same plan, with a wide veranda running en-

House of Refuge, haven for shipwrecked seamen (VAIL COLLECTION)

tirely around the building. The steeply pitched roof extended out over this porch, and afforded also a large, comfortable loft which could house approximately twenty iron cots. The first keeper of the Fort Lauderdale House of Refuge was Washington Jenkins, who remained there until 1883.

* * *

Contemporary accounts provide descriptions of the land and of the incredibly beautiful and clear river lined with tropical foliage. Fish and game were plentiful. James A. Henshall visited New River in 1879 and again in 1882, and on both occasions hunted and fished. His description of what he found was published in 1884. It follows:

New River, for six miles above its mouth, is the straightest, deepest, and finest river I have seen in Florida.

Rushing in and out with the tide . . . fishes can be seen by thousands, which snap at any thing, even a bit of rag tied to the hook and thrown to them by a strong hand-line. We took crevalle from ten to thirty pounds, always large ones here, never less than ten pounds. By anchoring a boat in mid-stream they can be speared or grained as they swim rapidly by, often pursued by sharks and porpoises. Mr. Jenkins takes them in this way up to forty pounds, and cures and smokes them.

We spent two or three days here, shooting ducks, coots, and snipe, and one day went out with Jenkins and his dogs for deer. "Wash" went

13

a mile above, on a neck of land between the North Branch and a creek, to drive, the rest of us taking stands across the timbered strip.

In 1876 New River had only one known inhabitant, John J. (Pig) Brown. He was raising hogs and living a hermit's life. That Reconstruction year, "Pig" was nominated without his knowledge to run for the state legislature against William H. Gleason, a carpetbagger who had been a lieutenant governor of Florida. Canvassers for Dade County, of which the New River area was then a part, declared Gleason elected, but the legislature voted to seat Brown. "Pig" later left New River for Tallahassee and there is no indication that he ever returned.

There are reports of the mails being carried down the beach of southeast Florida well before 1886, but the United States government did not establish regular mail service until that year. The "Barefoot Mailman" route, originally from Jupiter Inlet to Miami, passed up and down the beach. The local Houses of Refuge were regular stopovers for men who carried the mail.

Henry M. Field, in a book *Bright Skies and Dark Shadows*, published in 1890, remarks on a region so "destitute of inhabitants that the mail has to be carried by a man on foot . . . not a wagon road, nor even a mule path." Fields also recounts the death of James Edward Hamilton, one of the barefoot mailmen, who met his death at Hillsboro inlet. Evidence seems to indicate that a traveler had taken the boat Hamilton depended upon to carry him across the inlet to the other side, and left it there. Hamilton left his mailpouch on the beach and attempted to cross by wading and swimming. No trace of his body was ever found. Those who arrived shortly after Hamilton was reported missing saw that "the waters were dark with flow from the Everglades and swarming with 'gators." Charles Coman, keeper at the Fort Lauderdale House of Refuge, also noted that a stranger had spent the night at the house after claiming to have been rowed over the inlet by men he had met there. Today a marker at the Hillsboro Coast Guard Station off Pompano Beach commemorates the tragic death of Hamilton.

The days of the barefoot mailman were numbered. With the great internal conflict ended and the vast bitterness incurred forgotten, the vibrant nation was producing a new breed of restless adventurers. Here was a challenge.

In 1891 a United States post office was established at Fort Lauderdale with William C. Valentine, civil engineer and surveyor, as postmaster. Valentine homesteaded on land that subsequently was known as "Vreeland's Island," later as "Burnham's Point," and, finally, as "Harbor

"THE MAIL MUST GO."
IN MEMORY OF
JAMES E. HAMILTON,
U.S. MAIL CARRIER, WHO
LOST HIS LIFE HERE IN LINE OF DUTY
OCTOBER 11 1887.
ERECTED BY,
THE LAKE WORTH PIONEER ASSOCIATION,
1936.

(J. FLETCHER PHOTO)

Beach"—today an exclusive residential area. He might have seen the birth of the city had he not drowned in New River in 1903.

As the area's first bona fide resident since the great war and, as justice of the peace, he performed the first marriage ceremony in the budding community—that of Eva Bryan and Frank Oliver. Valentine performed the services from the small wharf as the young couple stood in a rowboat anchored close to Marshall's packing house, near the present residential subdivision of Idlewyld. W. O. Berryhill was their official witness.

Major Lauderdale and his men had used an overland route through the pine barrens to move troops from Fort Jupiter south as far as Fort Dallas, and at that time (1891) an effort was begun to build a road along this route. The capital of Dade County then was at Jupiter, and the *Tropical Sun*, a newspaper published at Lake Worth, made frequent reference to the project, particularly to proposed bridges.

Work begun on the bridge across New River was not yet completed. Late in 1892 the trail was opened without it. Almost at once the Bay Biscayne Stage Line went into operation, taking the mail contract away from the colorful beachwalkers. The round-trip stage fare was sixteen dollars; the one-way fare, ten dollars; board and overnight lodging were offered at New River for two dollars. The schedule indicated that the

15

FORT LAUDERDALE

The ferry across New River from 1893 until 1896

"Stage leaves Lantana, at the foot of Lake Worth, and Lemon City, at the head of Biscayne Bay, every Mon., Wed. & Fri., at 7 a.m., passing at New River where accommodations are provided for all passengers."

The stage route crossed New River near today's Tarpon Bend. Edward Moffatt ran a camp on the site of the Cooley massacre, and a ferry transported the stage across the river. On January 31, 1893, Frank Stranahan replaced Moffatt as operator of the ferry, acquired ten acres of land one mile west of the camp and moved the operation, and opened the Stranahan New River Camp and Trading Post. Both Moffatt's camp at Tarpon Bend and Stranahan's establishment near present-day Federal Highway on the north bank of New River were on land owned by Miami's William and Mary Brickell. The Brickells urged Stranahan to establish his camp west of Tarpon Bend. They wanted the road to cross New River at a place which would leave their choice hammock land to the east free for development. Their son William surveyed and supervised the change in the route of the road. The *Juno Tropical Sun* of March 30, 1893, observed: "The New River Camp, under Manager Frank Stranahan, meets with many encomiums for its conveniences and cuisine. 'A better bed I never slept on in Florida,' says one delighted passenger."

Other purchasers included the Florida Fiber Company, of which Duncan U. Fletcher, of Jacksonville, later United States Senator from

Stranahan's camp and trading post

Florida, was president. The firm bought thirteen hundred acres, hoping to grow sisal hemp from seed bought from Yucatan. By 1895 the venture had failed, owing to lack of labor, leaf wilt, and frost, but the company retained the land, platted it, and advertised lots for sale in what they called "Progresso."

The Florida Land and Mortgage Company made a deal in 1881 through which it bought two million acres of Florida land. This firm of Englishmen bought from Philadelphian Hamilton Disston, who had previously bought vast holdings from the state. The company was given its choice of unsold acreage, selecting, among other lands, sixteen sections in what is now Broward County. A portion of this land was along New River, west of the Lewis tract.

* * *

The first land platted for sale within the present city of Fort Lauderdale was "Palm City." Made up of Sections 16 and 21 of the present southwest section of Fort Lauderdale, Palm City was an 1887 dream of Arthur T. Williams of Fernandina. Lots were sold throughout the country, some for ten dollars each; others, larger, at two for twenty-five dollars; and whole blocks were offered at five hundred dollars. But Palm

City remained no more than a plat. No streets, bridges, or houses were ever built, and by 1900 the property reverted to the state for taxes.

Adventurers and investors were discovering Florida. By 1895 progress was universal in booming America, and this was the year that Fort Lauderdale acquired its shape as a definite settlement of planned permanence. Although most major speculations were centered around Lake Okeechobee, the lower east coast came into the circle.

Miami was a flourishing outpost. Henry M. Flagler, who had extended his East Coast Railroad to West Palm Beach, decided to continue it down the peninsula to Miami. Surveys for the extension were made in June, 1895. In a letter of Flagler to Julia Tuttle, April 22, 1895, now in the archives of the Florida East Coast Railway Company, he stated: "Included in Mr. Brickell's proposition was one hundred acres at New River . . . not that I expect to build up a town at New River, but I think it is good farming land, and I should hope to recoup myself to some extent, by the sale of property given to me in that Neighborhood."

That summer the first crew cleared the right-of-way to New River under P. N. Bryan, subcontractor in charge. With Bryan was Tom, his teen-age son, who recalls that the only inhabitants on New River when he arrived were Frank Stranahan; Captain Valentine; Captain Dennis O'Neill, keeper of the House of Refuge; E. T. King, who homesteaded because he had heard of Flagler's plans; and Mr. and Mrs. A. J. Wallace, who worked for Stranahan and cooked for the railroad crews.

William and Mary Brickell had bought approximately eight hundred ninety-five acres of the vast Florida Land and Mortgage holdings at a dollar thirty-five cents per acre in 1890. Two days before Flagler's railroad went through Fort Lauderdale they filed a plat for the town with the Dade County Circuit Court Clerk. This plat called for a town of one square mile. It was bounded on the south by today's 9th Street, on the east by Federal Highway, on the north by 4th Street, and on the west by a line varying from 8th to 9th avenues. Flagler's surveyors had hoped to run his railroad down the high coastal ridge adjacent to the old county road, but the Brickells again refused to sell land for the right-of-way. Thus the railroad was pushed westward. A look at a modern Fort Lauderdale map provides an interesting insight into the Brickell obduracy. One sees the railroad lines headed directly south through some of the city's highest and choicest lands, aimed toward but not crossing the river at Tarpon Bend. The Brickells' refusal forced Flagler wide to the west, north of the present Gateway Shopping Center.

Once the route was agreed upon, the Flagler-Brickell dispute developed into a more friendly relationship. An agreement was reached under which the Brickells gave the railroad rights-of-way. In return, the railroad platted the town at its expense and built a railroad station to make Fort Lauderdale a stop on the line. Contrary to his earlier statement to Mrs. Tuttle, Flagler also agreed to promote the new town in his advertising and publicity. He was to receive consideration from the Brickells for this expense; one-half of all lots platted were to become the property of the railroad or its real-estate subsidiaries.

Over-all charge of the platting was given to J. E. Ingraham, an official of the railroad, and the actual field work was under the supervision of A. L. Knowlton, a civil engineer. Platting and street building kept pace with the railroad construction and the undertakings were finished almost simultaneously. The railroad, renamed the Florida East Coast Railway, carried its first passengers into Fort Lauderdale on February 22, 1896. Among them was the family of E. T. King. Through service to Miami began on April 22, 1896. With this service, Fort Lauderdale became an established way station and shipping point.

Farm lands in the area had always been excellent, but the difficulties of reaching a market made planting impracticable. Now, with a railroad, the situation improved. Spurred on by railroad press agents, settlers and farmers began to arrive. In 1898 the *Miami Metropolis* conducted a survey of growers in Dade County. Found in the New River area were E. T. King, R. S. (Uncle Dick) King, O. L. Hardgrave, Andrew Jackson Wallace (the restaurant pioneer), William Marshall, W. B. Joyce, L. W. Marshall, the firm of Marshall and Marsh, P. N. Bryan, Sabato and Bravo, Captain W. C. Valentine, Thomas Powell, George Brabham, C. M. Corn, and W. S. Phillips. All produced for shipments to the North and many of these pioneer growers became lifelong residents of the future city.

According to a reprint of a letter from W. H. Marshall to J. E. Ingraham in the *Florida East Coast Homeseeker* of August, 1899, he wrote: "As you know I saved an acre of tomato plants by covering them with earth in the February frost. I want to tell you that I shipped 528 crates from that acre. I have cash returns from 481 crates to hear from."

The chief crop in the Fort Lauderdale area continued to consist of tomatoes, though at Pompano, eight miles to the north, "Uncle Pink" Pearce had planted the first bean, thereby founding a growing industry that was to become a giant in years to come. Farmers grew a variety of vegetables for local consumption; but as yet they found little market for cucumbers, squash, or peppers. Strawberries would grow but were too difficult to pack and ship. Irish potatoes would likewise "make" in the low-lying soil. Potatoes would keep in northern cellars, but there were no buyers on the dock waiting for them. Corn was consumed by insects before it could reach maturity. Tomatoes were always in demand. One of the worst features of the crop, as noted in a meeting of the Board of Trade, was the practice of dumping the culls into the river. In rotting condition they drifted through town creating a stench. This practice was to be ended.

There were a few scattered citrus groves in the area, but either the humid summers or the prevalence of insects caused the product to bear an inordinate amount of melanose and scale, and the fruit, though sweet and juicy, did not grade well on the market and commanded only moderate prices. During this period both dairy and beef cattle were considered to be impractical for the region.

Other little-known tropical fruits, including the avocado, had built no market in the northern cities as yet.

Among the needs of the new community had been a doctor. This need was filled in 1899 by a young farmer, Thomas S. Kennedy, a former druggist with some prior medical experience, who began to grow tomatoes along the north branch of New River. Though Kennedy had no license to practice, word got around that he knew medicine. An epidemic of yellow fever struck the settlement during the year of his arrival, and before it ended nearly every man, woman, and child contracted the disease. Kennedy cared for them, though he also was a sufferer, working his tomato fields during the day and doctoring at night. In his memoirs, written in 1936, Dr. Kennedy recalled that the epidemic lasted three months. He ordered his medicine from Miami and dispensed monumental doses of calomel, Epsom salts, and quinine to combat the fever.

Shortly after the epidemic ended, officials from the federal Bureau of Health came to New River on an inspection tour. At first they charged Dr. Kennedy with practicing medicine without a license. After he explained to the officials that there was no doctor in the area and that none had come from Miami or Palm Beach during the epidemic, and after they had personally examined every patient he had treated, he was told to make out a bill for his services and send it to the Bureau of Health office in New Orleans for authorization. He received payment for his services from the government, and with these funds and the receipts from his tomato crop he attended the University of the South at Sewanee, Tennessee, to complete his medical training. He returned to Fort Lauderdale to practice in 1901, becoming the village's first doctor.

Dr. Kennedy's effective work was done in the rough surroundings of the pioneer homes. He became one of the best-loved men in the community and the "miracles" he worked remain a legend. He served whites, Negroes, and Indians, and he hitched up his wagon and rode circuit. In his memoirs he recalled those early days of serving as the town's only physician after his return from medical school:

I started another crop, and went to practicing medicine full blast, without a horse, a row boat, or anything but my feet to walk on. I would get up every morning at four o'clock and walk a mile and a half to my field, work in the tomato field all day, and walk up and down both banks of the river, for a distance of two or three miles, and what houses and what people there were lived there near the river. They would take me back and forth across the river in their boats. I would "holler" when I came opposite a house and pretty soon some one would come for me. Then I got to practicing all over the county from Stuart to Miami; I have been from here to Stuart to see people, a distance of one hundred sixty miles round trip.

Dr. Kennedy had no hospital for his hardy patients on the swampy, malaria-ridden frontier, and he was often forced to perform surgery outdoors with his jackknife. It was said that, lacking other means of sterilization, he occasionally used tobacco juice. Once he amputated a man's leg with a carpenter's saw, and the man lived to tell the tale.

In the early days an itinerant dentist came regularly by schooner and filled or pulled teeth in its cabin. But until 1903, when Dr. Samuel J. Clark started his practice of over thirty years, an unplanned toothache necessitated a trip to Miami.

* * *

By the fall of 1899, when there were enough children in the little village of Fort Lauderdale to justify starting a school, E. T. King journeyed to Miami to urge the Dade County School Board to establish one. Told that a teacher would be sent when they had built a schoolhouse, King and his fellow citizens constructed a one-room frame building on South Andrews Avenue at what is now 5th Street. Dade County then sent Miss Ivy Cromartie to be the first teacher. She lived with the King family until the following year when she became the wife of Frank Stranahan.

The one-room school built by citizens in 1899 (COURTESY MRS. FRANK STRANAHAN)

By the time of his marriage in 1900, Stranahan was doing a brisk business with the Seminole Indians. They came down New River in their long narrow canoes with wives, children, dogs, pigs, pots, pans—everything they owned. As many as a hundred at a time would make the trip from across the Everglades and as far away as the Big Cypress to set up camp on Stranahan's property. The Indians brought otter skins, alligator hides and eggs, and fresh vegetables for trade; in return they got bright-colored calico, cooking utensils, ammunition, and a few staple groceries as well as money. The alligator eggs were hatched and Stranahan shipped the baby gators to Jacksonville for sale to tourists. There Stranahan obtained his supplies.

The Indians were peaceful and not dangerous, but they were against the white man's government, against Christianity, and against education. Because she was new and also a schoolteacher, Stranahan's bride was regarded with great suspicion even though her husband was liked and trusted. Gradually the compelling curiosity of the children led to shy observation, then to investigation, and finally to trust and friendship. When they found themselves welcome, the children learned to like and trust her, and the adults in time followed suit.

22

Group at great "lottery"; R. J. Boles, fifth from left

The Town Is Born

In 1900 the census taker found fifty-two people living in the village of Fort Lauderdale. This was a closely knit pioneer world and the inhabitants had begun the job of cutting a niche for man in what had been only unsurveyed and unexplored jungle and swamp. Most farms were located along the navigable streams to afford boat or barge transportation to the railroad docks on New River. Dr. Kennedy described his farming this way:

Chapter 3
1900–1911

We worked in our tomato fields getting them ready to set out tomato plants. All the work was done with a hoe. Farming down here in those days was quite a bit different from any place else in the world. One had about ninety days to make his crops and money, and that was all. I had an acre of tomatoes and it kept me busy working from daylight until dark.

23

Everything was done by man himself. Had to bring our fertilizer five and six sacks at a time in a rowboat up the river and then take it on our shoulders and carry it to the field and put it out by hand. When we gathered our crops that was all by hand also; pick the tomatoes, put them on your shoulders, take them to the packing house, grade them, make the crates, and pack them, then put them in a rowboat and row them to the dock.

Before the time of the Brickells, land transportation had been along sandy trails. Now a few narrow, white rock roads were built and wagons came into general use. "Pop boats" with two-cycle engines announced their passage up and down river by their irregular, explosive noises.

People discovered the pleasures of beach bathing and built a crude bathhouse on the beach, to which many came on Sundays. The beach could be reached only by a two-mile boat trip down the river. Women used the bathhouse to change into swimming togs and men used the woods. Sea grape trees and other varieties of tropical vegetation, including many plants with vividly colored flowers, grew profusely. On the bay side coconut trees lined the shore. Though the entrance channel at New River was unmarked, mariners sighted it easily by an exceptionally tall coconut palm known as the "Sentinel Palm," growing all by itself a few miles up the beach from the inlet. This tree was destroyed by the great hurricane of 1926.

Large yachts bringing hunters and fishermen to the rich game area came into New River Sound. The *Miami Metropolis* of October 24, 1902, carried the intelligence that "Mr. W. L. Archibald of Fort Lauderdale bought a nice, comfortable houseboat which lay near the Royal Palm docks and invited a party of friends to come down and join him on the return trip. Those of the party were Miss Bryan, Miss (St. Bernard) Montague, Mrs. Frank Stranahan, Mrs. E. T. King and Messrs. Beebe and Reed Bryan."

Fresh water for the village was obtained from shallow wells but it was hard and it discolored utensils and clothes. Soft rainwater was prized, and houses were supplied with gutters that drained rainwater into tanks mounted just below roof level. Pipes from the tanks supplied taps in kitchens and bathrooms. There was no electricity, so at night homes were lighted by candles or kerosene lamps. Many of the original homes were little more than tar-paper lean-tos; others were shacks of palmetto and cypress such as Dr. Kennedy built. He said in his memoirs:

We made ours twenty feet square, put four small-size cypress trees of fifteen feet in length in the ground at the four corners, and on the side facing the river, in the center, two more about three feet apart for our door, then one between each of the corner poles in the center.

We took some smaller cypress poles and made a V-shaped roof, and in the center of each side and opposite the door, left space for a window, nailed strips of boards about six inches apart over the whole thing, roof and all. Then we cut cabbage palmetto fronds and overlapped them closely and thickly over the whole shack. When we got through we had a rain-proof shack, a dirt floor, and we built bunks in it to sleep in. Did our cooking on a fire in front of the shack.

The villagers ate mostly game, fish, some canned goods, and home-grown vegetables. Since cattle could not thrive in the tick- and mosquito-infested country, the milk came in cans. Not the least of the hardships were the insects, particularly the hordes of mosquitoes that plagued the pioneers in the summer. Small fires topped with green pine needles and carefully placed to windward produced a smudge that brought some relief from the insects. But the smoke was a considerable nuisance in itself.

Most of the men farmed, and a few trapped for furs. The women cooked on kerosene or wood stoves and did the washing in big tubs out-of-doors. They carried stout sticks to use against snakes when walking to and from a neighbor's house. Locks on homes and stores were unknown, and so were thievery and other forms of crime.

Church life began in 1903 when a group of Methodists held meetings with an itinerant preacher in the schoolhouse. When they outgrew the one-room school building, the Methodists built the village's first church at the northwest corner of South Andrews Avenue and 6th Street. The construction took place in 1905 on a lot bought from the Florida East Coast Railway for thirty-five dollars. From these beginnings, new church buildings of other denominations paced other construction in the growing town.

As Fort Lauderdale continued to grow, a dream grew in the minds of the pioneers. Lying to the west were the vast Everglades. Underlying the shallow water and saw grass was rich black muck, or peat, known to be as productive as any other land on earth. If the Everglades could be drained—if! The dream was not a new one.

In 1907, Thomas E. Watson wrote in his *Jeffersonian Magazine:* "For several years the voters of the State of Florida have been kept in a state

Mrs. H. M. Forman (1910), with alligator she has just shot

Above: "Sentinel Palm," early landmark for seamen (COURTESY MRS. S. S. THOMAS)

Left: Thomas E. Watson, editor of *Jeffersonian Magazine*, statesman, and second owner of Las Olas lodge (GEORGIA HISTORICAL SOCIETY)

of agitation over the question of the drainage of the vast region known as the Everglades. *Can* this wild, weird expanse of marsh, saw-grass and quivering hammocks be opened up to a successful cultivation? How shall it be done? *How much* will the experiment cost and who will be the chief beneficiaries? *At whose expense* shall it be done? Each of these questions has been eagerly debated and opinions vary widely."

Drainage had been tried with some success many years before by Hamilton Disston, but the area immediately surrounding Fort Lauderdale was not included in his plans. In 1904, however, when Napoleon Bonaparte Broward was elected governor of Florida, Fort Lauderdale found a champion for the drainage dreamers.

Broward had become a national figure during the Spanish-American War as a result of his smuggling arms to Cuba in his steamer "The Three Friends." It is not known whether Broward visited Fort Lauderdale during these operations, but during the period he was closely associated with "Dynamite" Johnny O'Brien who captained "The Dauntless." This ship, similar to "The Three Friends," was active off New River at the time. A flat-bottomed stern wheeler, "The Biscayne," carried arms for Cuba loaded in New River near the railroad bridge and transferred them just outside the inlet to "The Dauntless." The *Miami Metropolis* of March 31, 1897, reports that a United States Treasury Agent, Benjamin F. Hambleton, caught "The Dauntless" and "The Biscayne" in the middle of an operation. Beaten by the crew and put ashore with a warning, Hambleton notified Key West authorities. The cruiser "Marblehead" was dispatched, and after a gun battle off Palm Beach "The Dauntless" was captured. The people of Florida and, apparently, government officials must have sympathized with the Cubans for there is no record of any punishment meted out to Broward, O'Brien, or Captain W. S. Spiers of "The Biscayne." Eventually "The Dauntless" completed her voyage to Cuba.

Meanwhile, the federal government had earmarked money for drainage projects and Broward determined to use some of these funds in Florida.

Plans for drainage were soon under way after Broward took office in 1905. He selected Reed A. Bryan to supervise the construction of two dredges and these craft were built in Fort Lauderdale near Sailboat Bend (South West 3d Avenue) in New River. The first, "The Everglades," was christened on April 2, 1906, with Governor Broward and his family present. According to the *St. Augustine Record*, the new vessel was the "largest and finest dredge south of Philadelphia." Miss Con-

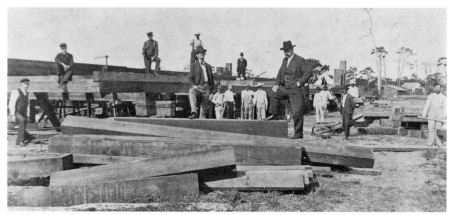

Governor N. B. Broward inspects construction of dredge "Okeechobee"
(GIFT, W. T. KENNEDY)

Captain H. T. Holloway (*left foreground*) on bridge of "Okeechobee"

stance Bryan was sponsor, and smashed a bottle of champagne across
the bow. "Okeechobee," the second dredge, was launched the following
October.

By midsummer of 1907, both dredges were cutting canals and drains.
The dredging contracts brought more people, most of them transients.

28

However, the drainage plan brought national attention, and land speculators and real-estate operators were quick to assess the moneymaking
possibilities. In order to procure additional funds for its project, the
state offered for sale large tracts of Everglades land at two dollars per
acre.

The largest sale of state lands under Broward's drainage program was
made to Richard J. Bolles. In December of 1908 he purchased five hundred thousand acres. Bolles' contract with the state contained the agreement that half of the million dollars was to be spent "solely and exclusively for drainage purposes." Meantime, Governor Broward had heard
of Bolles' farmland development in Oregon. While attending the Democratic convention in Denver, Broward got in touch with Bolles at his
home in Colorado Springs regarding the purchase and development of
Everglades land. Bolles has been described as "the most spectacular, most
ingenious, and most criticized promoter and speculator" in such lands.
Though Broward is given credit for not expecting the land speculation
which resulted from his drainage program, it nonetheless occurred, and
Bolles was one of the contributing elements. Land sales, however, added
impetus to the drainage program.

Richard Bolles divided his Everglades holdings into twelve thousand
tracts of ten to six hundred and forty acres (a section) and set up a
unique selling plan. He advertised nationally, and as an added inducement included a lot in Progresso, the subdivision of Fort Lauderdale he
had purchased from the Florida Fiber Company. Contracts for a minimum ten-acre tract, with a Progresso lot included, were offered for two
hundred and forty dollars each at the rate of ten dollars per month.
Thousands of contracts were sold. The purchasers were also to have the
opportunity, at a huge drawing to be held in Fort Lauderdale in March
of 1911, of acquiring as much as a section instead of the minimum ten
acres guaranteed by their purchases.

With speculative interest centered on the Everglades and lands to the
west of the village, the possible value of the beach as real estate was almost completely overlooked and ignored. As Lucy G. Morgan noted in
1931 in *The Story of Glen Helen*, there was one major exception: "In
the winter of 1893 Hugh Birch went to Florida. At that time the railroad
ended at Titusville at the head of Indian River. Further south and west
the state was almost a wilderness. By boat and on foot he explored most
of the wild coast to the south, looking for a desirable location for a
winter home. Wisely he chose the ocean front near Fort Lauderdale as
preferable to any other part of the miles of shore."

FORT LAUDERDALE

Hugh Taylor Birch and John MacGregor Adams bought approximately three miles of beach property from Mary MacDonald and Arthur T. Williams, the Palm City promoter. Sold in separate parcels for a total cost of thirty-five hundred dollars, it included other unspecified lands. The Birch-Adams purchase took in the present Hugh Taylor Birch State Park, the Birch Ocean Front Estates, and Las Olas-by-the-Sea. Mrs. MacDonald and Williams had acquired the property from the government in 1883 and 1884 for unspecified amounts, the deeds being signed by the then President of the United States, Chester A. Arthur.

In 1902 Adams and Birch had a falling out and divided their land. Adams took a south portion, Las Olas-by-the-Sea, which included the cottage he and Birch had first shared. Adams replaced the cottage with a hunting lodge, built by Ed King in the shape of a gun; and Birch had King build a second winter home for him. Shortly thereafter Adams died.

Palm grove at Las Olas-by-the-Sea (BURGHARD COLLECTION)

In 1905 Adams' widow sold the lodge and the surrounding land to Thomas E. Watson, who had been a candidate for President of the United States on the Populist ticket the preceding year. Watson, who edited the *Jeffersonian Magazine,* was later to be a United States senator from Georgia and father of the rural free delivery service. He and his family used the lodge as their winter home until 1914. In a tribute to Adams, former owner of the lodge, he wrote in his magazine: "This is Las Olas—he, Adams, called it so, in the indulgence of that fondness for giving pet names to those things which one especially loves. He had already grown old when he chanced upon this spot—old and rich—and the joyousness of boyhood had come back to him, and he found pleasure in nature and his fellowman."

The land south of the Watson property continued to be occupied by the House of Refuge, with Captain Dennis O'Neill in charge from 1888 to 1894. He was succeeded by J. H. Fromberger, who gave up the post in 1906 when Captain James B. Vreeland was made keeper. James B. Vreeland, Jr., eight years old when he arrived in Fort Lauderdale with his father, thus recalls the life he lived during those eight years his father served as keeper: "Every summer in May and June fleets of schooners would come into the bay west of the house and anchor. The crews would patrol the beaches at night catching giant loggerhead turtles as they came ashore to lay their eggs. The turtles' flippers would be tied or wired together, rendering them helpless, and, still alive, they would be put on the schooners for shipment to Key West."

Vreeland also recalls a number of wrecks off the coast, particularly one from the bad hurricane of 1909 when the entire crew of a wrecked Key West-bound schooner reached the beach safely. The men stayed at the House of Refuge until their passage home was arranged. On another occasion, according to Vreeland, a lumber boat was wrecked and the entire beach was strewn with railroad ties that had been destined for Cuba.

To the people of Fort Lauderdale, the beach was still a remote spot. With at least a mile of dense mangrove swamp, under water at high tide, between the town and the ocean front, little thought was given the beach other than as a place to swim or for social gatherings. There were murmurs about a road and a bridge to the beach, but only to give access to the recreation afforded there. The land had no apparent value and went begging for purchasers. Adams and Birch were able to buy Fort Lauderdale ocean front for approximately a thousand dollars per mile.

Although the work on North New River Canal was well under way, it was nowhere near completion when Broward's term as governor expired in 1908. But the canal-building activities brought growth to Fort Lauderdale. The 1910 census listed one hundred forty-three inhabitants in the village on New River. Activity continued to center around

31

Wall Street in 1909

the river or the railroad, and the town was preparing for the big Bolles land drawing and the crowd it would attract.

Although Stranahan's remained the leading place of business, handling all necessities of life, other stores began to spring up. Stranahan moved his store upriver near the railroad, erected a two-story building covered with corrugated iron, and incorporated. Besides himself, other stockholders were W. O. Berryhill, Bloxham Cromartie, and Frank R. Oliver.

P. N. Bryan contracted with Ed King to build the New River Inn just across the tracks from the railroad station. King built the inn of concrete blocks molded on the site. In 1909 the Keystone Hotel was built by Frank Oliver at Wall Street and Andrews Avenue. A packing house, built in 1902 for the Florida Vegetable and Fruit Growers Association, was converted into the Osceola Hotel on Brickell Avenue, now South West 1st Avenue, opposite Wall Street.

* * *

A milestone was reached on September 10, 1910, when the state granted a charter to the first bank, the Fort Lauderdale State Bank, with a capital of fifteen thousand dollars. Frank Oliver was named president. A prime mover in the bank's establishment was Tom M. Bryan. Before the opening of the bank, virtually all financial transactions had taken place at Stranahan's store. Although at first Stranahan opposed the bank since he was in fact already the village's banker, he soon be-

New River—Stranahan home (area's first "mansion") in background (KELCY
PHOTO)

came a stockholder along with Oliver, Bryan, H. G. Wheeler, and
others. The new bank opened in a small building near Stranahan's store.

The only theatrical entertainment had been local talent shows at private homes or in the schoolhouse. But then Frank Oliver built a theater
on Brickell Avenue, named it the Dade, and offered occasional road
shows and silent films. A perennial favorite was the Pickert family—a
father, mother, and three daughters—who performed in a wide variety
of presentations. Home talent shows continued to spice the scene and
the townsfolk turned out to applaud the efforts of the locals. Dances
were held in various homes, but most often upstairs in the Stranahan
store. Accordionist Charlie Root provided music, and later a fiddler was
added.

Another great step was taken in 1910. That year the Board of Trade
was formed, meeting in Oliver's theater, which had been renamed the
Lyric. The first session of record was held December 16, at which time
the name "Board of Trade" was adopted. Reed A. Bryan, who had been
appointed president at an earlier organizational meeting, presided at the
December meeting. As its first official act, the new body named E. T.
King and W. H. Marshall, the latter as secretary, as a committee to ar-
range for the entertainment of Governor Broward's successor, Albert
W. Gilchrist. Gilchrist was to visit the town to inspect progress on the

North New River Canal. Membership dues in the Board of Trade were set at three dollars initiation fee and fifty cents per month, with life memberships at one hundred dollars. Only one member subscribed for life at that initial meeting—J. L. Billingsley, Bolles' attorney.

The subject of incorporation of Fort Lauderdale as a town was brought up at the January 6, 1911, meeting, when it was suggested that incorporation would be the best way to provide the village with a need that greatly concerned the citizenry—sanitation. The actual motion to incorporate was made by William Heine and seconded by D. G. Tenbrook. It passed unanimously. W. H. Marshall, Stranahan, Wheeler, and Billingsley were appointed as a committee to "investigate and prepare and push completion of a plan of Charter."

The same evening it was also moved and duly carried that "all energetic ladies of the town be asked to meet with the board to form a civic organization." T. S. Wood, C. H. Slifer, and Henry R. Brown were appointed to extend this invitation, which was promptly accepted by the ladies. The board was notified at its next meeting by Mrs. Slifer that the "Women's Civic Improvement Association" stood ready. She obtained instant action on her request that the board furnish garbage cans to be "placed at convenient places about the most used locations in Fort Lauderdale," stating that "same would be of great benefit to the cleanliness of the town." The board agreed "to keep same clean." The women's organization, which soon became known as the Woman's Club of Fort Lauderdale, still exists, is most active, and has an impressive record of accomplishments.

Never had a community looked more ripe for incorporation, and never had one's future looked brighter. The vast Everglades were being drained and thousands of people, already on hand for the Bolles allotment, were ready to start cultivation. Commerce on New River would soon reach the rich Lake Okeechobee region and even the Gulf coast. With these big things in prospect, northern investors were interested and ready to provide capital for almost any venture. The road to unbelievable prosperity was open and waiting.

Downtown bridge over New River, 1910

Incorporation & the "Sanitary Mule"

Early in 1911 Fort Lauderdale was officially incorporated as a town, but there are several versions of when and how, each apparently so well documented and authenticated as to defy the historian's authority for an arbitrary decision. The Board of Trade definitely initiated the move, but the minutes of that body covering the period immediately preceding actual incorporation are either lost or undecipherable. It is known, however, that J. L. Billingsley, the one life member of the Board of Trade and the town's only attorney, was empowered to draw the papers necessary to incorporation under the general laws of the state.

The fifth issue of the new *Fort Lauderdale Sentinel*, a weekly newspaper published by Colonel George Mathews, carried a long account of a mass meeting at which it was voted to incorporate the town and at which officers were elected. The meeting was attended by forty-five of the fifty men who had been adjudged to be qualified voters; but Mathews noted that no charter or bylaws were voted into effect at the meeting, which set the town limits at one and one-half miles square.

35

FORT LAUDERDALE

William H. Marshall, Fort Lauderdale's first mayor (1911)

J. L. Billingsley, the attorney responsible, held that the meeting was legal and effective. The great confusion to the historian, however, stems from the fact that the date of Mathews' paper is April 7, 1911, whereas the minute book of the town council shows that the first meeting of that body was held on March 30 of the same year. The officers elected at the meeting were the same as those shown already seated and acting on the earlier date. Mathews notes in his story that Dr. T. S. Kennedy, who attended the meeting only briefly, objected to "all these secret meetings."

Whatever its official date, the minutes of meeting number one show W. H. Marshall as mayor, Ed T. King, president of the council, and Tom M. Bryan, W. C. Kyle, W. H. Covington, and W. O. Berryhill as councilmen. On June 2, 1911, the state legislature approved the charter of the Town of Fort Lauderdale. The limits of the town included that land platted and offered for sale by the Brickells and the Florida East Coast Railway in 1896, as well as land on all four sides sufficient to make the town one and one-half miles square. The charter further stated that

Tom M. Bryan, pioneer and far-sighted
developer

the officers of the town already elected should stay in office until a general election to be held in 1912.

The town council, meeting on April 3, 1911, agreed to hire Kossie A. Goodbread as town marshal. His salary was set at forty dollars per month with an additional fee of one dollar for each arrest and a maximum allowance of ten dollars per month for office expense. Mindful of the civic need which had prompted the move to incorporate, the council's first positive action was a motion, carried, either to buy or rent a mule or horse and wagon to perform the much needed sanitary duties. This work consisted of emptying privies and disposing of refuse. For the record, at a subsequent meeting the mule was duly purchased, complete with wagon, from V. W. Craig for two hundred and thirty dollars on a thirty-day trial. The duty of operating the department was assigned to the town marshal. In future entries in the city minute books the draft animal was referred to as "the sanitary mule."

The council was forced to take things easy at the beginning for lack of funds. The jobs of appraising property for tax purposes and establishing a budget and tax millage were not even started, but money could be borrowed to a limited extent and some revenue was realized from various fees and permits. In June, Mayor Marshall made the following appointments: H. G. Wheeler, treasurer; Kossie A. Goodbread, tax collector; and F. A. Bryan, tax assessor.

5/17/12.
Guy E. Phipps.

Gov. Gilchrist presenting to Mayor Marshall, shovel which opened gateway. connecting Gulf to Atlantic, Ft. Lauderdale, Fla. 5/16/12.

The Big Boom & the Great Fire

Chapter 5
1911–1913

The little village buzzed with activity. The big Bolles land allotments had taken place only two weeks before the town's incorporation and many of those who had attended were still in Fort Lauderdale, some to remain permanently. The "Tent City" in Progresso was still occupied and all three hotels were full. The town had grown from an estimated one hundred and fifty into a probable five thousand for the big event; this number by no means represented all the twelve thousand contract holders who had paid two hundred and forty dollars each for their minimum ten acres and a lot in Progresso.

In the July, 1911, issue of his *Jeffersonian Magazine*, Thomas E. Watson gave an interesting description of the situation:

Tent city for land purchasers in the Bolles "lottery" (GIFT, MRS. FRED HIXSON)

By the way, Fort Lauderdale is on a big boom. The little town is situated on New River, just two and one-half miles from the Atlantic Ocean; this river is made up from the waters of the Everglades. It runs right through the Everglades, and is a navigable river, large New York steamers could come right up to Fort Lauderdale if the channel through the inlet was deep enough.

Fort Lauderdale is on a boom at present, for the reason that a few capitalists bought all the land around Fort Lauderdale, besides millions of acres of the Everglades, with all the river frontage. This property was

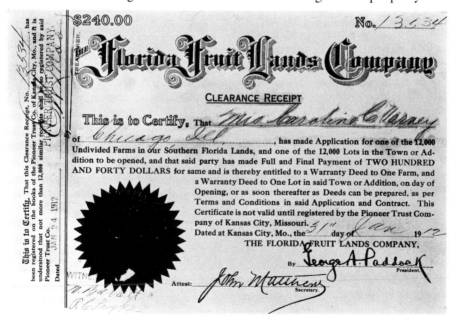

39

thoroughly advertised throughout the East and West for several months by parties having the management of the scheme.

Sale began March 15 and ran until about April 1. I was there when these bargain seekers (or, I might say suckers) began coming to Fort Lauderdale. One day, about March 19, I saw three long, heavily loaded trains come to the place; at one time they simply filled the woods, as there was not house room for one-fourth of the crowd in town. More than a thousand tents were put up through the piney woods between March 15 and 20. Fort Lauderdale two years ago had nearly 150 inhabitants, counting men, women and children and dogs.

The town had 5,000 inhabitants on March 20; I was there on the ground and counted. About 4,800 of these people came to this wonderful place to buy a small portion of the Everglades.

The Everglades is the best country in the whole world to raise alligators, rattlesnakes, mosquitoes and malaria. Alligator hides sell for $3.00 to $6.00 apiece; rattlesnake skins bring from $3.00 to $5.00, according to size.

The Seminole Indians have had a monopoly of the Everglades for years and it is my opinion that they will continue. I am quite sure they will during the summer months, as they are the only things that can possibly live there all the year round, except the alligators and rattlesnakes and mosquitoes.

I promised to tell you where our destination was, and I will say now that it was not Fort Lauderdale or the Everglades. We left the train and did stop longer in Fort Lauderdale than it was our wish.

It took us a week to get there and I was requested to run by the post office and get the accumulated mail that traveled much faster than we did. Knowing all the party was in a hurry, also hungry, as we could get no breakfast and now it was late dinner time, I was expected to get the mail and get down to the river dock by the time our motor boat was cranked up and ready to go.

When I arrived at the post office I soon learned that I had no chance to rush any further—a crowd was lined up and it looked very much like a desperate crowd making a run on a weak bank. All sorts and colors of people stood in this line; I stopped and looked on for a while; one end of the line-up reached into the post office and the other end going down the sidewalk about fifty yards.

I finally walked up and asked one man if they were making a run on a bank or what the trouble was? He replied that they were making a run on the post office and this line-up was a continuous thing every day, all day long, I asked him how long it usually took for a fellow to get his mail; he said it depended entirely upon the line-up—said I could take my position and get to the window in one and a half hours.

I did not take my position or get the mail, as I thought breakfast and dinner would be more pleasing to us all. I passed the little bank on the way down to the boat and saw the line-up there—almost equal to the post office; all this was on account of the sudden increase of population from 150 people to 5,000.

Land increased in value during the past two years from two and a half dollars per acre, to two and a half thousand dollars per acre. This latter, of course, being right in town.

Excitement ran high. The people were confident that the state's efforts to drain the Everglades would be successful, particularly now that it had received moneys for the sale of land to Bolles and other operators. Prosperity, hitherto undreamed, lay just around the corner; and as a result of the fulfillment of the obligations, Bolles and his associates were held in the highest local esteem. In many northern cities, however, the reverse was true. Their operations had, in fact, created a nation-wide scandal, stemming particularly from the localities where their sales had been heaviest. Such an uproar was raised that the federal government was moved to investigate and, ultimately, to bring charges. Bolles himself was indicted on a hundred and twelve counts of using the mails to advertise a lottery and of false advertising. J. L. Billingsley was also indicted. Other land companies were charged and some convictions were gained. Bolles remained steadfastly in Florida where the courts held that he had acted in good faith in believing that the lands he sold would be drained as the state had promised. He died in 1917, on a Florida East Coast train he had boarded at Palm Beach, without ever having been brought to trial.

Local people had always liked the small, dapper Bolles, who was gentle and courteous at all times. Many felt he was being persecuted unduly and that he had faithfully fulfilled his obligations in giving, as he did, good title to all the lands he sold.

In 1911 the completion of the canal system as planned under Governor Broward was still a year away, and drainage of the Glades was not expected until then. Many of those who came to the drawings decided to wait, and houses began to take the place of tents on Progresso lots. Most of the residential lots were only twenty-five feet wide. Many of these oddly built houses, with one room right behind the other, remain in the area today.

A race had got under way to establish the town's first newspaper. First to reach the streets was the *Fort Lauderdale Herald*, published by Professor William Heine, which actually printed the first issue in 1910;

but this newspaper was printed in DeLand and shipped to Fort Lauderdale. First to be locally printed was the *Fort Lauderdale Sentinel*, in March, 1911, published by Colonel George Mathews. Both were weeklies.

Frank Oliver installed an electric plant for the sole use of his Lyric Theater on Brickell Avenue, according to the *Florida Times-Union* of December 8, 1911. The only refrigeration in the new town was from ice brought irregularly from Miami by horse and wagon and stored in a shed near the Andrews Avenue bridge. In September of 1912 Tom M. Bryan, who had promoted the formation of the town's first bank, was given a permit by the council for the Fort Lauderdale Light & Ice Company, which proposed to put in an ice plant and an electrical power system. Of the two proposed services, the ice for carloads of vegetables being shipped to the northern markets was expected to be the financial mainstay. Power for running this machinery could conveniently be used also for generating electricity for public consumption. Most of the houses in the community were equipped with iceboxes, but hardly any were wired for electricity. A few of the downtown business places adopted the "newfangled" lighting almost at once.

Much of the town's new growth was in anticipation of the great day to come when the canals would be opened and the Everglades would start to drain—at long last.

Among the most ambitious projects was the Atlantic, Okeechobee and Gulf Railroad, a line projected to be built from Fort Lauderdale across the Everglades to Lake Okeechobee and on to the Gulf of Mexico. The town council granted representatives of the road the needed rights-of-way through the city. But the line was never built. Surveys proved the potential cost of laying such a line so staggering that the project was abandoned. It was one of the few early plans that never came to fruition, even in the lusher years to follow.

The council was also besieged by various companies seeking the rights for installing telephones. Dr. Kennedy was one of the petitioners, but he lost out in favor of Frederick A. Barrett, who was later joined by E. Luneman. The telephone system was eventually taken over by Tom Bryan.

Late in 1911 the town got its most pretentious new business building. This was the H. G. Wheeler structure on the corner of North West River Drive and Brickell Avenue, facing the river. Wheeler opened a general merchandise store which offered competition to the Stranahan store located nearby. Another store was L. M. Bryan's on New River near the railroad, operated largely by his sister Susie, who became postmistress when the post office was moved into the building. The Everglades Grocery Company, owned by W. H. Andrews, W. C. Kyle, and John T. Kelly, offered further competition in its line, as did the Dade Lumber Company, of which R. P. Paddison, Jr., was manager. In 1910 Berryhill and Cromartie had opened a grocery store on the corner of North West River Drive and Andrews Avenue—the first business on Andrews Avenue. They were followed shortly by the Lake Worth Mercantile Company, managed for a time by W. E. Compton. D. G. Tenbrook and I. K. Gordon operated a real-estate office on Brickell Avenue.

The *Florida Times-Union* of February 10, 1912, observed that "representatives of the Witham System, operating a chain of banks, will meet Thursday with local capitalists to organize a second bank. Mayor Marshall, T. O. Webster, of Webster and Kelly, W. O. Berryhill and Dr. C. G. Holland are among the interested." In the same year, the Fort Lauderdale State Bank had its first competition. The Witham chain, of Miami, opened the Dade County Bank. W. C. Kyle was president of the new bank. It would, in 1915, build its own building on Brickell Avenue (still standing) and become the Broward State Bank. Both grew rapidly, although the original retained the major part of the business.

The "great day" for which the town waited fell on April 26, 1912, when Governor Albert W. Gilchrist came to preside at ceremonies marking the opening of the North New River Canal to Lake Okeechobee. With every man, woman, and child in Fort Lauderdale in attendance on the river front at the foot of Brickell Avenue, he presented a gold shovel to Mayor Marshall. Realization of the vast, golden future, so freely predicted in speeches on that day, seemed imminent.

The bright dreams of the people were somewhat dimmed when, on the night of June 1, the entire business section burned to the ground. The *Florida Times-Union* noted as "wiped out" the Wheeler and Stranahan stores, Everglades Grocery, Fort Lauderdale Pharmacy (in the Wheeler building), *Fort Lauderdale Herald*, Pioneer Realty, Snyder & Hortt Real Estate, Gutchen's Bakery, Williams Bros., Jeffries' Meat Market, D. E. Johnson's Jewelry, Wheeler Garage, and the post office, the fixtures of which were owned by Susie Bryan. The huge frame Osceola Inn miraculously escaped, saved by dynamiting intervening buildings. It was to burn in solitary grandeur a year later.

On the day before the fire, real-estate partners W. B. Snyder and M. A. Hortt had proudly posed for pictures on the steps outside their

Fort Lauderdale power plant in 1913 (GIFT, MRS. W. J. REED)

Above: Stranahan store still smoking (*left*) and gutted Wheeler building (*right*) after 1912 fire (MRS. WALTER HOLLOWAY PHOTO)

Below: Zouaves in front of Osceola Hotel, 1912 (GIFT, SUZANNE T. COOPER)

new building. The next day only the steps were left, but Snyder and Hortt, with grim humor, posed again.

The 1912 fire kindled more than just a giant conflagration. It confirmed in the minds of the citizenry the determination to be prepared for such emergencies and to provide proper facilities needed if the town was to continue to grow. During the big blaze, fire departments from Miami and Palm Beach responded to the call for help, but they arrived too late. The bank had been saved by the only fire-fighting method the town had; a bucket brigade which dipped and passed water from the river. At the next meeting of the town council a large majority of the townsfolk was present to demand a fire department and, along with it, city water and sewers for the great and growing town.

The town council voted unanimously to establish a volunteer fire department. Authorized, forthwith, was the purchase of a gasoline-operated pumper and fifteen hundred feet of hose. Councilmen Bryan, Covington, and Kyle were appointed as a committee to organize volunteers. Samuel L. Drake called a meeting for June 10, 1912, to organize the volunteer fire department. George G. Mathews was made chairman, and Charles E. Newland was elected chief. Fort Lauderdale was beginning to function as a city.

The first tax collection had netted the town seven thousand dollars. This amount was far from sufficient for the improvements planned, and a forty thousand dollar bond issue was forthwith approved. It provided not only for fire-fighting equipment and a water plant, but also for a fire department and some streets. The "sanitary mule" was doomed. Plans for replacing the burned-down buildings were well along before the embers had cooled.

Although the council was unanimous in its vote for improvements, other matters caused contention. One of these was the purchase of a site for the new water plant and a permanent city hall. Council meetings were being held in a room rented at seven and a half dollars per month in the Tenbrook-Gordon Real Estate building. A committee headed by Councilman Bryan recommended that a site at the corner of Las Olas Boulevard and Andrews Avenue be purchased, and the group finally voted three-to-two to go ahead. Mayor Marshall, however, did not approve. He felt that the purchase of "such an expensive" lot (twelve hundred dollars) without acquiring with it a site for a water-front park on the river was unjustified. He contested the decision and the town attorney finally ruled that Marshall should have a voice in such an expenditure. A compromise was finally worked out under which the city

Vegetable docks at Fort Lauderdale, 1915

bought three lots at the corner of South East 2d Street and Andrews Avenue (the present site of Burdine's Department Store) for six hundred and fifty dollars. The site served for many years as the location of the water plant, the fire and police departments, the city hall, the Chamber of Commerce, and the library when it expanded beyond the facilities of the Woman's Club building.

Marshall's demand for water-front property was significant. He envisioned Fort Lauderdale as a port and felt that the city should own and control the water front. Completion of the waterway to Lake Okeechobee had brought a booming trade with the fertile area surrounding the lake. Stern-wheeled boats, including the "Lily," the "Napoleon Broward," and the "Suwanee," were put into service taking passengers and supplies to the lake region and returning with cargoes of winter vegetables ready to be loaded on trains and sent to northern markets.

The "Suwanee" was exclusively a passenger boat and sailed each week on Thursday, reaching the east coast on Saturday. It left on a return voyage on Monday, and reached Fort Myers on Wednesday. Fare one-way, including meals and berth, was fifteen dollars; round-trips were twenty-five dollars. Mrs. Frank Oliver, writing a column, "Pioneer Days," for the *Fort Lauderdale Free Press* on January 22, 1937, recalled a trip taken aboard the "Suwanee": " . . . such a grand trip it was! We had our meals on the boat. We left Fort Lauderdale late in the

The "Suwanee," stern-wheel passenger and freight steamer (PHIPPS PHOTO)

afternoon and arrived at the lake next morning. We began our stops at the different farms. At that time sugar cane was three times as high as a person, and the vegetables and flowers were gorgeous. We came back down the canal in daylight and saw thousands of beautiful birds. It was a treat for tourists, and many made the trip across to Fort Myers and other points."

Another development resulting from the canal opening was the establishment of fishhouses along New River. The waterway made it possible to send boats out of Fort Lauderdale to the huge lake, where an abundance of fish, principally catfish, in the shallow waters made catches an easy matter for seiners. They brought the fish to tin fishhouses, which lined both banks of the river, to be packed in barrels and iced for shipment to various points in the North. These fishhouses were both unsightly and unsanitary, many of them having open toilets which emptied raw sewage directly into the waters of the river.

The Fort Lauderdale Fish Company shipped from eighty to a hundred and fifty barrels of fish a week. Others did as well. The river, with the constant digging at its headwaters, had changed from a crystalline stream to an opaque brown. The presence of these fishhouses violated the sensibilities of the members of the Woman's Club, who objected on both sanitary and aesthetic grounds. At a later date their objections were to be heeded.

Florida East Coast crossing at New River

Dreams of Grandeur

By the dawn of 1913 Fort Lauderdale had recovered from the effects of both the great fire and the Bolles land boom. The latter had created a sizable increase in population and many who had come for the so-called "lottery" remained to become permanent residents, though most engaged in work other than that originally planned. A big majority of people still firmly believed that the Everglades would be drained and would become an area of vast productivity, second, perhaps, to none in the world.

Business leaders now envisaged two major steps forward as being of prime importance. They wanted to pry loose from Dade County and form a county of their own, and they wanted a deepwater harbor. Fort Lauderdale had many able, proved businessmen, and they all felt quite capable of administering their own affairs. They simply did not like, or trust, Dade County. They thought that they, as northernmost residents, were being neglected. The few lawyers in the town complained of the long and arduous trip to Miami to file any kind of legal document.

Dreams of Grandeur: 1913-1914

The deepwater harbor, long a cherished dream of Mayor Marshall, was seen as necessary for the future transport of the vast produce that would flow from the Everglades. The railroad could take a limited amount to the North, but rates were high and Fort Lauderdale was looking at markets all over the world. There were more than two million acres of rich land lying just west of the town, quietly draining. The dream was so great that it almost engulfed the civic leaders; they intended to be ready for reality when it came.

A committee met at the office of Mayor Marshall to discuss county division. Mr. L. W. Brobeck was made chairman and Mr. Heine secretary, according to the *Sentinel*. Present were Tom Bryan, Frank Oliver, W. H. Marshall, Mr. Brobeck, Wm. Heine, E. C. Parker, G. G. Mathews, Frank Bryan, and Ed King. The intention was to apply to the next legislature for the new county, to be called, perhaps, Everglade County. Wealth and fast population increases anticipated would excite the wonder of the world, the enthusiasts predicted. Colonel Mathews, editor of the *Sentinel*, stated in an editorial that the new county should be named either Broward or Everglade.

On May 9 Colonel Mathews, W. O. Berryhill, M. A. Marshall, and Reed A. Bryan went to Tallahassee to promote passage of the act. But back home opposition was developing. The Miami Board of Trade went on record strongly opposing the move and sent a telegram, signed by Edward C. Romfh, acting president, to its legislative delegation. The message declared that the people outside Fort Lauderdale opposed the division of Dade County and reminded legislators that its body contained four hundred and eighty members—all, presumably, voters. Despite this opposition the bill passed in the house of representatives on May 16. As proposed, the new county would include Fort Lauderdale, Dania, Zona, and Hallandale—comprising, in all, about eight hundred square miles of land.

It had first been proposed that Pompano be included, but Pompano, in neighboring Palm Beach County, objected, preferring to remain as it was. The Dade-Palm Beach county line was approximately that of the present Oakland Park Ocean Boulevard. Opposition to the new county also developed in towns south of Fort Lauderdale. Dania sent A. C. Marshall, of that town, to Tallahassee to work in opposition. Despite the fact that nearly one hundred enthusiastic people from Fort Lauderdale attended a mass meeting in Dania later in May, results were discouraging. Mayor H. P. Tubbs of Dania presided. Speeches were made by Col. G. G. Mathews, A. C. Marshall, Q. Bryan, Samuel Drake, and Guy Sherman.

All listened attentively and enjoyed the Fort Lauderdale band, but it was very plain that Dania was not in favor of Broward County.

Fort Lauderdale leaders, in desperation, now offered new inducements. Their city, they maintained, should be the county seat, and they proposed, at Fort Lauderdale's expense, to furnish the new county with a building to house the new county offices until a courthouse could be built. A further blandishment was an agreement that all county officials, for their first two terms, would be chosen from the towns of the southern portion—Dania, Hallandale, and Zona. A new petition for the county, containing these provisions, gained a hundred and nineteen signers.

On June 4 the new county bill passed in the state senate, but there was a major hitch. It provided for a county divided into three districts, each containing a major town, that is, Fort Lauderdale, Dania, and Hallandale. The bill also contained a local-option provision providing that the vote in each of these districts must favor the new county or the law would be void.

Held in July, the election results showed Fort Lauderdale in favor, two hundred eight "for" and three "against." Dania voted only sixteen "in favor" and fifty-seven "opposed," and Hallandale ten in favor and twenty-nine against. The measure was defeated under the terms of the bill, although had it been left to a simple majority the county would have been approved by two hundred thirty-four to eighty-nine. Fort Lauderdale leaders were disheartened but by no means permanently defeated. The legislature would meet again two years later, and their determination was as strong as ever.

With this issue decided, at least temporarily, the citizenry turned to the other great project, the deepwater harbor. The agitation continued to grow. Deep Water Harbor Company was incorporated with capital stock to be five hundred thousand dollars. Fifteen were named as incorporators: Fred Barrett, Frank Stranahan, Frank Oliver, H. G. Wheeler, Guy Sherman, W. H. Marshall, E. T. King, C. P. Weidling, W. C. Kyle, Miamian Dr. J. L. Holmberg, W. M. Heine, C. M. Davis, Tom M. Bryan, Dr. C. G. Holland, and W. O. Berryhill. Marshall was elected president; Wheeler, vice president; Heine, secretary; and Stranahan, treasurer.

Among the early activities of this organization was a lively correspondence with the United States Corps of Engineers. It was argued that when the Everglades were finally drained and their millions of acres of fertile land were in full productivity, the one single-track railroad could not provide adequate transportation and, in any case, would serve only markets in the northern United States. Fort Lauderdale was shooting for markets throughout the world, and these could be reached only through shipping. Hence the need for a deepwater harbor.

There were whispers that the Everglades drainage was not proceeding very well; but engineers had assured the people that all would be well, and a favorite "shusher upper" for blowhards at that time was echoed: "Rave on, Everglades, we'll get you drained some day."

Plans for the new harbor were essentially complete as to the location and the facilities to be included. The inlet to the ocean, at this time, was several miles south of the House of Refuge, at about the present location of the Port Everglades entrance. It was planned, however, to redig the inlet back at its former location beside the House of Refuge, and to use the wide bay between the House of Refuge (now Bahia Mar) and the west bank (now Idlewyld) as a turning basin in much the same manner that Lake Mabel was finally used in the construction of Port Everglades. Digging of the turning basin was thus to provide fill for the mangrove swamp that comprised much of the west (Idlewyld) side of the harbor. Ships entering could thus proceed straight up New River, then much deeper than at present.

W. H. Marshall owned the property on the landward side of the proposed port and farmed there. He entered into a tentative agreement with the harbor company for use of the land. A firm agreement was never to be finalized. The Board of Trade offered to arbitrate a dispute between Marshall and the company, but there is no indication that this offer was accepted.

This project was so overwhelmingly important to the public that it was "immortalized" in song. C. P. Weidling had written a home talent production called the "Music Master" which was duly produced as a benefit for the Eastern Star on the stage of the town's theater with almost every person in the county in attendance; home talent shows remained tremendously popular despite the advent of the newfangled movies. Colonel Mathews proved his versatility by writing a review of the show. "The entertainment Wednesday night by local talent has never been surpassed in our town," he said. Carl Weidling, as singing master, was splendid. Mrs. Herbert Lewis and Mr. Weidling were encored several times. They sang a parody on the then popular "Reuben, Reuben" about the deepwater harbor project. Mr. and Mrs. Frank Kozla and Mrs. H. G. Wheeler, who had a well-trained voice, were also enjoyed.

The Fort Lauderdale Harbor Company apparently died on the vine.

The *Sentinel* makes no further mention of either the company or the project. The only certainty is that the harbor was never built.

The town was still smarting from the failure to establish Broward County, but, in October of 1913 a new election was coming up. This was a referendum to determine whether Dade County would be wet or dry under local-option prohibition laws. It was obvious that Miami, with its tourist business, wanted to go wet. Local leaders, therefore, began a campaign to get the county to vote dry. Colonel George Mathews, himself a man who liked his dram now and then, editorialized in favor of the drys. Tom M. Bryan, who frankly told his listeners that if he wanted a drink he would have it, spoke at meetings in favor of the drys. The WCTU joined in, as did most of the advocates of women's suffrage. The election came to a storybook finish. The final tally of votes was 978 dry and 868 wet. The Fort Lauderdale precinct vote was 138 dry and 31 wet. Dania also went dry. The wets would have won by three votes had it not been for Fort Lauderdale's opposition. This vote was the factor that carried the election.

It was generally believed that this convinced many in Miami and vicinity that it was "time to get rid of those north county 'blue noses.'" Among these were many of the members of the Miami Board of Trade who had so vigorously opposed division of the county the year before.

In September, 1913, local voters approved a bond issue to pay off twelve thousand dollars of the town's debts and build a new city hall, but they rejected an additional four thousand dollars for extension of the water and sewer systems. It was during this year, also, that D. C. Alexander, who with his real-estate partner H. E. Fine had taken over the operation of the Fort Lauderdale Development Company, purchased the Las Olas-by-the-Sea property, consisting of thirty-three acres, from Tom Watson. They subdivided it into one hundred lots and advertised "some lots as low as $500." Sales boomed and in less than a month forty lots were sold. The property, however, could be reached only by boat, and houses were slow to be built. The Alexander interests turned the old Adams-Watson hunting lodge into an inn.

It was in 1913, also, that Fort Lauderdale got its second movie theater. E. C. Marine leased the lot on North West River Drive between Berryhill and Cromartie's grocery store and Lee A. Spear's Ice Cream Parlor for an "airdrome" theater. It was truly an "airdrome"; it had no roof. There was a front wall, a small projection room, and the ticket booth; at the other end was a screen. The area was "rocked" and benches were placed for spectators. This would seem to offer little protection against

Las Olas Inn

the clouds of mosquitoes, but smudges were set in the center walkway, and in the still walled-off air they proved effective as mosquito control, although disagreeable in other ways. Marine later incorporated with A. C. Heldt, and still later they bought the old Dade Theater and moved it to Wall Street to make way for Tom Bryan's new two-story brick building on the northeast corner of Brickell Avenue and Wall Street. They remodeled the old Dade Theater and renamed it the Rex. Marine later sold out to Heldt.

The last scars of the fire that had destroyed the downtown section were erased in 1913. Oliver Brothers, who had taken over the old Stranahan store, had opened their new building on Brickell Avenue. On February 17, 1913, the new Gilbert Hotel, also on Brickell Avenue, was opened with great fanfare. The hotel adjoined the new Wheeler store building and covered half of the east side of the block, ending at Wall Street. In March of the same year the new Wheeler store was officially opened. Wheeler's old store, standing next to his new one and still a fire-blackened shell, was shortly thereafter converted into a garage.

On July 17, with the first of the produce buyers just beginning to arrive, the Osceola Hotel—the only major structure to escape the 1912 fire—burned to the ground during the night. The newly formed fire department was commended for its efforts to save the structure and for

New fire fighting equipment (BURGHARD COLLECTION)

The Osceola Hotel destroyed by fire in 1913

preventing the spread of the fire. The three-story frame building, however, provided a tinderbox that was consumed almost in minutes. The
hotel on the west side of old Brickell Avenue, and directly opposite
Wall Street, was the last vestige of the old downtown section that existed in the original era of growth. When the ashes had thoroughly
cooled, Ed Caruth built a hamburger stand on the site, which was one
day to become the first Hector's Supply Company home office, and
then the final home of Brown's Good Food restaurant.

54

The hamburger was then comparatively new and Caruth, a tall man with long, fierce-looking mustachios, was an impresario who presided over the premises with a swordlike knife. He used this implement to turn hamburgers, slice buns, and, perhaps, to smite an occasional unwary cockroach. If his customers objected to this lack of sanitation, the shiny knife was enough to muffle any violent protest.

One of the most popular customers was Duke, a long-haired setter belonging to "Papa" Joe Atchinson, catcher on the baseball team. Joe would wrap two nickels in a piece of brown paper and put them in Duke's mouth. The dog would then trot over to Caruth's, drop them on the counter, and the restaurateur would cook and wrap two hamburgers. Duke would return with the paper wrapping unbroken in his mouth, though an unwritten law provided that one of the two was for the faithful messenger. In later years, when his ball-playing days were ended, Atchinson became a noted professional animal trainer. Duke performed many other notable tricks and, in his own way, was a tourist attraction for the occasional visitor who came through the town en route to Lake Okeechobee and adventure.

Another attraction was provided by the Seminole Indians, who comprised a large portion of the population. They set up a sawhorse at the end of the Oliver buildings which faced the river. From near the river front they would shoot arrows at a dime placed in a groove on top of the sawhorse, with the one knocking it out getting the dime. The wily Indians had learned that a dime would buy a vial of lemon extract; this was 80 per cent alcohol and palatable to their aboriginal taste.

Another crueler form of entertainment was occasionally held at the firehouse on a Saturday night. The firemen had built a cage about six-feet square. Trappers often brought in wildcats, whose hides were worth only a pittance. The cats would sometimes be tossed into the cage with an English bulldog, the firehouse pet, and the resulting carnage was as spectacular as it was bloody. The practice was condemned with horror by the Woman's Club.

The *Fort Lauderdale Sentinel* of May 23, 1913, contained the following news: "The new 75,000 gallon tank for the city water system has been completed (northwest corner of intersection of S. Andrews Avenue and 2d Street) and accepted by the city council."

The Board of Trade, which had been formed in 1910 and had been responsible for incorporation of the town, had been almost abandoned and forgotten. By 1913 demands were being made for reorganization and President Tom M. Bryan called a meeting to be held on October 14.

The body was completely reorganized and an election of officers was held. Robert J. Reed was elected as president; E. S. Randall, vice president; Frank Stranahan, treasurer; and Samuel L. Drake, secretary. Directors included Colonel George Mathews, Will H. Marshall, Tom Bryan, C. C. Ausherman, and J. N. Oliver. The board was active thereafter. It was eventually to father the present Chamber of Commerce.

What had started as only an ugly rumor was now growing in magnitude to a mighty grumble and finally to an almost perpetual newspaper outcry. The Everglades were not draining as scheduled. The summer rains still covered them with water to depths of several feet. Even the dry winter season left them in no condition to be cultivated. The hundreds of buyers who still had faith in the project, and they were scattered throughout the nation, felt that the state was dragging its feet on the project. They accused it of breaking faith with the buyers of the land.

Bolles was still in Florida. He was, however, no longer the chief scapegoat. The drainage project had been undertaken by the state; let it get on with it. Engineers still expressed confidence. New canals were added to the original one. Water flowed down them bringing with it silt that settled on the bottom of the river, making it shallower. Once considered a salt-water stream, it changed to near-fresh in nature as the Glades water poured out; but the vast Everglades remained a swamp. The newspaper outcry continued. Probably the most insistent demands came from Thomas E. Will, of South Bay, the leading protagonist of the future glory of the Everglades and eloquent both in speech and with his pen.

By January of 1914 Mary Brickell was in complete charge of her deceased husband's estate. She maintained that she owned the riparian rights along the river, and sold and leased to the fishhouse operators "strips of land of indeterminate width between the city streets and the river with full riparian rights." Mrs. Brickell's claim to the riparian rights was well recognized. Most of the town's leading citizens had bought river-front property and most of them had paid Mrs. Brickell for the rights in front of their property even though the street intervened.

In December of 1913 Jacob F. Bunn had been appointed town attorney. Bunn began looking into the question of riparian rights, and his investigations led him to the conclusion that Mrs. Brickell did not, in fact, own these rights. He believed that they were vested in the city. He persuaded the town council to permit him to institute suit. Probably Bunn himself had not realized what the reaction would be. The town was immediately split asunder. Those who had bought riparian

Right: Colonel George G. Mathews, *Sentinel* publisher and active participant in civic and state affairs

Above: Dr. Thomas E. Will, leading protagonist and critic of Everglades drainage project

Right: Carl P. Weidling, well-known attorney, publisher, and legislator

rights wanted them and believed them necessary. They also argued that, although ugly, the fishhouses were an economic necessity. But people who had bought property not bordering on the river wanted access to the stream which was, at the time, the main artery of traffic through town. They argued that the fishhouses were not only ugly but even a menace to sanitation. Carl P. Weidling, Bunn's young law partner, joined him in his action. Mrs. Brickell hired J. L. Billingsley, the former town attorney, as her lawyer.

Bunn had to amend his bill of complaint three times before it was accepted by Circuit Court Judge H. Pierre Branning. The Judge, however, subsequently ruled down many efforts to have it thrown out of court, and finally a Special Master was appointed and the taking of testimony began. Bunn and Weidling called what they considered their two best witnesses first—H. C. Davis and J. H. Gearing. They were civil engineers and their testimony was identical. They declared that the plat from which the entire town of Fort Lauderdale had been sold showed no indication of any reservation of riparian rights on the part of the property owners. The designation of North and South River streets, the two in question, was by a single straight line on the land side of the street. On the water side the line was the undulating one that designated the edge of the waterway itself. Both said that had the street been of the definite forty-foot width claimed by the defendant, then it would have been so marked by a second line scaled to this distance from the first one. Davis also remarked that there was no indication in the dedication, signed by both William and Mary Brickell, of any such reservation.

This was telling testimony, but it was refuted by a parade of the town's leading citizens. Stranahan, Will Marshall, Tom Bryan, and his father, P. N. Bryan, all testified that the two streets involved had been intended to be forty feet wide and that when the right-of-way was cleared it was cleared only for this width, leaving the strip along the river untouched. The Dade County clerk and tax assessor W. E. Norton and James J. Jaudon testified that taxes had been levied and collected on the strip of property on the water front.

Then Mary Brickell took the stand and delivered a bombshell. She declared that she and her husband had had nothing to do with platting the town; it had been done by Mr. Flagler. In charge of the platting, actually done by A. L. Knowlton, a civil engineer, had been James E. Ingraham, a vice president of the Florida East Coast Railway. Ingraham was called to testify. He stated that, in the platting, it had been his "hope" the downtown section of the river front would be used for quays and docks and that the residential areas would see it beautified. He had not contemplated that it would fall into private hands. He was followed to the stand by Dr. Kennedy, who said that his attorney, Fred Worley of Miami, had informed him that he knew the situation and that Kennedy, buying property that was not on the water front, still had a right to use the river front. He said he bought property upon this advice.

J. A. B. Shippey, who followed Kennedy to the stand, declared he was an expert on these matters and that he had also bought property away from the river, from the plat, in the firm belief that it plainly showed that the riparian rights belonged to the public. Finally, on June 3, 1916, almost a year after Broward County had been formed, Branning handed down a Final Decree in favor of the town. The final solution was delayed for two more years by an appeal to the State Supreme Court, which affirmed Branning's decision. The ruling made possible the city docks which were to become nationally famous and to attract thousands of fishermen and yachtsmen to this area. Bitterness that had flared throughout the long trial calmed down and was forgotten.

Fort Lauderdale was growing. Tom Bryan built a two-story brick building on Brickell Avenue north of Wall Street, on the west side of the street. It housed the post office, which was moved from the south end of the Oliver building to make room for Tillman's (later Windham's) confectionery and the Fort Lauderdale State Bank, which was moved from its original quarters on River Drive.

The Hector brothers, Clarence J. and Harry H., found their old quarters on the river front not only too small but condemned by the results of the suit against Mary Brickell. They built new quarters on the site of the Osceola Hotel, forcing out Ed Caruth and his hamburger stand. Caruth built an elegant new hamburger stand, of brick, on Wall Street across from the new location of the theater. C. P. Weidling, who had bought the *Herald*, constructed a two-story building on Wall Street to house it. Andrews Avenue remained, for the most part, residential, though it was the Dixie Highway, the through street, and had the bridge. The Berryhill and Cromartie store was on its corner at River Drive. Crim's Variety store and the Keystone Hotel occupied the two corners on Wall Street, and S. S. Price had a bicycle shop behind the Berryhill and Cromartie store. The telephone office, the two-story frame *Sentinel* building, and the Lake Worth (later Palm Beach and then Fort Lauderdale) Mercantile building were other business houses.

First of the telephones, under the new franchise, went into use early in 1914 and quickly became a popular feature, particularly with the women, who could now order groceries on these newfangled instruments. Groceries were always delivered by the store's delivery man. The telephones, however, proved a blessing of a rather informal sort. Callers turned a crank on the side to reach the operator. When the operator answered, the caller usually said "Hello, Claudia," whereupon the village gossip was repeated, more often than not, to a considerable audience who had heard the ring on the party line and joined in.

On one occasion, Mrs. Will J. Reed, wife of the town's mayor, saw "Shirt Tail" Charlie, an Indian who according to local legend had been condemned by the tribe to wear shirttails because of a minor tribal infraction, taking a bath in New River in front of her house. Charlie was a well-known character, usually drunk, but utterly harmless. The fact that he was taking a bath was real news. Mrs. Reed notified the community via telephone and many of the unbelieving ladies witnessed the spectacle from a distance.

With the building and the new telephone system and other forms of progress came civic pride in yet another field. Baseball was the national pastime and many citizens felt that "every good town ought to have a baseball team." Accordingly, on May 21, 1913, a mass meeting of citizens was held for this purpose. Enthusiasm was fired when Frank Stranahan offered to donate ground for use as the ball field and further offered to clear it himself. The ground thus donated by Stranahan (for public use only) was that which eventually became the athletic field for the old Fort Lauderdale High School, lying on the west side of what is now Federal Highway between Broward Boulevard and South East 2d Street.

A baseball committee was formed with James N. Oliver, president; E. C. Parker, secretary; and W. O. Berryhill, treasurer. Volunteer baseball players were called for, and duly reported, and the team was ready for its first contest by July Fourth. It turned out to be a great day. The team beat Stuart in both ends of a double-header.

Such rivals as Stuart, Palm Beach, and Fort Pierce were fine for fun, and good sportsmanship always prevailed; but with Miami it was different. Miami was the "enemy" and this was red meat. There was no sportsmanship, the team had to win. By September 19 the newspaper was able to report that the locals had beaten Miami in five straight games to capture the championship of the East Coast League. It was another satisfying measure of revenge against their fiercely hated southern neighbors.

The spirit was to continue, along with the East Coast League, for many years. The game became so popular that the local Negroes also

Above: Tony Tommy, beloved Seminole chief, poles canoe for member of movie troupe

Left: "Shirt Tail" Charlie, familiar Seminole character (GIFT, MRS. HALE TALBOT)

formed a team as, in fact, did the Seminole Indians who were still encamped in what is now downtown Fort Lauderdale.

Many of the Seminoles were known in the community, a fact due largely to Tony Tommy, a young Indian who broke tribal precedent by entering the local public school. Tony was a warm and lovable person, much admired by both Indians and whites. Legend has it that he was a chief, but there were no official tribal chiefs, the Indians being governed by a council. Tony was highly influential, and his influence was important to both races. He induced the Seminoles to form their baseball team, which occasionally played games against the white "town team." Seminoles, reserved and dignified people, were a familiar sight on the streets throughout this era. The *Fort Lauderdale Sentinel*, November 21, 1913, reported that "Tony Tommy, the Indian boy who is attending school here left this week to attend the Carlisle school in Pennsylvania. It is pleasing to see one of that race become ambitious. We hope that he may prove a success."

The women of the tribe seldom spoke to white people in public, or even looked at them directly. They wore colorful but cumbersome dresses, yards of beads about their necks, and impressive hair styles. The men continued to wear striped shirts with flowing sleeves and tight cuffs, but wore conventional trousers and sometimes even shoes. They were encamped on New River at Sailboat Bend and their canoes were familiar sights as they moved up and down the river.

Hamilton M. Forman (left), Fort Lauderdale's first fresh-milk producer

The County Is Born

The *Fort Lauderdale Sentinel* of April 2, 1915, contained the following news: "A county division with our town as county seat will again be brought before the approaching session of the legislature. . . . Petitioners are out and a canvass will continue until every voter has been visited. . . . The new county will embrace a portion of the northern territory of Dade County and a portion of the southern confines of Palm Beach County. It will extend along the east coast just south of Hallandale, in Dade, to a point south of Boca Raton in Palm Beach County, and from the Atlantic Ocean to the western borders of the present county."

In 1915 the climate for a drive for a new county was different from that of two years earlier. The attitude of the interested members of the state legislature was favorable. This may have been due, in part, to a desire on the part of Miami residents to get rid of those who had voted Dade County dry in the 1913 election. But Tom Bryan, who led the delegation to the state legislature, believed the legislators "wanted to be fair" and that they realized the justice of the request. This time, also, the people of Dania and Hallandale favored the project, and those in Pompano and Deerfield were quite ready to divorce themselves from Palm Beach County.

FORT LAUDERDALE

A mass meeting was held at Dania, then almost as large as Fort Lauderdale, at which the Fort Lauderdale Board of Trade and Dania and Hallandale interests voted to provide three hundred dollars to defray the expenses of Tom and Frank Bryan to serve as advocates of the new county before the legislature. The two reached Tallahassee in good season, but Frank was almost immediately recalled to Fort Lauderdale by the death of his sister, Mrs. Fred Fisher. Anticipating little difficulty, Tom stayed on alone, saying he would "call on Frank" if he were needed.

Bryan found the Dade County delegation cooperative throughout the session, but the Palm Beach representatives, headed by a man named Carmichael, remained obdurately opposed to part of the plan—the question of the county line between the proposed new county and Palm Beach County. The Hillsboro canal, two miles south of the 47-48 township line, was agreed upon as the boundary on the eastern portion, but the new county group wanted this line to continue to the North New River canal and thence follow its diagonal course to Lake Okeechobee. This would have given Broward County a portion of the shore of the big lake and would have included in it the small settlement of South Bay. Carmichael insisted that the line should continue westward along the same straight line all the way across the Everglades. Bryan argued in vain that if this were the dividing line, should the canal be bridged, the two counties would share the expense.

Bryan telegraphed his fellow citizens stating what he was offered, and the answer came back for him to accept. This he did, and the bill was duly passed as a local bill by unanimous vote. The new county included the towns of Deerfield, Pompano, Fort Lauderdale, Dania, and Hallandale, as well as the communities of Davie, Colohatchee, and Progresso. The population was estimated at eight thousand. The outcome caused the *Fort Lauderdale Sentinel* of April 30, 1915, to comment with satisfaction: "The creation of Broward County gives to Florida's greatest governor a fitting monument. The Gate City will make rapid growth under influence derived from the new county."

The county extended southward for twenty-six miles from the above-named line and extended from the ocean on the east, westward for approximately forty miles, thus enclosing something over one thousand square miles instead of the eight hundred proposed two years before. It should be remembered, however, that only a comparatively narrow strip of coastal ridge along the eastern edge of the county was habitable. The rest was Everglades swampland, still undrained and intermittently flooded.

Flag raising at opening of the new Fort Lauderdale school, 1915 (BURGHARD COLLECTION)

The county was divided into five commissioner districts from north to south, and Fort Lauderdale was named as county seat. It was to have one representative to the state legislature of its own, but was to continue as part of the senatorial district that also included Palm Beach County. Since Palm Beach County was then much more heavily populated, it was a foregone conclusion that Broward County would have no state senator. It did not, in fact, until 1945 when districts were reallocated on the basis of the census of that year.

Selected to serve Broward County in its first general election of 1915 were Will H. Marshall, state representative; J. F. Bunn, county judge; Frank Bryan, tax assessor and clerk; A. W. Turner, sheriff; D. E. Clune, engineer; D. G. Tenbrook, supervisor of registration; F. L. Neville, chairman of the board of public instruction; J. M. Holding, school superintendent; J. G. Ewing, treasurer; and A. B. Lowe, J. J. Joyce, I. I. Hardy, C. E. Ingalls, and W. L. Bracknell, members of the county commission.

An immediate problem of housing for the new county offices, and one which might have been expected to pose difficulties, was solved rather readily. On March 25 in that year, the town of Fort Lauderdale had held a celebration to mark the laying of the cornerstone of a new school. Completion of this building came in plenty of time for the opening of school in September; and when Governor Park Trammell spoke at its dedication on September 16, the old schoolhouse on Andrews Avenue was vacant and ready to house the county offices.

Fledgling Broward County, in common with the rest of Florida and the other southern states, was overwhelmingly Democratic in its politics. Nomination to office on this ticket was tantamount to election, with the general election a formality, although political lines might be crossed on national issues. Republicans seldom bothered to nominate candidates for state or local offices. When they did (only Democrats voted in the all-important primary), the ensuing campaign was not taken seriously by either party. Usually most newcomers, even though Republicans in their former homes, registered as Democrats since this was the only way in which they could have a voice in local politics.

This, however, was not the case with two stalwart Republicans. Both Sam Gillian, a lumber dealer who had come here in 1913, and C. C. Ausherman, a real-estate broker who arrived at about the same time, adamantly registered their party affiliation as Republican. Though they had little influence in local politics as represented in state and county offices, the two were of tremendous help in national affairs when the administration was Republican. Gillian, in particular, had strong party ties in Washington. In later years he was to play a major role in obtaining a sorely needed new post office for the city. Partisan politics had no place in city elections, a fact demonstrated by Gillian's election in 1918 to the city council by an overwhelming majority. Ausherman also benefited from his party affiliation, serving as postmaster from June, 1922, to January, 1925. Many other Republicans were to follow Gillian in winning city elections during the period in which the state and county remained solidly Democratic.

It should be noted that Europe was already at war when the county was formed and the United States was becoming more and more embroiled. The great war seemed far away, indeed, from Fort Lauderdale; but feelings against "Kaiser Bill" and his plans for aggrandizement were spreading. In 1915 local plans and ambitions, however, far overshadowed such feelings. In this year Fort Lauderdale first gained fame in a completely new field—high school athletics. The high school did not graduate its first class until that June (1915), the graduating class consisting of five boys, Charles Crim, Martin and John Davis, Dale Redman, and Raymond Russell. The school was not large enough to muster enough ablebodied youngsters to form a football team or even a baseball nine. It had, however, a basketball team which played in Baker's Hall, over a garage on South Andrews Avenue at New River. The ceiling of the hall was only twelve and a half feet high and the height of the basket was ten feet. Learning to make baskets under those conditions became a local skill and the team won all home games.

The one sport in which the school, lacking a fitting gymnasium, could seriously compete was track. In 1915 the track team achieved the goals of defeating Miami High School in a dual meet and finishing third in the state meet at Gainesville. In the following year a team composed of five boys, Keith W. (Watty) Gordon, Cyril Mitchell, Fred Blosch, Jennings Howard, and Walter Brock, beat all local competition and won the state meet as well. Their feat became a local tradition which, for many years, saw prime emphasis on sports in the local school centered on track. It should be mentioned that debating was then a part of the meet and Brock was the local debater.

Although the new school was dedicated with appropriate ceremonies that September, one feature of it was not yet completed. This was the fine auditorium, the floor of which remained flooded throughout the ensuing rainy season. When finally completed that winter, the facility added much to the social life of the town. It had a fully equipped stage and dressing rooms, and home talent shows were now readily possible on a far larger scale than before. It also enabled students to produce their own class plays, which soon became a tradition. All such entertainments drew capacity crowds.

On June 18, 1915, the White Star Line was officially put into operation. This was a bus line which operated between Palm Beach and Miami using White (manufacturer's name) openside buses. It was locally owned, with W. C. Kyle, George Crim, J. N. Oliver, and W. H. Andrews listed as officers. There were two buses, one driven by Charles Swaggerty, the other by "Tex" Woodward. Each made the complete circuit once each day. The line was the local predecessor of the Greyhound Lines and was later sold to that company.

In August of 1915, with the county assured and the date for actual establishment near, Fort Lauderdale's first abstract company was organized. The Broward County Abstract and Title Company had ten thousand dollars in capital stock, with W. Q. Bryan as secretary, treasurer, and chief stockholder. Other members of the firm were Robert J. Reed, president; M. A. Hortt, vice president; and C. P. Weidling, director. The firm opened for business in October in the old Fort Lauderdale State Bank building on River Drive, with A. L. Joiner in charge of the office.

Progress was in the air. The Woman's Club was plugging for a new project, a hospital, though there were, even then, only three doctors active in the town—Thomas S. Kennedy, R. S. Lowry, and J. A. Stanford.

Among other items considered to be signs of vast progress was the opening of the Dixie Highway, the first connection by auto with the rest of the nation. The first car passed through Fort Lauderdale over this interstate route on July 22, 1915. Few realized at the time the magnitude of the milestone thus passed. In retrospect a historian could easily call this the beginning of things to come. It should be recalled that this highway passed through many old Spanish grants in its course down the Florida east coast. The owners of the grants gave permission for the highway only in return for the privilege of establishing tollgates and charging motorists a fee for passage. The road, by today's standards, was far too narrow, twisting, and tortuous to be considered more than a barely traversable trail.

Although it has been noted that the land here was productive of most green vegetables, young children still were forced to drink evaporated milk taken from cans and diluted with water. The climate and soil were considered unsuitable for cattle raising, particularly for dairy herds. In 1914, however, a young man from Illinois, Hamilton M. Forman, had arrived here with his wife Blanche. He had bought ten acres of land in the Davie area, sight unseen. He and his wife made the trip from the railroad station to the property up the North New River Canal on Captain Rossi's barge. Rossi landed them at the site and pointed out the particular tract. There was not a house to be seen and it was late. Forman had a tent, but no time to pitch it. The two slept on the ground.

Within a year Forman had built himself a house with his own hands (the house still stands on land south of State Road 84 and east of Davie Road) and he was winning prizes at the fairs in the area for his fine vegetables. In 1916 he was to sell one thousand bushels of potatoes on the vegetable dock at two twenty-five a bushel, though in 1915 his first sale netted him but three hundred sixty-four dollars. Forman was far from satisfied. He had graduated from an agricultural college in animal husbandry and he wanted to go into the dairy business. Bankers advised him sternly against it, but he was determined to see for himself. By the time Forman produced his first milk for sale he found few customers. People had been on the "tin cow" so long they had forgotten how good fresh milk was. Forman took milk to town on his Model T Ford truck and walked the streets with a tray on which was a bottle of milk and a glass. He urged all he met to "try it and see." Most of those who yielded

Hamilton C. Forman, with prize animal

became customers of Forman's Sanitary Dairy. Fresh milk became part of the town's diet. Forman had been a member of the University of Illinois track team, running in the two-mile event. This stood him in good stead in operating his one-man dairy. When he had milked and cared for his cows, and chilled and bottled the milk, he loaded it on his truck and went to town. He stopped the truck as near as possible to homes where he made deliveries and ran with the bottles to the doors. By running he saved time and gasoline, for the truck engine was left running. It did not crank easily.

Winter vegetables, grown on the marginal lands, remained a big and thriving industry; but transportation to Lake Okeechobee was definitely threatened and the sobriquet "Gateway to the Everglades" was no longer completely fitting. The fishhouses, doomed in any case by the outcome of the city's suit against Mary Brickell, were seeking new locations. Most of those who had come for the big Bolles lottery had left or were leaving, and another big bubble of dreams had burst.

But in another direction things were beginning to stir. By June of 1914 underbrush and trees were being cleared on the beach for a new bathing pavilion. Messrs. Alexander, Ralph Horton, and other local men formed the Las Olas Beach Company to build a resort at the beach. A pavilion seventy-four by forty feet, double-decked, provided floor space for a dancing pavilion, rest rooms, and a refreshment stand. The bathhouse had seventy-four dressing rooms and there were shower baths. A plot of ground was converted into a playground for children. The

69

pavilion opened the following Labor Day amidst much fanfare, to the joy of the entire populace.

Now, at long last, local businessmen began to eye the tourist business, already thriving in Miami and Palm Beach. It was realized that two things were essential: a road to the ocean beach and a suitable tourist hotel. A golf course was a third and highly desirable need in the eyes of some. The primary objective, the road to the beach, was a county problem since the area was then outside the city. Although in 1914 a group of Fort Lauderdale citizens had formed a company to build a boulevard to the beach, plans were abandoned with the realization that this would become a responsibility of the new county. Work was begun on the boulevard to the beach in early December, 1914. A stock company, composed of Frank Stranahan, Tom Bryan, Dave Oliver, W. C. Kyle, Frank Bryan, and Fred Barrett, was organized to build the bridge. Mr. Alexander donated a block of land on the Las Olas tract and made an agreement with them to complete the boulevard and put in the bridge.

In January, 1915, the Las Olas Bridge Company applied for a charter. This company was formed with a capital stock of fifteen thousand dollars and its purpose was to construct the road. Contract for the subgrade and approach bridges was let to Scott Holloway. Alexander was to bridge the bay. Much of the work was actually done. Mrs. Mary Brickell built the road through her property in Colee Hammock and Holloway dredged a canal beside the site for the new road. A bridge was completed over the Sospiro Canal, but there the work ended.

Youngsters who were bold enough to brave the stingaree-infested bay could walk down the canal bank to its edge and, from there, alternately wade and swim their way to the beach. There they found little company. During the winter season Hugh T. Birch, the recluse, resided at his home a half-mile north, but Birch forbade trespassers. Seldom were there people at the big lodge. Until the bathhouse was completed and tended, there was only Captain A. C. Skogsberg and his family at the House of Refuge. On Sunday the excursion boats brought bathers and picnickers. On other days of the week it was a lonely place, wildly beautiful, alive with the chirping of birds and the antics of sandpipers, which were always present in large numbers on the beach. Downtown seemed far away; and of future destiny there was not an inkling.

The problem of bridges to the beach could not be solved individually, for every community in the county that lay along the coastal ridge needed the same facility; and Davie, to the west, needed an access road with consequent short-span bridges. The county, of course, had no

The first Keystone Skimmer Scoop south of Jacksonville; owned and operated by S. P. Snyder (*at controls*) (GIFT, BYRON SNYDER)

money in its infancy, and the city was in almost as bad shape. In the face of these events, the new county voted a bond issue totaling four hundred thousand dollars with which to build roads and bridges to the beaches and to build an overland access road with the necessary bridges to serve the Davie area. Most difficult of the beach access roads was the one at Fort Lauderdale, which had nearly a mile of dense mangrove swamp to be crossed, as well as the wide bay at the eastern end.

The *Fort Lauderdale Herald* of September 22, 1916, announced: "Engineer H. C. Davis is of the opinion that the bridge to Las Olas Beach will be completed and ready for use by the first of the year. He also states that the road to Dania Beach should be finished within the next thirty days. This will give us three beaches in the county that are accessible, Fort Lauderdale, Dania, and Pompano. Deerfield and Hallandale will also receive roads and bridges and it may be that they too will be finished by the first of the year which would give Broward County five beaches. This ought to put us on the map when it comes to entertaining and interesting tourists who like ocean-front property."

Contract for building the road across the swamp went to Bryan and Snyder, with Walter (Scott) Holloway as dredging contractor. Barges brought in fill for the road. Mules, used to haul rock and fill and pull the graders, were forced to wear muck-shoes on the job. Inasmuch as contracts let for fill and paving included all the various projects, no

FORT LAUDERDALE

First bridge to the beach was hand-operated, 1917 (GIFT, CHAMPION BRIDGE COMPANY)

breakdown of the cost of this one roadway is possible. The contract for the drawbridge over the East Coast Canal was let to the Champion Bridge Co., of Wilmington, Ohio, which firm agreed to build and install the structure for sixty-four hundred and fifty dollars. The single land span called for the use of sixty-four thousand pounds of steel, fabricated and erected in workable condition on the site. Replacement of this facility in recent years cost the state more than a million dollars.

Commenting on the progress, the *Fort Lauderdale Sentinel* of December 22, 1916, said: "Fort Lauderdale's beach stands in natural attractions far ahead of any other on the Atlantic, and the privately owned portion of the peninsula will no doubt soon become a city."

The bridge and road to the beach were opened to the public in January of 1917, marking a day of days in the calendar of progress. There were, of course, speeches and a motorcade, which included nearly every usable vehicle in the town, including the volunteer fire department. The approach to the drawspan was made of wood. The draw itself was a single-lane, wooden-decked structure supported on each side by steel trusses and set on a turntable that could be turned by operation of a large key inserted into the mechanism through the center of the deck. It was opened by hand, with the bridge-tender, Benjamin F. Bailey, furnishing the manpower. It was also Bailey's duty to tend to the kerosene lights that served as warnings and signals to boatmen passing on the Intracoastal Waterway.

The opening brought an immediate burst of activity to the beach. Now, at long last, Alexander began to sell lots in earnest. Records show more than twenty sales in that year. Las Olas-by-the-Sea became more

72

than a name on a plat. J. E. Hasbrouck, of Modena, New York, a regular visitor, had foreseen the event by building in 1914. Kenneth Mitchell of Chicago now built, Alexander built also, and a number of small wooden tourist cottages began to appear. The old wooden casino, which the city had so proudly opened in 1915, was used originally only on Sundays when excursion boats, such as Captain Dick La Vigne's "Excelsior"

Above: The "Excelsior," Captain Dick La Vigne's excursion boat to beach (VAIL COLLECTION)
Below: Pontoon bridge used during construction of Broward's first lift bridge over Andrews Avenue

FORT LAUDERDALE

Las Olas Boulevard crossing East Marsh mangrove swamp (KELCY PHOTO)

made their regular runs. Now it was open daily. The new road also made practical the use of the dance floor on the second story of the casino. Dances were held there often.

The *Fort Lauderdale Herald* of December 15, 1916, announced: "Ground has been broken and construction work begun on the erection of the Woman's Club and Public Library building on the Dixie Highway." Another landmark was added to the city with the building of the new Woman's Club building on land (in the downtown area) donated by Frank Stranahan. The concrete building, which was to house the club and its library, was built as a public project, with much of the labor and material donated. It was, and still is, located on Andrews Avenue between Broward and South East 1st Street, in an area now known as Stranahan Park.

* * *

There was, however, a distraction from the local scene. American ships were being torpedoed by German submarines and war fever was spreading fast among the people. In Washington, President Woodrow Wilson was solemnly proclaiming the necessity of "making the world safe for democracy." Other excitement revolved around the suffragettes, who demanded voting rights for women. Daily newspaper cartoons depicting red-nosed "John Barleycorn" were screaming the cause of

World War I volunteers at Fort Screven, Georgia (GIFT, MARTIN R. DAVIS)

prohibition. The people of Fort Lauderdale were not greatly concerned over these noble causes. Will Marshall, representative to the state legislature, openly favored votes for women and in so doing reflected the general sentiment of his constituents. Mrs. Frank Stranahan was named state president of the Woman's Suffrage Society. On the prohibition question little interest was shown since the town was legally "dry."

By 1917 Fort Lauderdale filled the necessary population qualifications by having more than three hundred registered voters, and the state legislature approved its new charter as a city on June 4, 1917.

Fort Lauderdale stood ready to do its part in quelling the ambitions of "Kaiser Bill" Hohenzollern, the German Emperor. When the United States entered the great war in April local boys were ready, and on April 6, nine of them volunteered. First to sign up was Keith Brown, but the others, including Dale Redman, Jennings Howard, Lloyd Parker, James Hendricks, Vance Mahannah, Ralph Ebner, Raymond Sechy, and Martin Davis were in line right behind. The boys had to make the trip to Miami to enlist.

Gertrude Mason was president of the Fort Lauderdale School graduating class of 1917. Other members were Edward Viele, vice president; *Watt Gordon, secretary-treasurer; Alma Grant, Irene Jones, Irene Morrison, Thelma Marshall, *Cyril Mitchell, *Darrell Smith, Arthur

FORT LAUDERDALE

Coast Guard Base Six (BURGHARD COLLECTION)

Anderson, Reynold Gabrielsen, Eugene Holloman, and *Jennings Howard. Students with asterisks before their names had enlisted, but were to be awarded their diplomas.

There were the usual spy scares. Captain Will Reed, perennial baseball umpire and often mayor of Fort Lauderdale, was put in charge of the Home Guard, which drilled on the school athletic field with wooden rifles. Some foods became in short supply, notably sugar, but otherwise life went on almost as usual. Before the war ended nearly all homes had "service flags" hanging in their windows with one or more stars, each signifying a close relative in service. A gold star denoted a soldier who had died in the conflict.

The House of Refuge at the beach was taken over by the Coast Guard, which began to patrol the beach regularly on a motorcycle, usually ridden by Wallace King. In charge was former keeper Charles Skogsberg.

* * *

The war affected the city's two banks. Purchase of Liberty Bonds became so popular that savings were withdrawn at a rapid rate and the Broward County Bank was forced to merge with the Fort Lauderdale State Bank. Will C. Kyle of the former institution stayed on as president of the merged banks.

Captain James B. Vreeland, Jr., gaffs bonita for movie star Dick Barthelmess

A Bid for Tourists

Through the grim anxiety of the war years a harsh fact was borne home upon the people: the Everglades were not going to drain. The vast, superbly productive "garden" that was to build an empire in southeastern Florida was only a dream and in actuality was to remain an almost inaccessible marsh. Not only that, the canals that were providing a means of commerce between Fort Lauderdale and Lake Okeechobee were growing ever more shallow and causing boatmen great difficulty.

Chapter 8
1918–1922

A dim ray of hope was the measure of response to the city's rather timid bid for tourists. Alexander, who remodeled the old Las Olas hunting lodge and opened it as an inn, often found it filled during the winter season. Other property on the beach was developed in groups of small tourist cottages, usually of frame, that also proved popular with an in-

FORT LAUDERDALE

West side of Las Olas Beach in the 1920's

creasing number of winter visitors. From December on throughout the winter strangers appeared on the streets in such numbers as to become commonplace. Storekeepers noticed an upsurge in business in these months and one occasionally heard references to "the season," meaning the tourist season.

By midsummer of 1918 the tide of war had definitely turned against Germany and the nation looked forward with confidence to the day when the boys would come home. Finally, on November 9, a report reached Fort Lauderdale that an armistice had been signed. The schools turned out for the event and flag-waving children paraded the streets. The report proved false but the youngsters at least got a day off from classes. Two days later the armistice report was confirmed, touching off a celebration that very nearly started a new war locally. Most of the city's leading male citizens gravitated as if by magic to the back room of Johnny Schroeder's Feed Store in the old bank building on North West River Drive, and there the "jinks" were high. Pent-up emotions and war tensions were let off in an orgy at which liquor flowed freely. The party grew to heroic proportions as citizens sought to erase in one sudden explosion the frustrations and hardships of the past two years.

Neither the momentous event that justified the alcoholic "hurrah" nor the joyous abandon of the celebrants were immediately appreciated

78

by the wives of the participants. To them it had been a brawl; long, loud, and disgraceful. The returning "Dove of Peace" was greeted locally by families in which a stony silence was apt to be the rule between husband and wife, and many a mother openly wept over the fate of her children fathered by a spouse referred to as "that sot." The big Armistice Day party may well have served as a requiem for red-nosed John Barleycorn, for national prohibition was hard upon the land. While the AEF was still engaged with the Kaiser the nation had voted. The women had gained the vote while the men had lost their booze; or at least, so it was supposed. As expected, prohibition had little immediate effect on a town that had never had a saloon. As the years passed, however, it was to become of vast significance—so much so that it brought about a change in the entire social and economic structure. From the start, the comparatively few regular drinkers in Fort Lauderdale experienced little difficulty in finding a spot or so of liquor when they thought it was needed.

For the most part the citizenry released its war tensions in another way. The urge to combat was still upon them and the opportunity to experience it without the drastic effects of actual bloody warfare presented an appeal out of proportion to the importance of the events themselves. "Beat Miami" was still the battle cry, and the contest was baseball, played at the high school's Stranahan Field. As in the period preceding the "War to End Wars" the sport still had great fascination. Now, however, the sport became an obsession; and Miami, scapegoat for many of our past ills, was the "enemy" and always the prime target.

The league was not a part of organized baseball and any player was eligible. Although it started out as an amateur team, all in the league began hiring players, "ringers" if you will. Some of those obtained were former "Big Leaguers" who came from the outlawed "Million Dollar" league; others were players banned from organized sport. But many were players who had simply drifted down to Florida. On the afternoons when a ball game was being played, every store in the city closed and downtown was utterly deserted. It was often remarked that a smart thief could have come with a wagon and unnoticed carted the city away.

Perennial manager of the team was Herb (Pop) Lewis, a former professional catcher. "Cap" Reed served as umpire with autocratic urbanity that permitted no argument. The business manager was almost always A. J. Beck, who had moved from Ocala to open a Brickell Avenue drugstore. Lewis developed a star pitcher, Lester (Sugar) Sweetland, who could usually answer satisfactorily the prayer to "beat Miami." Sweetland later went to the major leagues but lasted only a few years. His alter ego on the mound and almost as effective was lefty Oran (Squirrely) Swearingen.

The end of the war brought about a resurgence of civic consciousness. Businessmen were more than ready to take up where they had left off in creating a tourist community, and the two remaining "most urgent needs"—the tourist hotel and the golf course—were not forgotten. The city had visitors now and people liked what they saw and stayed. Often they invested in property—and the city grew.

When a customer of real-estate man Hortt asked what he could do for the city, Hortt had a ready answer: "Help us build a tourist hotel." The benefactor, George E. Henry of Winchester, Massachusetts, studied Hortt's suggestion for a structure on a site available for a hotel. Henry had August Geiger, Miami architect, draw plans and Hortt advertised for bids. Henry had warned that if the bid exceeded one hundred twenty-five thousand dollars he would not build. The lowest price was one hundred forty thousand dollars. Noting the deep gloom into which the city sank, Henry made another proposal whereby citizens could participate. The terms included the gift by Henry of the plans, sale of the site on Andrews Avenue at Las Olas Boulevard to them for exactly what he had paid, and the raising by the city of forty thousand dollars as part of the construction costs of a two-story building, rather than the planned three-story structure. The citizens were to put up the first and the final twenty thousand dollars needed.

The Henry offer was accepted enthusiastically by the Board of Trade. Notes were pledged in the required amount to be used as collateral for a bank loan—and the goose hung high! But there was a hitch. Banker Kyle advised that some signatures were not acceptable as collateral. Then Clarence E. Rickard, lumber dealer, came forward with the suggestion that Hortt be sent to Boston to see Henry to determine what further could be done. Specifically, he asked Henry to advance ten thousand dollars of the sixty thousand dollar Henry share of the one hundred thousand dollar building fund. Henry agreed.

The Citizen's Committee finally raised twenty-three thousand dollars of the forty thousand dollar balance, but when this and Henry's sixty thousand dollars were spent, the building was still incomplete and the additional seventeen thousand dollars needed simply could not be raised. The method used to get a large portion of this money illustrates both the ingenuity and the determination of the citizenry. Frank Stranahan, then president of the city council, had about decided to deed Stranahan

Hotel Broward under construction (VAIL COLLECTION)

Park to the city. Now, with money needed so desperately for the hotel, the idea occurred that he might sell it. The city could not under law make any donation to, or investment in, a private enterprise. Stranahan could, but another hitch arose. As council president, Stranahan could not sell anything to the city. On July 5, 1918, therefore, he deeded the property to John Sherwin for one dollar. Sherwin sold it to the city for six thousand dollars and promptly turned the money over to the hotel building fund.

In final desperate conferences, Hortt persuaded Henry to accept the money invested by the townspeople as a gift, and Henry in turn completed the hotel to the three stories originally planned. It is worthy of note that the money raised represented fortunes to the average citizen-

Richard Barthelmess and Creighton Hale with actors in "Classmates"

contributor. Many, to advance their city, contributed large parts of their yearly earnings. The building of Hotel Broward is reported at length because it demonstrates the spirit, fight, and foresight which were to make the city great.

Hotel Broward was finished in time for the 1919-20 winter season. Furnishing, however, was not completed when the first guests—and they were important people—arrived. First to sign the register was David Wark Griffith, top motion-picture producer of his day. He had come with his entire troupe, including actors Richard Barthelmess, Creighton Hale, and Ford Sterling, as well as actresses Clarine Seymour and Carol Dempster, other lesser players, camera and property men, and technicians.

Griffith knew of the excellent jungle scenery in the area. His manager, Gerritt Lloyd, had accompanied lawyer C. P. Weidling on a quiet survey a month before. Here Griffith was to film the "Idol Dancer." New hotel manager John W. Needham was chagrined. His kitchen equipment had not yet arrived. But Griffith blandly assured him that this company had come prepared. There was a portable kitchen with his other voluminous movie-production gear which was promptly set up.

From its earliest beginnings big and unusual events happened in Fort Lauderdale. Now the city was really agog. Almost the entire population watched as the movie scenes were shot. Griffith, employing Seminole Chief Tony Tommy as interpreter, engaged many local Indians as extras for the South Sea Island picture. Other locals were employed to act the parts of savages and to appear in the occasional more civilized scenes. Captain James B. Vreeland, Jr., the deep-sea fisherman, was engaged to transport the troupe to and from the island location and up and down New River. "Jimmie" Vreeland learned much about movie work and became a skilled camera-man himself.

The company proved relaxed and sociable. Many, Barthelmess in particular, were well liked and were frequently entertained in local homes. So well did they get along with the townspeople that prior to leaving Griffith engaged an orchestra and arranged a bountiful farewell party in the Hotel Broward lobby. Weidling, charged with making up the guest list, ran into trouble. All five thousand residents wanted to attend, and the list was limited to two hundred! He did his best but remained unpopular for months after. Many crashed the party without difficulty.

The "Idol Dancer" was a success. Griffith and his coproducer, Ralph Ince, made other pictures in Fort Lauderdale. Barthelmess starred in Ince's "Classmates" filmed in what Barthelmess considered "his" town.

Fishing had always been good in the surrounding waters and the phenomenon of Tarpon Bend in New River had long been spectacular. The Bend, in Colee Hammock, was often alive with rolling and leaping fish, some of them of great size. Here, seven years later, Hal Ryder and W. H. DeBold were to catch the largest game fish ever taken within the city limits of any American city—a 195-pound tarpon. Inland waters were alive with mangrove snappers, snook, and jack crevallé. But fishing as a tourist lure had not been considered important. Fish were taken to eat. This attitude toward fishing was to take a dramatic change.

One day in 1919 Captain Vreeland and W. L. Kester, a wealthy angler from Virginia, had gone fishing on the ocean. They returned with six magnificent sailfish, caught on hand lines. These fish, with the tremendous dorsal fin which raises from a slot, were complete oddities and Vreeland brought them to the Board of Trade. There Al Hortt saw them and realized the possibilities. He tied the great fish to the sides and fenders of his car and took off for Miami where he stopped in front of Bayfront Park. There he almost broke up the daily concert for tourists being given by Pryor's band. Of the hundreds who crowded around to see the fish at least one, Frank Mooney, is known to have become a Hortt real-estate customer, buying the land that later became known as Mooney's Point.

Prior to this time there had been a few fishing boats available for charter at the downtown docks. They were captained by Vreeland,

Right: Movie stunt man Charles Hamilton with Mayor Will J. Reed and family

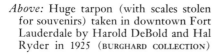

Above: Huge tarpon (with scales stolen for souvenirs) taken in downtown Fort Lauderdale by Harold DeBold and Hal Ryder in 1925 (BURGHARD COLLECTION)

Right: Commodore A. H. Brook, ardent civic booster, arrived in 1919 (GIFT, LAUDERDALE YACHT CLUB)

Flavius Van Gosen, Otto, and a few more. Fishermen used hand lines, and the edible kingfish was the prize among catches. Fishing, however, was to attract increasing attention, and soon a number of boats equipped for "sport" fishing appeared at the public docks along the river front. Captain Vreeland and his series of Kingfisher boats continued at his private dock off Las Olas Boulevard on the beach. He kept pace with new equipment, eliminating the old "knuckle-buster" reels and improving other facilities used in the sport. A knuckle-buster was a reel which had no free-spooling mechanism, and with a big fish on the handle it spun so rapidly it could inflict serious damage to the hand of a careless angler. Outriggers, which caused controversy among the anglers themselves and were to lead to the removal of boats from the river dock to Bahia Mar, were still in the future.

The year 1919 saw the arrival of Commodore A. H. Brook, retired manager of the Thomas H. Cusack Outdoor Advertising Agency of New York. Brook fell in love with the town. In him Fort Lauderdale had a new booster, and one highly skilled in publicizing its charms. Brook, short in stature, informal in dress, and with a large sandy mustache, was a vigorous and vital force in civic affairs from that time on.

The Board of Trade had continued to thrive after its success in its first big project—incorporation of the city. When the town was rebuilt after the fire of 1912, the board had established headquarters in the Wheeler building on Brickell Avenue (South West 1st Avenue). By this time the ebullient and indefatigable Samuel L. Drake was secretary.

When the new Hotel Broward was completed new quarters were sought; but the board, by this time, also aspired to a new status. Under the presidency of C. E. Rickard it applied for membership in the United States Chamber of Commerce. The membership was granted on February 14, 1920, and by the time the body became officially the Chamber of Commerce it was moved to a new office in the Broward. In October of 1920 the Chamber moved again—this time into a frame house formerly occupied by W. O. Berryhill on Andrews Avenue across from the dead-ending of Las Olas Boulevard. The property included a large yard where horseshoe courts were built for the increasing number of tourists as well as for the locals who had time for such recreation.

On March 1, 1920, the Security State Bank was opened in the building on Brickell Avenue vacated by the merger of the Broward and Fort Lauderdale state banks. President of the bank was C. J. Hector, whose supply company was just next door. Other officers included D. T. Hart, vice president; J. S. Hinton, cashier; and W. L. Dillard, assistant cashier.

FORT LAUDERDALE

Clarence E. Rickard, lumber dealer and first Fort Lauderdale city manager (BURGHARD COLLECTION)

Organization of the First National Bank was well under way January 7, the next year. The principal promoters were Harry Crim, Ray Bailey, W. B. Snyder, Fred Barrett, L. T. Hunt, and several others. Capital stock of a hundred thousand dollars, a substantial portion of which was already subscribed, was called for as was a new building, probably on the corner where the Crim Variety Store was located.

Feeling that a bank identified with the Federal Reserve System meant quite a safeguard for depositors, the directors of the Security State Bank made successful application to the Comptroller of the Currency at Washington for the conversion of the bank into the First National Bank of Fort Lauderdale. In 1921 the First National Bank opened in the Security Bank building. Officers of the First National included Fred A. Barrett, president; E. N. Hawkins, vice president; J. A. Stanford, vice president; and from the Security Bank, J. S. Hinton, cashier; and W. L. Dillard, assistant cashier.

A move was on to build a golf course, spearheaded by C. D. Kittredge and Weidling. Many felt the city was not big enough to support

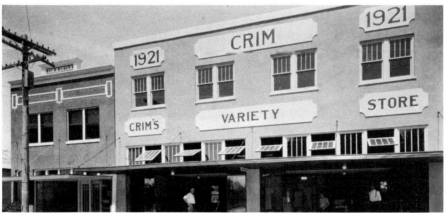

Top: Chamber of Commerce, former home of W. O. Berryhill (GIFT, MARY TALBOT)

Center: Crim's Variety Store on Andrews Avenue at Wall Street (BURGHARD COLLECTION)

Right: First National Bank on Brickell. First the Dade County Bank and then the Broward County Bank, it is now a typewriter salesroom

FORT LAUDERDALE

Right: President-elect Warren G. Harding on new golf course in 1921 (BURGHARD COLLECTION)

Below (left to right): James S. Rhine, Philip Weidling and C. P. Weidling on links

such an expensive luxury. The city council, after long consideration, was persuaded to buy forty acres of land fronting on the Dixie Highway south of the city and to engage a Miami golf architect to design a nine-hole course. The site is now part of the Fort Lauderdale-Hollywood Airport. The resulting course was necessarily short and by today's standards not a difficult test of golfing skill. But it was on good marl land, the fairways were well grassed, and it was a pleasant, though easy, course to play.

Norman Sommers, fresh from the AEF in France, was hired as club professional. Golf immediately became popular with the local residents, many of whom had heard only vaguely of the game. Among those who frequented the old nine-hole course were D. C. Alexander, who had long been a tennis fan; Tom Bryan and his son Perry, who was later to become a fine tournament player; Weidling, Kittredge, Hinton, Ira Dresbach, Harry Crim, Bob Chapple, Ray Bailey, Wade Morrow, C. E. Farrington, C. G. Rodes and his son Charles; the two banking Parker brothers of Dania, I. T. and William S.; "Windy" and Paul Windham; Hortt, and many others. Located directly on the main highway (Dixie), the golf course drew the attention of tourists on their way to Miami. Among those who stopped to play and eventually made Fort Lauderdale their winter home were Henry Oosterhoudt and Irving Hornbeck.

But the big day for the golf course came during its first year of existence when it was played in 1921 by President-elect Warren G. Harding. There are several versions of President Harding's first visit to the city. The following account is that of M. A. Hortt, as presented in his memoirs. Miamians, hearing of the President-elect's impending visit, attempted to have the yacht on which he was traveling, owned by Senator Joseph S. Frelinghuysen, go through on the Intracoastal Waterway to Miami. Thomas N. Stilwell, an Indiana Republican, heard of it and informed a group of men including Commodore Brook, who was later to become chairman of the Inland Navigation District. Mysteriously, a large dredge ran aground blocking the channel of the Intracoastal Waterway; and, lo and behold, on the other side of the dredge was the Brook yacht "Klyo" waiting to rescue the presidential pary from the mosquitoes by taking them to Fort Lauderdale. According to Hortt, the dredge had been dispatched by Brook and Stilwell to "meet" the yacht.

Needless to say, the President-elect and his party were entertained with all that the city could muster. Among the diversions offered was a game of golf on the brand new golf course. Harding was an enthusiastic, if inexpert, golfer and gladly accepted. Although he scored a, for him, mediocre 18-hole 110, he expressed admiration for the nine-hole layout. Harding enjoyed his golf in Fort Lauderdale, and on his return trip from Miami played the course again. Norm Sommers was selected as scorekeeper and Harding's total, when tallied up, was so remarkable that his chief opponent, Ambassador Henry P. Fletcher, objected.

"Surely," said Harding blandly, "you don't suspect Norm of cheating."

Norman was a burly six-foot-two; Fletcher hastily agreed that this was unthinkable. Fort Lauderdale was to play host to many Presidents and other great and famous men in the years ahead.

Center parking on Brickell Avenue, now South West 1st Avenue

Bootlegging & a Boom

Chapter 9
1922–1924

The end of World War I brought many upheavals in the American way of life, some of which were of prime importance to southeastern Florida.

One, workingmen's salaries, in the boom that followed the war, reached proportions never before contemplated—in the new assembly-line world of manufacturing. Another, which was to have a major impact on the entire nation, was Henry Ford's development of what soon became known as the "Tin Lizzie"—an automobile so cheap that the average man could afford it, and so dependable that even long overland journeys were not only possible but also practical. The nation was on wheels and eager to investigate new fields. Romantic Florida, known to most northerners as a "faraway" land, now was accessible by cheap "Tin Lizzie" transportation.

Bootlegging & Boom: 1922–1924

The influx of money into the pockets of the nation's citizens had spread downward to the workers; upward to management, bankers, and stockholders; and outward to farmers and merchants. Thousands had capital which cried for a suitable outlet for investment. Industrialization, moreover, had provided more time for vacationing. The nation was ripe for some new, big adventure. It seemed, at times, as though its people had decided, as a group, that this was "it."

There were, of course, few accommodations in south Florida for the thousands who poured in. But that was no drawback. The visitors brought their own. Ground was provided for tents and portable shacks in a further development, the first tourist camps, which usually offered rest and wash rooms. The somewhat disdainful name for these travelers, as applied by the locals, was "tin can tourists"; this because of the suspicion that many even brought their own groceries. Whatever the sobriquet, these people played a big role in what was to come, for they carried north with them tales of the wonders of the Florida climate, and of its beaches, fishing, and recreational possibilities. These stories spread throughout a booming nation.

Tourist camps were now scattered throughout Broward County. Prominent ones in Fort Lauderdale included the lot on South Andrews Avenue at the river, where the Maxwell Arcade was to rise a few years later. Largest was that owned and operated by the city. It occupied the two blocks on South Andrews Avenue between South West 7th Street and South West 9th Street, and extended westward from there to the Florida East Coast tracks and provided toilet and laundry facilities.

With new faces appearing in the city every day it did not seem odd when a group of well-dressed men rented the Frank Oliver home on New River at South East 1st Avenue. It was a spacious two-story house and close to downtown. These well-dressed men proved to be good spenders. They drove high-powered cars, and most of them joined the golf club and displayed a free-handed disposition to tip well. They used the latest in fine, all-leather golf bags and expensive clubs. Before long rumors began to float about town concerning their activities. They never invited any of the local citizens into their house. Somehow the name "wire tappers" became associated with them. Eventually they were arrested by a posse of local men organized by an officer of the state.

Eugene Kelcy, a newspaper man and a member of the raiding party, said that some citizens had appealed to Governor Cary A. Hardee at Tallahassee. He promptly sent a special investigator, Bob Shackleford, brother-in-law of Mrs. H. L. Shackleford of Fort Lauderdale, with power to deputize as many citizens as needed to carry out the surprise raid. Chosen were W. C. Kyle, M. A. Hortt, Morgan Bryan, Lucian Craig, James Oliver, and E. M. Kelcy. The time was February 19, 1922. On the green cloth-covered table the raiders found seven thousand dollars in cash which the wire tappers had been unable to salvage.

All of the gang, except two who managed to escape, were herded to the old courthouse jail on South Andrews Avenue. The bond of $18,000 set by Judge E. C. Davis was quickly given their lawyers, C. E. Farrington of Fort Lauderdale and Price & Price of Miami. The arraigned men gave their names, mostly fictitious, as J. J. Knox, E. J. Sellers, C. Watson, William Fenton, John Ford, Albert Ross, Tom Tracy, John Moore, John Adams, Mike O'Flannagan, Harold Rosen, James Bowden, and H. Cowen. They were mostly middle-aged, well-dressed New Yorkers, not the type commonly associated with racketeers.

The hearing before Judge Davis, when bail was set and furnished, was humorous in the extreme as all the defendants pleaded innocent and one could sense their assurance that they would escape any serious prosecution. And that is the way it turned out. When bail was provided, all in cash, the men were set free and that was the last they were seen in these parts. The beautiful woman companion of the gang's leader, who was active in luring "customers" to the Oliver house, was not held as no specific charge could be placed against her.

When the case was called to trial by Circuit Judge E. B. Donnell of Palm Beach, only the defendants' lawyers were present. They entered guilty pleas for their clients and Judge Donnell fined them $18,000, the exact amount of their bail. It is understood that this money was used as part of the cost of establishing a hospital at the location formerly occupied by the Pine Crest School on East Broward Boulevard.

The report was widespread and it may have been the intention of the county to use the forfeit money for that purpose. No record has been found to verify that this was ever done. However, a Special Enabling Act, sponsored by Representative Weidling, was passed by the state legislature in 1923, empowering and directing the Broward County Commission to buy a hospital or buy real estate to be used as a hospital site, and to erect and own and operate a hospital; to provide a method of taxation; and to provide issuance of interest-bearing warrants of said company or other evidences of indebtedness not exceeding $18,000 for the purpose of borrowing money to carry out the objects of that act.

It was shown that the men had only claimed to be wire tappers. They had set up a fake horse-booking place and the decoys would lure unsuspecting but avaricious visitors by claiming that they had tapped wires giving horse race results. The victims would bet on one of two of these "sure things" and would be allowed to win according to the results posted in the fake bookie room. The greedy victim then would usually send north for a really sizable sum of money and the horse would "win" at large odds. It would then be explained that it was necessary to go to the headquarters of the syndicate in New Orleans to collect the huge winning. The wire tappers would send a man with the victim to New Orleans, but he would slip off the train en route. Because he himself had been cheating, the victim seldom complained to the law.

The gang had, however, contributed, so it was thought, $18,000 toward a much-needed new hospital. In the pioneer days of the city babies were born at home, and emergency operations were performed by Dr. T. S. Kennedy, with or without outside help and usually on kitchen tables. There were hospitals in cities nearby but transportation was, by today's standards, primitive and more dangerous to the patient than even the makeshift arrangements that could be made in the home.

As the 1920's dawned, however, the need for a local hospital was both obvious and urgent. A beginning was made by Dr. Scott Edwards, son-in-law of the Idlewyld developer, Thomas N. Stilwell. Edwards had opened an office in the Wallace apartments on East Las Olas Boulevard between 5th and 6th Avenues in 1921. In 1922 he converted a portion of the building into the city's first hospital. In 1923 James Allison, an Indianapolis financier and a patient of Edwards and Dr. Leslie Maxwell, agreed to finance a modern hospital if these two doctors would take charge. A site on East Broward Boulevard was donated by Mr. and Mrs. Frank Stranahan and the Edwards-Maxwell Hospital was completed in the fall of 1923. After a year of operation, Maxwell sold his interest to Edwards and the institution became known as the Edwards Hospital. In 1925 Edwards moved to Allison Hospital (now St. Francis) on Miami Beach. Dr. Elliott M. Hendricks, an Ohioan, became superintendent of the Fort Lauderdale Hospital and in 1926 Edwards sold it to Doctors R. E. Repass, D. E. Carter, and Maxwell. The name was changed to Memorial Hospital.

In early May of 1927, Fort Lauderdale voters gave a decided 16.5 to 1 negative vote on the proposition that the city purchase Memorial Hospital for $65,000. Of the total vote of 660, there were 616 against, 37 for, and 7 spoiled ballots. The citizens did not desire city ownership of the hospital and made that fact clear and emphatic. The county medical society had suggested the purchase by the city. Some months later, in November of 1927 the hospital was again sold—this time to Dr. S. P. Brush of Jamaica, Long Island. With the depression well under way it was a losing proposition and Brush closed the institution in July of 1929. By this time, however, the Broward Medical Society had bought hospital equipment from the Hollywood Gulfstream Hospital, also closed.

It opened General Hospital in the Mozelle Hotel in the 800 block on South East 2d Court. A few weeks later the Memorial Hospital closed and a year later so did the General Hospital, with most of its services rendered on an "on the cuff" basis. For several weeks the county again had no hospital. Into the breach stepped Mrs. Juanita Gentry Clay, an experienced hospital administrator from Miami. She bought the old Memorial in 1930 and reopened it. It was under her management until 1937.

Charter members of the first Civic Club. (*Front row left to right*): David D. Oliver, Alfred J. Beck, Commodore A. H. Brook, Maxwell Baxter, Dr. John A. Stanford, James S. Rikard, Wm. C. Kyle; (*back row*): John D. Sherwin, M. A. Hortt, Dewitt T. Hart, Asbury D. Marshall, Ed. Hart, Hiram G. Wheeler, Clarence E. Rickard. *Not shown*: Clinton D. Kittredge and John W. Needham (BURGHARD COLLECTION)

By 1922 Fort Lauderdale had been large and interested enough to support its first civic and luncheon club. The Fort Lauderdale Rotary Club received its charter at the Hotel Broward on March 15. It was distinguished by the fact that the Fort Lauderdale Rotary Chapter was located in the smallest city in the country where Rotary clubs then existed.

In 1923 the usually lazy summer saw many strangers on the streets of the city most of whom appeared interested in real estate. Many local businessmen were ready to admit that "things looked good." Both

Casa Sonrienda (house of smiles), luxurious river home of Ida Erkins (GIFT, A. W. ERKINS)

weekly newspapers, the *Herald* and the *Sentinel,* were publishing twice a week, and Colonel George Mathews of the *Sentinel* toyed with the idea of going daily.

A. W. (Bert) Erkins arrived with his mother, Mrs. Ida A. Erkins, and both fell in love with the town. Erkins almost at once began investing in real estate. One of his investments was in building the Towers Apartments on Himmarshee Canal, the city's first large-scale venture in this field. Of perhaps even greater significance was his joining with Hortt in the construction of a new, modern, downtown theater. The new movie house, the Sunset, directly across Andrews Avenue from the Hotel Broward, was opened on Christmas night of 1923 in a blaze of glory. Speeches were made by Mayor R. G. Snow, by R. G. Beekner (Erkins' father-in-law and the lessee of the theater), and by Erkins. Featured picture was "In the Palace of the King" with an all-star cast, and featurettes included a "Felix the Cat" specialty and the latest "Our Gang" comedy. The theater seated eight hundred and was fully equipped for stage productions, including an asbestos curtain replete with a painting depicting Ponce de León discovering the Fountain of Youth. Dressing rooms, lighting, and stage scenery were included and, needless to say, this new facility immediately became a social center and gathering place.

It was reported that Erkins' interest had been aroused by his boating a huge sailfish on a trip from the local docks, a story which Erkins does not seriously dispute. Big game fishing was becoming an increasingly important facet of the winter scene. Another fisherman who landed a big sail at about this time and who remained to become an important part of the town's development was John B. Lochrie. Lochrie caught the fish on his first trip out with Captain J. B. Vreeland. He then purchased from D. C. Alexander beach property overlooking the Intracoastal Waterway for construction of a winter home.

In other fields progress was on the march. The Fort Lauderdale State Bank had grown apace. As banking quarters in Tom Bryan's brick building on Brickell Avenue were too small, a fine new building was erected on the corner of Las Olas Boulevard and Andrews Avenue. The construction job was taken over by the Fuller Construction Company of Boston, one of the nation's largest. At the time of moving, the name of the bank was changed to Fort Lauderdale Bank and Trust Company.

"We are getting in too much of a rush here. City life too fast for me," Frank Stranahan wrote to G. C. Varney on February 24, 1923. The city's rapid growth was, as always, a mixed blessing. Schools were inadequate, traffic was too much for the old narrow streets, and pressure in the city water pipes was distressingly low. The original single-lane bridge over the waterway at the beach was an aggravating traffic bottleneck. New and enlarged facilities were needed in every category of city services and these needs expanded much faster than the increase in tax collections.

Broward County was in a like situation. New roads were imperative. At least one more high school was needed to augment the Fort Lauderdale School, still alone in the county. New elementary schools and a greatly enlarged school bus system were also a necessity. There was an answer—the one reached by most civic bodies in similar situations. Bond issues could be floated for enough money to provide all these present needs and for the foreseeable future. All boards began studies of this possibility.

* * *

National prohibition which had hit with great impact in the North was beginning to be felt. It became increasingly apparent that the Bahama Islands, the closest only fifty miles away, were still British and very wet indeed. It was an easy trip by boat and a few enterprising boatmen started making the run regularly, bringing back cargoes of illicit booze. This fact became known not only to local residents but also to a new breed of lawbreakers throughout the nation, the "bootleggers." With more and more people coming from the North the locals found it easy to sell liquor that cost ten dollars a case on the islands for three and four times that amount.

Drinking in public—frowned on in Fort Lauderdale during its early existence—now began to be fashionable, and nearly every party featured cocktails and highballs made from imported liquors. Women began using their new-found freedom to join the fun. This was the beginning of the "roaring twenties" that were to be populated by "sheiks" and "flappers" wearing, respectively, bell-bottomed trousers and knee-length skirts. Appearance on movie screens of Rudolph Valentino, a well-shaped, slick-haired, dark-eyed Italian with a smouldering expression, was causing women to swoon.

Bootlegging was now a full-scale industry. From a haphazard start it had grown in scope and importance. The local market for "booze" was good and getting better, but was comparatively unimportant. Prices locally were cheap, but in the parched northern and midwestern states good liquor was bringing fantastic premiums. New ways to ship it to the North were constantly devised. One method used successfully for months was that of disguising an entire railroad carload as a shipment of beans. The bootleggers would buy a carload of the winter vegetables and pull it onto a siding beside another railroad car. They would then buy extra hampers and pack them full of booze and place them in the center, with enough beans around the outside to disguise the shipment. Bottles were stuffed into the original bean hampers to replace the beans that had been removed. The cars would then be consigned to a northern vegetable broker who was "in" on the deal. The ruse worked fine until one day when one of the cars got a rough jolt which broke a number of the bottles in the Philadelphia railroad yard. The odor was enough to bring throngs and a great deal of undesired publicity.

Increased bootlegging activity led inevitably to increased efforts on the part of the Coast Guard to apprehend and stop the rum-runners. In 1924 the old House of Refuge property, which had been taken over by the Coast Guard during the war, became United States Coast Guard Base Six, greatly enlarged to accommodate a full crew. That year the Service redug the inlet at its old location and put in protecting jetties. Coast Guard Base Six was located on the southern end of the Fort Lauderdale site, north of the New River inlet, cut through in 1922. The base was established in accordance with Coast Guard Headquarter's letter of June 9, 1924, and was occupied by thirty-three men from the Coast Guard cutter "Yamacraw" in September, 1924. The muster roll shows that the first commanding officer was C. G. Porcher. Shaw and

FORT LAUDERDALE

House of Refuge at beach was taken over by Coast Guard during World War I (VAIL COLLECTION)

Chief Gunner Thrun were Porcher's assistants. Captain P. W. Lauriat succeeded Commander Porcher. There were eight picket boats and four patrol boats, 75-footers. The base was on the houseboat "Moccasin." In February, 1926, the "Moccasin" was towed to Fort Lauderdale and made fast to the wharf, then just built. In September, 1926, the hurricane blew the "Moccasin" across the sound and wrecked it.

Opening and deepening of the inlet was a real boon to the charter boat fleet, now just coming into its own. The old inlet at Lake Mabel Cut, south of today's Port Everglades inlet, had been shallow and treacherous. The new one made practical the use of larger, better boats. The 75-footers of the Coast Guard were slow and cumbersome and the guardsmen were unfamiliar with surrounding waters. They interfered with rumrunning, but by no means halted it. Profits from this "importing" industry were so high that it continued to attract many with capital to acquire fast boats.

* * *

During this period baseball, which had been semipro, became, with few exceptions, all professional, though the team still was not in any officially organized league. The American Legion, after a poor start, had reorganized, and had amateur football and basketball teams on the field. M. Lewis Hall, a young lawyer who had been a college athlete of note, starred in both sports and helped both teams become habitual winners. In 1923 the high school senior class published the first volume of *The*

Part of "Flying L" team that beat Miami in 1925. (*Top, left to right*): Buck G. Geiges, Delmar Portwood, Perry Bryan, Robert Blount, Tom Berryhill, Carl Folsom; (*center*): M. L. Hill; (*bottom*): Robert L. Clark, Sam Marshall, Leonard Jeffrey, Orville Chesire, Charles "Hooks" Gordon (BURGHARD COLLECTION)

"*Flying L.*" It was dedicated to Miss Mary Frances Dawson, English and Dramatics teacher, who was to become Mrs. M. Lewis Hall.

On the baseball field "Sugar" Sweetland was still a top performer. An illustration of the grip he held on the populace is an incident that occurred at the old Westside Ball Park in which the games were then played. Charles Swaggerty, the old White Star Line driver, owned and operated a taxi service consisting of two Model-T Fords. It was the year Ford was advertising his second million cars on the road. On Saturday night Charlie's two cars met head-on on a remote road near Davie, and he was out of business.

It was Sunday and he knew that W. C. Leaird would be at the baseball game. Leaird, a partner of John Pellett in the Ford dealership, was indeed there. The ensuing conversation went about like this: "W. C., I got to have a car. I'm out of business. Let's go over to the garage for just a few minutes and get me one."

"Charlie, we're playing Miami and Sweetland's going to pitch. I'm going to see this ball game before I go anywhere."

99

The discussion ended with Leaird handing Swaggerty the keys to the garage. "Go take any car you want and bring me back the keys— I'll see you after the game."

Elsewhere in town another industry was a-borning: yacht storage in fresh water. Captain George J. Pilkington ran newspaper advertisements about his fine facility, saying among other things that "ferrets were kept to exterminate rats." He claimed accommodations for boats of any size.

In 1923 Broward's first county judge, J. F. Bunn, died and his post was filled by his assistant, Fred B. Shippey. Weidling took a former Ohio schoolteacher, C. N. McCune, into law partnership and they in turn made Carl A. Hiaasen a partner. Weidling had been elected to the legislature in 1923 and served through 1925. He sponsored the first law in the state that made a cattleman responsible for accidents caused by his cows roaming at will across the highways. The bill was passed by the small northern counties merely to humor Weidling. It applied only to Broward—which had then, in effect, no range cattle.

Tom Bryan and S. P. Snyder dissolved partnership and Bryan was now engaged in contracting work in Palm Beach with his new partner, Captain Hampton T. (Hamp) Holloway. The firm was building Connors Highway, which was soon to supplant the last of the boat traffic to Lake Okeechobee. The fastest of the lake boats between Fort Lauderdale and the Lake, Clint M. Stone's "Passing Thru," had made its last regularly scheduled trip on Christmas Eve of 1921, with Lawrence E. Will a passenger.

* * *

From the time of its incorporation, subdivisions had been added to the city of Fort Lauderdale, but until the 1920's they had been of modest proportion. The first big subdivision was Rio Vista. Clarence J. Hector, who with his brother Harry started the Hector Supply Company during early trading days with residents of the Lake Okeechobee region, had acquired title, after a series of lawsuits, to the vast area bounded on the north by New River, on the east and south by Tarpon River, and on the west by 6th Avenue, now Federal Highway. It was high pineland and Hector laid out a huge addition containing twenty-seven blocks and approximately seven hundred lots, many of them river fronts. The subdivision was an almost immediate success.

But of even greater significance to the future of Fort Lauderdale was the development of Idlewyld. This subdivision comprised the easternmost section of the vast mangrove swamp lying along the west shore of New River Sound that separated the city from the beach. The property had been purchased by M. A. Hortt and R. E. (Bob) Dye.

Then Hortt, while bathing at the beach, met Thomas Neil Stilwell of Anderson, Indiana. He pictured to Stilwell the wonders wrought by Carl Fisher at Miami Beach in filling in swampland and suggested to him that the same could be done here. The two made trips to Miami Beach to inspect "Fisher Land," and finally Stilwell agreed to go into the project with Dye and Hortt if his partners in Anderson, William Morsches, Ernest Hill, and Rex Kaufman, were willing. He wired them and they made the trip to Fort Lauderdale. After discussing the proposition and reviewing the land, they agreed and a six-way partnership was formed. This was the first experiment in Fort Lauderdale with "made" land, which for the first two years was only a moderate success. Lots sold slowly. But in 1923 the project "caught fire," and nearly every lot was sold. Until that time the only houses built were those of the partners, but soon nearly all lots were occupied.

At about this time Joseph W. Young announced that he would build a complete city eight miles south of Fort Lauderdale. People were polite about it, but somewhat skeptical.

It was the success of Idlewyld that led to the most significant development in the history of the city. Charles Green Rodes had been a seed-store operator, farmer, and real-estate investor in Fort Lauderdale for years. Among his investments was a parcel of land lying between East Las Olas Boulevard and New River bounded on the west by Sospiro Canal. He decided to become a developer and to fill this land, which was impenetrable mangrove swamp under water at high tide. Rodes found that neither the river nor Sospiro Canal could supply anything approaching the amount of fill needed for his purpose. Therefore he resorted to "finger islanding." This meant dredging a series of parallel canals from Las Olas southward to the river. Thus he created a series of long peninsulas between the canals filled by the spoil taken from these man-made waterways. By putting roads down the middle of each peninsula he evolved a subdivision composed of water-front lots, each with a degree of privacy hitherto unknown, since all streets dead-ended at the river. Rodes did not claim that the idea was original with him. It had, he noted, been used in Venice, Italy, a hundred years before. But it was new here. Rodes fittingly named the subdivision "Venice."

Rodes' system worked perfectly and was largely followed, not only in Fort Lauderdale but elsewhere in Florida and the nation, in subdivisions where low-lying lands had to be filled. Its value in the local scene

Idlewyld and Stilwell Isles, south of East Las Olas Boulevard (BURGHARD
COLLECTION)

was vastly increased because it offered a sound and economical means to
drain away salt marshes, for years prime breeding ground for mosquitoes and sandflies. The plan had the added advantage of being comparatively inexpensive since no floating equipment was needed for the
dredging process. Where Idlewyld had employed suction dredges which
cleaned out the bay bottom to a depth of thirty feet, Rodes used drag-
lines for all except his sea walls. Although his subdivision was platted as
"Venice," Rodes himself unfailingly pronounced the name as "Venus."
It nevertheless gave Fort Lauderdale a new sobriquet, and one well de-
served in the years that followed. Still used in city advertising is "The
Venice of America."

* * *

On December 29, 1911, a dredge working on the canal between Fort
Lauderdale and Lake Okeechobee had churned up the body of a Seminole Indian named De Soto Tiger. Investigation showed that he had
been murdered. Further investigation revealed that Tiger had left the
lake for a trip down the canal to Miami with a load of otter skins and
that he had been accompanied by a young man named John Ashley.
This same John Ashley had later sold twelve hundred dollars worth
of otter skins to Girtman Brothers in Miami. The skins, it turned out,
were the property of the Seminole tribe. A great deal of pressure was
exerted and Sheriff George Baker, of Palm Beach County, sent deputies
to arrest Ashley.

102

Ashley had moved into southeast Florida from Lee County several years before with his father Joe, his mother, four brothers, and four sisters. The family had lived at various places, among them Pompano, where Bob Ashley had already been in minor trouble with the law. Now the entire Seminole nation was aroused and the outcry became so great that John Ashley fled. He stayed in the North for several years but finally returned and, after an exchange of messages, was escorted to jail by Fred Cabot, then a storekeeper at Hobe Sound, and his brother Bill. Ashley was taken to Miami, where his trial for the killing of De Soto Tiger was to be held. This move was made necessary by the fact that after a two-day endeavor the court at Palm Beach had been unable to secure a competent jury.

The Ashleys, who had awaited the result of the trial with confidence, were horrified. Miami was a strange and unfriendly town to them. John broke jail, and the "Ashley Gang" was fast becoming a reality. Their first job was the robbing of the bank at Stuart. Though the job netted the gang forty-three hundred dollars, John was accidentally shot in the jaw, which resulted in the loss of an eye. Forced to hover close to town for medical attention, he was captured and taken to the Dade County jail. On June 2, 1915, Bob Ashley went to Miami to help John again break out. He first went to the home of Deputy Sheriff Wilbur Hendrickson and murdered the man for his keys; but he never reached the jail. In a running battle with police, he and one officer were killed. At this juncture the city of Miami, at large, was threatened with retribution by the Ashley gang if John were not released forthwith.

Meantime, the *Miami Herald* reported that two condemned men in the Dade County jail were busily engaged in chronicling the deeds of Ashley. H. E. Fine of Fort Lauderdale (later acquitted on appeal) and John Ashley were condemned murderers in the county jail awaiting execution. They decided to devote the remaining days of their lives to giving the world a history of Ashley's life. Fine wrote and Ashley dictated, going into the details of his life as an outlaw and bandit. When their story was completed it was to be edited by Deputy Sheriff W. A. Hicks, subject to the approval of Sheriff Dan Hardie. Partial arrangements for publication had been made with a St. Louis publisher. Hicks, appointed to the position held by the murdered deputy sheriff, was to figure prominently in Broward County activities later.

John's trial, strangely, miscarried. Tried in Palm Beach for the bank robbery job, he was sentenced to life imprisonment and sent to Raiford. By 1918 he had escaped, with the help of the gang, which was enlarged from time to time by renegades from other parts. It terrorized the lower east coast for years. They robbed banks, including the one at Pompano, bootlegged, and hijacked. Oddly enough, at some periods there seemed to be a sort of "scared truce" when members of the gang would venture freely into town. Since their hide-outs were in the Everglades, Fort Lauderdale was convenient and they often shopped at local grocery stores. John Ashley himself occasionally came into Fort Lauderdale to "fetch" Dr. Kennedy back to the hide-out to treat members of the family or of the gang.

Perhaps respect was accorded John Ashley on the basis of his expertness with a rifle. Firsthand testimony from such local residents as Tom Bryan and Dr. Kennedy indicated that he was as deadly with this weapon as a man could be. The gang was finally wiped out by an ambush at Sebastian River bridge November 1, 1924, when John Ashley, Hanford Mobley, Ray Lynn, and Rob Middleton were all killed as they "went for their guns."

Left: Dr. Thomas S. Kennedy, first doctor in area, and one of Fort Lauderdale's leading citizens during his long and vital career (GIFT, W. T. KENNEDY)

Right: Frank Stranahan, pioneer and city's first permanent resident. His name stands as a monument to his role in the development of today's Fort Lauderdale (BURGHARD COLLECTION)

Draining of the Everglades was forgotten and the dream of grandeur from this source was laid aside to make way for newer aspirations. Some of the pioneers even foresaw the day when the area between Fort Lauderdale and Miami would be "built up solid." Remembering the debacle of the great Everglades dream, the scoffers—grown fewer—continued to scoff.

Evidence of "frontier frugality" was the policy of letting school athletic teams furnish their own uniforms, via the family route. By 1923, however, the school furnished the uniforms and the students were able to adopt officially the Flying L emblem; one popular on the homemade uniforms of the past. The school had had an athletic field from the start, but it was not until 1919 that a wooden gymnasium was built. This enabled the school to charge admission to basketball games, thus providing funds not hitherto available for the athletic programs. The instance of the athletic uniforms was only a small intimation of the departing spirit of frugality, for the great "boom" was on and like the rest of the nation Florida was in a prime mood to "live it up."

Fort Lauderdale had received a certain amount of national notoriety over the "wire-tapping" incident and various other events but had not really been in the news on a national scale since the great Bolles land lottery debacle. Now, however, northern newspapers were taking note of the area. An aura of excitement, unexplainable at first, crept like some sort of strange hypnosis into people of the region and into visitors who came. A phenomenon, maybe a miracle, was on the verge of coming to pass and the populace could sense it.

Charles G. Rodes (*right*) and part of group he took on coast-to-coast tour

The "Era of Wonderful Nonsense"

Chapter 10
1924–1926

The great Florida "land boom," a phenomenal example of mass hysteria, at times reached such a point that buyers actually battled in frenzy to buy Florida land, any Florida land, anywhere in the state, often sight unseen. The frantic situation puzzled many who lived here, even though they believed wholeheartedly in the area's future. Bewildering to them was the fact that people came, not because they had found a place where they could live a longer and more pleasant life, but actually only for the indiscriminate buying and selling of land for profit. Often real estate was sold several times before the original purchase transaction was actually closed. Many local residents succumbed to the compulsion of overwhelming, unreasoning optimism and joined in the vast speculation which became known nationally as "Florida Fever."

Southeastern Florida had at that time one single-track railroad, the Florida East Coast Railway, and one narrow winding road, the Dixie Highway. The highway was jam-packed with passenger cars and buses bringing tourists and would-be land buyers. Railroad trains ran ten, twenty-four, and thirty-six hours late; freight shipments piled up on the sidetracks. The Inman yards at Jacksonville were filled to capacity with goods sorely needed here. Much of it was never to be forwarded.

Hotels and rooming houses overflowed with tourists and speculators. Tent cities were commonplace. Many newcomers were forced to sleep in cars or on the beach. Florida real estate had suddenly become "the thing to buy," and Yankee dollars flowed in a tidal wave. Promoters and pseudo-developers appeared as if by magic. Some were honorable, some completely unscrupulous. They bought and platted land indiscriminately, sometimes land so low that it was intermittently under water. They sold and resold, sometimes even to each other.

N. B. Cheaney, head of the Broward County Title Company, then the Broward County Abstract Company, recalls that ninety days were required to get an abstract ready for closing, and that he had a backlog of two thousand orders waiting to be serviced. But that did not slow the selling. "Most buyers bought on a sales contract with five or ten per cent down and didn't expect to wait until closing," Cheaney said. "They expected to sell at a nice profit, and to turn over the contract to the new buyer." These contracts were called "binders" and those who dealt in them were known as "binder boys." Prices skyrocketed to undreamed of levels. Cheaney recalls that in 1922 or 1923 he purchased for ten thousand dollars a lot across from the Broward County Court House. Two years later he sold it for fifty thousand dollars. Progresso lots, which sold for a hundred dollars in 1922 and 1923, brought fifteen hundred to two thousand dollars in 1925.

A fifty-foot lot on Las Olas Boulevard at 2d Avenue, having a twenty-five hundred dollar shack on it, brought one hundred and twenty-five thousand dollars from Dr. Dorsey Lewis and his associates. Cheaney said that a forty-acre tract on the ocean front at Pompano Beach which sold for thirty thousand dollars in 1924 commanded over a million dollars by mid-1925. Such sales and such price jumps, were the rule, not the exception. He also pointed out that the Pompano Beach acreage was back down to thirty thousand dollars by 1928-29.

But in the heat of the boom, with riches awaiting in the real-estate field, it is small wonder that it was difficult to find labor for any other kind of work. Almost everyone became at least part-time real-estate

Above: New River home of Mayor W. H. Marshall

Below: Thomas N. Stilwell's home in Idlewyld

Below: Intracoastal waterway home of John Lochrie of Windber, Pa.

Early scene at beach (KELCY PHOTO)

salesmen. Many made fortunes. Most eventually lost them. Harry Mills, a Fort Lauderdale High School student, made twenty thousand dollars one afternoon in a land deal. In this instance he did not wait to lose the money. He spent it.

Northern banks became deeply concerned over vast withdrawals of money for Florida. But these were the "roaring twenties" and the people of the nation were "Charlestoning" their way down the primrose path. That many Floridians developed delusions of grandeur is not surprising. An example was the announcement on December 10, 1925, that the Elks were planning a one hundred and fifty thousand dollar bond issue for a home. William Hicks, exalted ruler, said it was to be located on Valentine (now 3d) Avenue at South River Drive next to the Marshall home. It was never built, except in the enthralled minds of the planners.

Boom-time living in Fort Lauderdale was a far cry from the hard life experienced by the pioneers, in many cases the same people. Now many who had lived in the tar-paper shacks along New River moved into luxurious, if not palatial, Spanish-style mansions. The "dry skiff" that had been standard means of water-borne transportation was replaced by a fine yacht, with shiny brasswork, rich mahogany and teak, and soft lounging pillows. Sleek speedboats whisked, from place to place, the plutocratic old-timers who had had the forethought to buy property, and swank new roadsters, notably that "slick new Chrysler," took the place of the mule and wagon. If residents pinched themselves to see if it

The Angler's Club (KELCY PHOTO)

were real or just a dream, the gladsome message came back that this was only the beginning. Even greater things lay ahead. This was it. This was what they had known must happen.

Of course, there were problems. Rapid growth always brought them. The *Fort Lauderdale Sentinel* of March 14, 1924, reported that "the laying of water pipes through New River sound, or bay, to Las Olas was begun the first of the week. Las Olas has not only the distinction of being the most beautiful beach on the Atlantic, but it also makes Fort Lauderdale the only ocean city on Florida's east coast. . . . On the ocean front, Atlantic Boulevard has been widened to 45 feet from Sunset Avenue [South East 5th Street] to Palm Drive [South East 1st Street] furnishing an ideal auto parking place. . . . John Lochrie's $75,000 residence, the most elaborate in the city, will be started on the ocean end of the avenue within ten days."

Probably the most flamboyant demonstration of wealth was the grandiose project undertaken by Charles G. Rodes, the doughty entrepreneur of the "finger island" system. Rodes chartered a complete Pullman train and invited his relatives to tour the United States from coast to coast. Forty-six responded and were escorted on a trip that included the Grand Canyon, a portion of Mexico, many of the cities of the far West, Yellowstone Park, and other points of interest. E. M. Kelcy, local newspaperman and photographer, accompanied the party to handle publicity for the trip, which began on July 7 and ended August 20, 1925. "The Grand Tour" attracted national publicity, with particularly vivid descriptions in the cities where the caravan stopped.

Another demonstration of wealth was the handsomely constructed Angler's Club on the south end of Mola Avenue overlooking New

River. The club was headed by Commodore A. H. Brook. Almost the entire membership was local, made up primarily of newly rich families. Although it was the scene of many gay boom-time parties, the club became a casualty of the great hurricane and the ensuing depression. The building was eventually purchased by R. H. Gore and remodeled into a home.

Night life, of course, was correspondingly gay, though participants were forced to bring their own, readily available, whiskey. "Big names" abounded in the clubs. Van and Schenck, Sophie Tucker, Paul Whiteman, Blue Steele, Gilda Gray, W. C. Fields, and a host of other top performers entertained.

It was in this period that southeastern Florida gave birth to a professional football league. The money-flush gentry of sporting bent employed the redoubtable Bo McMillan, of the Centre College "Praying Colonels," and many other college stars to play exhibition games. Horse and greyhound racing were introduced in Dade County early in the boom and Pompano was to have a short-lived horse-racing track in 1927.

Golf tournaments were staged with prizes that unfailingly drew most of the greats of the day. Gene Sarazen, Walter Hagen, Jock Hutchison, Bobby Jones, and like company toured the available courses.

Slot machines, though not legal on a money-paying basis, paid off in redeemable merchandise checks and were everywhere. J. A. Portwood and U. S. Cayot of Fort Lauderdale were operators. Portwood was one of the owners of the local poolrooms. Cayot, a building contractor, became interested because of a friendship with Portwood dating back to boyhood days in Kansas. For those who wanted table gambling the Casa Grande was available in nearby Hallandale and ran "wide-open" but, strangely, without sensational play.

South of Fort Lauderdale, Joe Young's mammoth Hollywood-by-the-Sea development was well off the ground. He had completed the Great Southern and Parkview hotels, a golf course, and a number of business buildings and homes, all of which sold like wildfire. The huge multimillion dollar Hollywood Beach Hotel was well under way.

The three-masted schooner "Richmond" tied up at the local docks with three hundred and twenty thousand feet of lumber in early December, 1925, and was delayed five days getting through the inlet at Las Olas sound, because of her deep draft. The "Richmond" was to be a casualty of the great hurricane a year and a half later.

Building was greatly hampered by material shortages. The lone railroad track simply could not supply the demand for freight delivery and

Above: Gulfstream Park in the making. (*Left to right*): Sheriff Walter R. Clark, Promoter Joseph Smoot, Attorney Robinson R. Saunders (GIFT, MRS. R. R. SAUNDERS)

Below: Three-masted schooner sails up New River with building supplies during boomtime freight embargo

Large vessels travel up New River to city docks during boom

still bring in passengers. It was like an army that moves too far ahead of its supply lines. Scores of well-intentioned projects were planned. Many were started. Most were delayed, some even canceled, because of lack of materials. But in the field of real-estate development the city was moving.

W. F. Morang & Son, in a 1923 real-estate sales brochure, waxed almost hysterically eloquent describing Fort Lauderdale: "Here we reach the very apex of scenic climax. Here Mother Nature ceased her efforts to excel herself in the land of tropical luxuriance; for it was here she broke her mold and threw away her palette and easel and stands forever pointing with unerring index finger to the city divided by New River as the Masterpiece of Her Skilled Creation."

William F. Morang, a developer who dreamed on a truly vast scale, came to Fort Lauderdale and at once took over what he could get of the beach. D. C. Alexander had almost sold out, and Morang and his associates joined a group that acquired the property that became Lauder-Del-Mar and helped develop it with great success. From Lauder-Del-Mar Morang moved to Rio Vista Isles, where he dredged canals and built roads and bridges. He also dredged, but did not succeed in completing, what are now the Nurmi Isles extending northward from Las Olas Boulevard.

One of the most unusual of the boom-time events took place on a Sunday morning, when things were otherwise quiet. The Morang company, busy with the construction of Rio Vista Isles, had a huge corral on Ponce de Leon Drive at about South East 8th Street. The corral held upwards of a hundred mules that were used each day in the construction work. On this Sunday one of the mules kicked enough boards out of the fenced enclosure to allow himself and his cohorts to escape. By noon that day the entire population of the city had been alerted and most of the men were engaged in a vast mule hunt and chase. Whether all were safely recaptured and returned was never officially reported.

Meantime, Alfred G. Kuhn was developing Victoria Park. According to the 1925 publicity for the Croissantania Hotel, announced in 1925 by G. Frank Croissant, "A million-dollar hotel—perhaps a two-million-dollar hotel before the plans are finally and officially completed and adopted, of a type different from any other now in existence in America, will before the end of the year be under way in Croissant Park—Fort Lauderdale. Plans are now being prepared under the direction of one of America's most famous architects."

Thomas E. Hoskins, who later became mayor, and a group from Chicago, known as Woods, Hoskins and Young, purchased the vast area south of town and joined with their developer and sales manager, G. Frank Croissant, in platting it. In Croissant Park, at the insistence of Hoskins and his wife, they put in one-hundred-foot streets, rivaling those Young had built in Hollywood.

E. J. (Ned) Willingham, the Georgia pecan and peach grower, joined with M. I. Anglin in the development of Lauderdale-by-the-Sea. In 1923, W. F. Morang & Son, then headquartered in Miami, were the exclusive sales agents for the Willingham properties on Lauderdale Beach. Wilton Manors and the Wilton Manors Boulevard, an extension of Fort Lauderdale's North East 4th Avenue, derive their names from their builder-developer, Willingham.

In the height of the real-estate development on all sides, what is now Harbor Beach was neither neglected nor overlooked. It was an island cut off from the rest of the beach by the old inlet to United States Coast Guard Base Six. Tom M. Bryan had sold the property to Morang, taking back a first mortgage. One of Morang's last projects was to be a bridge at South East 15th Street which would link the prime area of today's Harbor Beach, then part of Lauderdale Harbors, with his Rio Vista Isles. This bridge and causeway would cross the Intracoastal Waterway. The contract for the bridge was awarded to the Champion Bridge Company, and to Hugh Quinn and J. S. Powell, subcontractors, for seventy-five thousand dollars. The fill and causeway approaches were not included in the contract. Powell recalls that when the contract was let in 1925, Morang had thirteen million dollars in his bank account. When the bridge was completed Morang was broke. Powell pointed out that at the time bridge contracts were sometimes let before design and engineering work were completed, and that a bridge was frequently not ready for use for a year or a year and a half after the contract was received.

The 15th Street span was completed, and with both ends of the bascule open and pointing skyward it stood as a marine-type monument to the bursting of the boom. The "bridge to nowhere" stood gaunt and

Lonely bridge spanned Stranahan river at South East 15th Street (GIFT, HUGH LANGSTON)

alone, its approaches and causeway never completed. Finally, the deepening and widening of the Waterway weakened the foundations. One side collapsed and the government paid Powell to remove the structure. He received only one-third of his contract price for erecting the bridge, but a decade and a half later he was paid to remove the structure.

The one piece of choice land that remained untouched was the two-mile stretch of ocean frontage owned by Hugh T. Birch. Birch, a semi-recluse, had created a wonderland of natural beauty on his property but hated intrusions. He adamantly refused to discuss selling. He did grant, reluctantly, a road right-of-way along the front or ocean side of his property; but when it came time to put in the light poles he rebelled. During the daytime Birch and his loyal servant "Old Jeff" patrolled the area with shotguns. The work had to be done at night. Birch, white-bearded and usually genial, bitterly resented these encroachments and later found a way to make the fact known.

In the meantime, Arthur T. Galt, another Chicagoan and son of Birch's law partner, had bought eight thousand acres of land, most of it across the Intracoastal Waterway north from Birch's holdings, but including a mile of ocean front. Galt now sold it to the American British Improvement Company, a firm that included in its directorate members of the British nobility, Lords Thirlestane and Boulton, and such socially prominent Americans as Mrs. E. T. Stotesbury, Mrs. Horace Dodge, James H. R. Cromwell, and Samuel Vauclain. Most of this group wintered in Palm Beach.

Here is the way the *Morning Sun* of February 18, 1926, told of a cornerstone laying: "A large gathering of persons prominent in the winter social world of Palm Beach and Fort Lauderdale witnessed the laying of the cornerstone of the Floranada Inn, on the Plaza Algre at Floranada Club, at 4 o'clock, Wednesday afternoon. . . . The Countess of Lauderdale, Mrs. Horace E. Dodge, and Mrs. E. T. Stotesbury assisted laying the foundation of concrete for the cornerstone, while the stone itself was put into place by Lord Thirlestane and James H. R. Cromwell, president of Floranada Club."

A new town to be called Floranada was designed. A golf course was laid out and brought to playable condition. Clubhouses were built and much survey work was done. Speedboats were purchased for use in waterways yet to be constructed. A narrow-gauge railroad was ordered. At that point, the project died away. A few lots were sold but the money was eventually refunded to the purchasers.

The end of this "era of wonderful nonsense" was heralded, according to N. B. Cheaney, by an action of N. B. T. Roney, who had built the Roney Plaza Hotel in Miami. Roney purchased land on the ocean near Hallandale and platted it as "Seminole Beach." When it was offered for sale, the "binder boys" bought up about a third of it on their usual contracts. A month later Roney lowered the prices on his lots, leaving the binder operators with contracts to pay more than the prices at which lots were being publicly offered. This marked the end of the "binder boys." They disappeared, and not long behind them in leaving were the unscrupulous developers and the high-pressure salesmen who had sold lots to hopeful speculators all over the nation, often using only a beautifully drawn plat of what "was to be" for the sales pitch. Although eventual catastrophe erased much of the credit for it, the great land boom produced many innovations and developments that were needed and well designed to promote the progress of Fort Lauderdale.

Among these was the formation of the first Planning and Zoning Board on December 8, 1925. The board, originally composed of five members, was formed upon the insistent request of the Chamber of Commerce. The members were: Clarence E. Rickard, Mrs. Frank

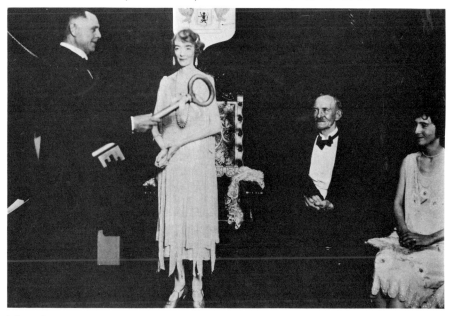

The Countess of Lauderdale receives key to city from Mayor John W. Tidball

Stranahan, Commodore A. H. Brook, E. N. (Chief) Sperry, and E. J. Willingham. It was a significant forward step for the city.

Duties of this board were extended in 1940 to include the group's sitting as a board of adjustment to pass on cases in which variances in the zoning laws were sought. The usefulness of this board since its original establishment has rarely, if ever, been questioned. Among the first moves taken was recognition of the need for a definite city plan for future expansion. This was accomplished through the employment by the city of Richard Schermerhorn to draw up a master city plan, the city's first.

Less than a year after the board was formed, the 1926 hurricane demonstrated not only the value of adequate planning but also the need for implementation of a strict building code. But the planning and the building code had little effect during the actual boom and bust.

Part of the sudden demise in land speculation was due to the unrelenting pressure from northern banks. Newspapers in the North joined with them. N. B. Cheaney tells of being in Pittsburgh for the World Series of 1925 when the boom was at its height. He was surprised to see a newspaper with a banner headline reading: "Florida Fears Slump."

He still had his backlog of 2,000 customers waiting to get closing papers on lands they had purchased. But by July of 1926 indications were

Magnificent Spanish-style clubhouse at golf course, 1927

much plainer. He found his office posting 60,000 pieces of property on which taxes were unpaid.

* * *

By a vote of the people, Fort Lauderdale on June 9, 1925, had adopted the city-manager form of government. A little later "high-powered" Blanchard J. Horne, a professional city manager, was employed at an annual salary of $10,000. Horne and the city's engineers completed a survey of city needs under the new plan and came up with a proposed bond issue to cover everything. The total amount called for was $3,340,000.

On August 3, 1926, the freeholders voted 717 to 63 in favor of the issue which Mayor J. W. Tidball and the commission had authorized. Sums earmarked included: $1,500,000 for sanitary sewers; $515,000 for a water plant and extensions; $75,000 for a sewage disposal plant; $50,-000 for an incinerator; $150,000 for streets; $250,000 for docks; $125,-000 to replace the old Las Olas drawspan with a double-lane bridge, and to build a causeway to replace the old wooden bridge leading to it; $175,000 for a golf course and parks; other improvements, some of which had been begun under previous issues, were also provided for.

Included in the projected improvements were a new beach casino and the golf course clubhouse, designed by Francis Abreu, a top expert on Spanish-style buildings. Only the exterior, the exquisite upstairs dance hall, porches, the men's locker room, and the dining room of the golf club were completed according to Abreu's plan. The club was west of the city and is today's Fort Lauderdale Country Club.

The end of speculation and the consequent decline in property values did not greatly concern the more substantial elements of the city. As they saw it, the fervid buying of the "quick buck" operators had not produced permanent profit to themselves, and the eventual growth of the city was not materially affected. The conditions that brought about the boom in the first place still existed with almost all facilities greatly improved. If people from other places wanted to live in a community where they could enjoy a better way of life, then every necessary element was at hand.

A major advancement came about when the new steel bridge spanning New River at East Avenue, the Federal Highway, was thrown open for public use on August 26, 1926. It was to be operated by Broward County as transportation facilities were improved.

People as a whole remained confident. They reasoned that perhaps a little breathing spell until they got the double-track Florida East Coast and the new Seaboard railroads and the water and sewer systems and the new golf course would be just what was needed. All these projects and additional street improvements were now under way but materials were still in short supply.

The "Prinz Valdemar," a steel yacht once reputedly owned by German Kaiser Wilhelm, mysteriously sank across the mouth of the harbor at Miami. This disaster effectively shut off a major entry source of building materials. Even old square-riggers and "Chesapeake Bay Ram Schooners" had been pressed into service to bring lumber to southeast Florida. Now they lay to helplessly off the Miami coast, unable to reach the docks on the last commercial voyage most of them were to make.

With passenger traffic slowed up, the railroad brought in some, though not enough, building supplies. As the summer of 1926 advanced, most of the city and county improvements were well under way or completed.

Several large hotel and apartment projects were still in the offing. These included William H. Marshall's Wil-Mar Hotel (now the Governors' Club) at South East 1st Avenue and Las Olas. The steel and concrete skeleton was up and the floors were in, but there matters rested. Work on the Wil-Mar halted, not only because of the lack of materials, but because payments due Marshall on lands he had sold were not coming in on schedule.

Another hotel at the east end of Aqua Vista, to be built by Morang in his Lauderdale Isles, was as far along as preliminary foundation work and a huge pile of lumber on the site. The Croissantania had walls up but no roof. Churches were hit by the same material shortages.

Cost of labor and building materials began to lessen. Many buildings erected during the height of the boom were substandard because of the lack of materials and competent labor. These conditions were now easing.

The city outgrew its old quarters and a new city hall was built on the property immediately north of the old one on ground now occupied by Burdine's Department Store. The library, having outgrown its space in the Woman's Club, was moved into the old city hall building.

In Fort Lauderdale, Southside, Eastside, and Westside Elementary schools were built and the original school was renamed Central School. Southside and Westside fire stations were added.

The dream of a deepwater harbor to serve Fort Lauderdale had stirred residents of the area from the beginning of the great Everglades drainage project. Along with the prospect of vast agricultural production had come a realization of the difficulties to be overcome to gain proper transportation. As early as 1912 Samuel L. Drake had appeared before the town council with a plan to induce the War Department to construct such a harbor. Drake then contended that what the city needed as inducement was ownership of water-front property, and Mayor W. H. Marshall had offered 300 by 300 feet on the north bank of New River as a donation. But the effort died a-borning.

The dream persisted even after it became apparent that draining of the Everglades was not to be immediately accomplished. It was brought to fruition in 1926, largely through the efforts of Joseph W. Young. Under the plan developed, the cities of Hollywood and Fort Lauderdale were each to issue $2,000,000 in bonds to be used in the project, and the Young interests were to underwrite the balance at a cost not to exceed a total of $6,000,000.

This was an unusual tripartite agreement between two corporate bodies, Fort Lauderdale and Hollywood, and J. W. Young, an individual. The two bond issues were to be taken over by a port authority to be established by an act of the 1927 legislature.

On August 3, 1926, Fort Lauderdale freeholders voted approval. Hollywood already had taken similar action. The site of the new port was to be Lake Mabel, about halfway between the two cities, as then constituted, and one that had been recommended to Henry Flagler by E. T. King before the turn of the century.

Lake Mabel (so named by M. W. Williams and his son Arthur T.) was a natural body of water, roughly 2,700 by 3,400 feet and was separated from the ocean by a narrow strip of land varying in width to a maximum of 200 yards. The lake was shallow and would need dredging, but since fill was urgently needed for the swampy shore line this was a "natural." Much of the land surrounding it was owned by Young and was to be contributed by him as part of his share of the cost.

The port was to be dug to 35-feet minimum depth at low tide, with jetties, turning basin, and one slip to be built in the exact center so that one side would be in Hollywood and the other in Fort Lauderdale. Signing the agreement for Fort Lauderdale were W. C. Kyle, J. W. Tidball, Tom M. Bryan, and Horace C. Stilwell; for Hollywood, I. T. Parker, Harry B. Hutchison, Frank C. Dickey, C. C. Freeman, and L. O. Casey. Young signed as an individual and as president of Hollywood Land and Water Company, Home Seeker's Realty Company, Hollywood Development and Harbor Company, and Hollywood Dredging and Construction Company.

Plans were drawn by F. C. Dickey, Hollywood engineer. They were duly approved by the War Department and work got under way. In 1926 the depression was already being felt along the lower east coast. To combat this was one of the stated objectives of the port; it would offer much needed work and "stabilize land values."

More years lay ahead before the port could be put to actual use. Plans included a completely workable harbor with direct access to the Florida East Coast Railway. Besides its minimum depth of 35 feet and turning basin 200 by 1,200 feet, it had a slip with 2,700 lineal feet of dock space, an adequate all-steel warehouse, and an entrance channel 200 feet wide. All these were convenient to near-by shipping lanes.

* * *

Local developments continued. The First National Bank building was to be finished about July 1, 1926. Tom M. Bryan had sold his Light and Ice Company to Southern Utilities. He had later repossessed and sold it again to the Florida Power and Light Company. A force of 500 men was working steadily on the mammoth power plant of the Florida Power and Light Company, four miles west and south of downtown Fort Lauderdale.

Ulric J. Bennett, to become principal of the Fort Lauderdale high school, arrived in town in June. He later became superintendent of education for Broward County.

121

Board of realtors arranged tours of Port Everglades development

Fort Lauderdale was growing in spite of the slowdown in property sales, but it was going deeper into debt. In addition to the roughly $3,500,000 owed on municipal bonds, the city, which then occupied more than half the taxable property of the county, owed its share of what amounted to more than half of a total $7,500,000 bonds in issues of the school board, county, and new port authority. Other taxing entities, which included the city, were the Everglades Drainage District and the Napoleon B. Broward Drainage District.

The amount was not considered too high in the light of vastly increased property values, which had gone up even faster than the city's debt in the preceding two years. Bonding houses that handled the issues considered them sound and recommended them to their customers.

The City Bank of Fort Lauderdale, which had opened June 2, 1925, closed its doors just over a year later. The closing stimulated the following reassuring editorial from the *Fort Lauderdale Greetings:*

The day of real test always comes to an individual, a city, a state, and a nation. That test came to Fort Lauderdale last Saturday, following the suspension that morning of the City Bank.

The First National Bank and the Fort Lauderdale Bank and Trust Co. experienced small runs for the first two hours Saturday morning, but by eleven o'clock the nervousness had appreciably calmed down, for all demands of depositors were cheerfully met and the officers of both institutions handled the situation with admirable good sense.

The closing of the City Bank is thoroughly regrettable, but the situation has been and will be wisely handled, and its reopening is highly probable; at any rate, the interests of depositors will receive the most careful consideration.

Shrewd businessmen such as Bryan, Hortt, Dye, and others realized that property values had gone too high and that a further decline might be expected, but they saw no reason to fear the future. Both of the city's banks were apparently in excellent shape and their loans amply secured—on paper at least.

The Broward Building and Loan Association, which had been established in 1922 with R. E. Dye as president, C. P. Weidling as vice president, and A. J. Merrill as secretary-treasurer, was equally "secure," handling only first mortgages on developed property. By June of 1926 the First National Bank had moved into its new building, the city's first skyscraper and today's Sweet building.

It was during the boom that Fort Lauderdale reached the peak of its size, geographically. Vast plans for the future indicated the necessity for expanding the city limits; ground was annexed in all directions with the incorporated limits finally reaching a·peak of 43 square miles in 1926. This represented nearly 30 times the original 1.5 square miles and was well nigh 50 per cent above the present-day 30.7.

Local businessmen felt that cessation of the wild speculation by no means meant that they had "builded a house of straw." But by September of 1926 many of the developers were low on ready cash. Young, for instance, who was continuing his development of Hollywood at full speed, went to New York in mid-September to negotiate a loan of $7,000,000. He intended to go to Philadelphia to see the Dempsey-Tunney fight. He reached an agreement with the bankers on the loan by September 17. The fight was September 23. There was no hurry. W. F. Morang, with millions in assets, shut down some of his development programs pending a return to "normalcy." Other developers were feeling the squeeze to a greater or lesser degree and some were in real trouble.

One of the new buildings that had reached near completion was that of the Pioneer Department Store. This firm had bought out the old Oliver Brothers store on Brickell Avenue, which for so many years had competed with H. G. Wheeler and Company and, later, Free and Lehrman, for the town's clothing and equipment business.

The new Pioneer, headed by Dr. J. A. Stanford, J. S. Hinton, and Lamar Thistlethwaite, built a four-story building on the southeast corner of South East 1st Avenue and Las Olas (now the Radio Center building) and opened for business on May 13, 1926.

In the meantime, D. D. (Dave) Oliver of Oliver Brothers and his brothers, Frank and Jim, had joined E. R. Heimburger of the Fort Lauderdale Mercantile Company in the start of today's Peninsular Supply Company, a wholesale plumbing firm. The firm was first called South Florida Builders Supply Company. D. D. Oliver eventually bought out his brothers' interest in the firm, which was to become the largest of its kind in the state.

Colonel George Mathews had stepped up publication of his *Sentinel* to twice a week, a step likewise taken by Weidling and John Sherwin of the *Herald;* but in late September of 1924 Mathews had taken the big step and the *Evening Sentinel* became a daily. Shortly thereafter, Mathews changed the name to the *Fort Lauderdale Daily News and Evening Sentinel.* The paper was printed in a two-story building Mathews erected on the back of the lot occupied by his home on South East 1st Avenue at South East 5th Street. Mathews continued to publish for several months before selling the paper to the Galvin brothers of Lima, Ohio, who bought out the *Herald* and combined it with the parent paper, moving the operation into the new Sherwin building on South East 2d Street at 2d Avenue. During the early days of the newspaper both advertising and circulation were listed as "more than satisfactory."

Now the hand of fate was to turn against the still high-spirited optimists of southeastern Florida. The carefree gayety that had reigned for so many months was already gone, but now hope itself was to be dealt a mighty blow. The stage was set, but this time tragedy was to tread the boards.

South Andrews Avenue business section after hurricane

The 1926 Hurricane

All but unnoticed were ominous headlines proclaiming that a mighty storm was hovering over the near-by Bahamas and threatening the Florida coast. What had been called a "hurricane" had hit the area only a few weeks before, but the name was misapplied to merely a severe summer squall or "tropical disturbance" with winds that reached briefly some seventy miles per hour. This experience served to increase the feeling of security held by the townspeople. Most were newcomers who had never seen a hurricane. But old-timers, who *had* seen them, were almost equally undisturbed. They remembered precautions taken in the past but did not comprehend that conditions were different. Their old frame houses with pitched roofs were well designed to withstand high winds, but now there was newer "jerry-built" construction. Moreover, although a light hurricane had moved across the state south of Fort Lauderdale in 1913, there had been none since. Memories fade. As the fateful day approached life was moving apace and the people were moving with it.

Chapter 11
1926–1928

125

FORT LAUDERDALE

M. A. Hortt, pioneer real-estate man, had made so much money that he was sure he would never have to work again. He had spent the summer of 1926 honeymooning in Europe and returned home to Fort Lauderdale with his bride the morning of September 17.

Emmett Dye—son of Hortt's partner, R. E. Dye—had just come home to the city from a hitch in the Marines, largely spent in the Orient. Emmett was the proud possessor of his first property, a lot on North East 3d Avenue. "Aside from that," he told friends, "I'm standing in the middle of my trunk."

Tom Bryan had gone to Baltimore to inspect dredges proposed for work on Port Everglades. He planned to join J. W. Young later in New York and to go to Philadelphia with him to see the Dempsey-Tunney fight.

Sara Mathews, daughter of the publisher and the town's first girl reporter, had married Charles Crim, a young lawyer, and they had proudly moved into a new bungalow in "Venice."

The D. C. Alexanders, with their young daughter Betty Lou, had returned from Ohio to reopen the house they had built on the ocean in their almost sold-out Las Olas-by-the-Sea. When they arrived they took delivery on a brand-new Chrysler sedan, drove it home, and put it in the basement garage. That afternoon, September 17, 1926, Mrs. Alexander, while watching her servant clean windows, noticed gusts of wind becoming stronger and more frequent. The sky was a sodden heavy gray. But, busy with house cleaning, she paid little attention to the weather. Home radios were not commonplace and such a thing as a hurricane did not enter her mind.

As the Alexanders sat down to their evening meal they realized that the intensity of the storm was increasing. They were still up at midnight, listening to the wind howling and shrieking about the house, when abruptly the electric power went off. Soon they heard glass breaking. Thirty-four of the thirty-six windows in the house blew out. The front door burst open and swung violently on its hinges, the doorknob knocking a large hole in the plaster wall. Rain and sand swept through the downstairs. "We'd better get out of here," said Mr. Alexander's father. The homeowner grimly pointed out a window. Water had risen above the level of the ground and no land was in sight. Only the tops of wildly swaying trees and a few roof tops were visible. Leaving the house was out of the question. The family went upstairs and found Betty Lou's room still comparatively dry. They waited there for what might happen. Daylight came with sullen reluctance and winds still blew strongly though now from the opposite direction and subsiding. The house had stood. It and its furnishings were badly damaged, but it withstood the hundred and twenty-mile wind without structural damage. The Alexander's beach tennis court was buried under several feet of sand.

Sara and Charlie Crim and their one-year-old daughter Patsy were not so lucky. The little home in Venice could not withstand the wind and they fled in terror, reaching her parents' home in safety. This stronger house, a two-story building, was of sturdy frame with a hip roof. The family was forced by high water to seek refuge on the second floor. During the height of the storm a portion of the roof blew off and they spent the remaining hours of the storm packed together in a clothes closet.

C. P. Weidling had bought a house built by Ed King many years before at 515 South East 6th Avenue. It was of reinforced poured concrete and more than eight inches thick. Quickly, it became a makeshift storm shelter and neighbors from all directions found haven there.

The *Fort Lauderdale Daily News* of September 19, 1926, said that "following the declaration of martial law by Mayor Tidball, all available food was commandeered, and taken to the Masonic Temple where it was dispensed to those who were in need, on requisitions issued at the city hall. Prepared food and coffee and milk for children were also distributed." By noon of September 18 the sun was shining benignly and the southeast breeze was gentle and balmy. The storm had ended, but the nightmare was just beginning.

In his Philadelphia hotel room Tom Bryan read a headline in his newspaper: "Southeastern Florida Wiped Out." He tossed the newspaper to his companion, City Attorney M. Lewis Hall. "Looks like they had another hurricane down there. These newspapers sure have it in for us. I've been through lots of hurricanes—they don't wipe things out." Hall was more concerned. He sent out for more papers and all confirmed the hurricane story. "We'd better get back home," said Hall. They waited for another batch of papers before returning to New York to see Young, only to find that his private train had already set off for Florida. His seven-million-dollar loan negotiations had been canceled. Bryan and Hall started home, bribing their way for space on a train.

Seven identified and one unknown dead were counted in Fort Lauderdale after the hurricane. Ultimately fifteen dead at Fort Lauderdale, twenty-five at Hollywood, nine at Dania, and fifteen hundred injured were reported at Fort Lauderdale. The seven identified dead and one unidentified dead lay in the temporary morgue established at Griffith &

New clubhouse hit by hurricane while under construction

Philbrick Undertaking Parlors on East Avenue (Federal Highway) Sunday morning and a number of others were taken to temporary morgues established about the city, according to the *Fort Lauderdale Daily News* of September 19, 1926.

Fort Lauderdale residents were out viewing the wreckage, picking up their dead, and succoring the injured. One of the saddest of the tragedies occurred at the small church at South Andrews Avenue and 6th Street. Several families had taken refuge there and the concrete block structure was blown down, block by block. Many were injured and some were killed in the church.

Owing to the lack of power in Fort Lauderdale and the damage to the *Daily News* plant, the type for the September 20 issue of the *Daily News* was set at Lake Worth through the courtesy of the *Lake Worth Leader* and *Lake Worth Herald*.

Emmett Dye was one of the lucky ones. A house blew onto his vacant lot. He later dug a septic tank, piped it to the bathroom, connected wiring, and lived in the "found" house for years, never once hearing from the former owner. Tom Bryan's seaplane was found in the middle of Idlewyld under a seventy-five-foot Coast Guard cutter, and furniture from Idlewyld homes was discovered in Colee Hammock. The houseboat of the United States Coast Guard, the "Moccasin," was torn from its moorings, dashed across the sound and piled on the ground half way out of the water on the bulkheading in Idlewyld.

The great mystery was how so many people had managed to survive. Houses were blown down, washed off foundations, and some rolled over and over. Loose lumber from the many building projects had flown

Wreckage left by hurricane (KELCY PHOTO)

through the air in wild profusion. Practically every house and building in town suffered damage. Live electrical wires swayed crazily in the wind before the master switch was cut.

Mayor John W. Tidball, issued the following proclamation: CAUTION —Boil all drinking water. City water to be had at the following stations: City Hall; East Side, West Side and Central Schools. Get chloride of lime and directions for use at City Hall. Keep children from wading water and mud. Have all wounds treated immediately by physician. Report uncared for, injured and dead at Masonic Temple. Report missing persons and description at City Hall. Burn refuse and vegetation, first obtaining permit from Fire Department.

It was a situation in which even next door seemed remote. Each household had only the briefest time to decide whether to stay at home or seek better shelter. The number of houses completely destroyed was mercifully low. Most homes, even those without roofs, provided a modicum of shelter from the vicious wind with its burden of rain, salt spray, and flying fragments of debris. Stories of heroic action were many. For example, Dr. Leigh F. Robinson said, in a story about Broward County doctors and their medical society:

FORT LAUDERDALE

Until the storm abated, those of us whose houses had not been blown away and who still had roofs over our heads, had no idea of the extent of property destruction. When we could venture out without being blown away, we found great havoc. On the street just north of us, one of our closest friends was alone with her three-year-old child and her Dominican maid. She was pregnant and within two weeks of term. Her husband was away on business and as soon as it was humanly possible I went to investigate how they had fared. As I approached the house, mostly on my hands and knees, I saw most of the roof was gone and the front windows were out. The door was jammed so I entered through a window. I found the mother, the child, and the maid huddled in the kitchen which fortunately, still had a roof, and while the water was inches deep and more was coming in, there was none from the ceiling. I remained with them until the wind subsided enough to take them to our house. Before leaving, the mother told her maid to gather up all the clothing she could carry, and follow. But the only thing she brought with her was the husband's golf trophy which she explained by saying he had told her no matter what happened, never to let it out of her sight. This incident brought us out of our doldrums and we all had a good laugh. But the poor husband never heard the last of it.

Some of the millionaires of 1925 had found an outlet for newly found wealth in building the Rainbow Roof Garden at 3d Avenue and East Las Olas Boulevard. This roof garden, where Lady Lauderdale was lavishly entertained during her visit from Scotland in more auspicious days, was blown away. The Angler's Club, gathering place of the elite, was so badly damaged that it was never reopened. The city had had a new theater, the Garden Court, in the 300-block of East Las Olas Boulevard, opened in August of 1926. Hurricane damage caused it to close a little more than a month later.

None of the bridges over the river could be opened, because of lack of power. Only slight damage was done to the new East Avenue (Federal Highway) span. The Andrews Avenue bridge lost most of its guard railings and the traffic control systems; and the control house, which rested at the south span, was blown over and wrecked. None of the three spans of the pontoon bridge was washed away, but all were damaged.

The bridge across the New River Sound to the beach was impassable by automobile. The loss of trees and shrubbery was great. Mountainous waves which swept Las Olas Beach during the worst hours of the hurricane Saturday morning failed to wash down any of the beach residences, and claimed only one life. The thirty-year-old grove of coconut palm

Ocean front took a beating in great storm (BURGHARD COLLECTION)

trees, which made the historic Las Olas Inn one of the most picturesque spots in Broward County, was blown down and uprooted. Australian pines back of the Inn were also destroyed. Waves swept through the lower part of the Inn building destroying practically everything on that floor. A four-inch deposit of sand was left on the upper floor. Small fish were swept through the lobby and out the rear. The Sentinel Palm, the landmark at New River Inlet, was downed. Fallen trees and utility poles made roads in all directions unusable.

Train service was restored on a limited basis by the nineteenth, but wire communications were cut off completely for several days. Looting, mainly for food, began almost at once. The police force went on twenty-four-hour duty but was entirely inadequate. Into this breach came the Coast Guard with scores of armed men. County and city crews worked clearing roads.

Doctors in the community organized themselves into a relief unit with a territory assigned to each man. By this time, the city's population had divided into groups to eat and sleep in the least damaged houses and to work together clearing debris and repairing damage. Red Cross relief trains began to arrive as the nation rallied to assist the stricken area.

A check of the water front revealed that few, if any, boats along the city docks escaped damage. The "Billy, Jr.," W. C. Kyle's yacht, was sunk. Captain Mortensen's "Arab" rode out the storm practically un-scathed. Lying in South Andrews Avenue one hundred fifty feet from the river bed was a twenty-five-foot power cruiser. The "Gadfly" rested on top of Henry Brook's sailboat "Seamew," and other power cruisers were smashed. The "Arletta" lay high and dry on her starboard side on the North River Drive docks. The Sea Scout's yawl "Companion" had

FORT LAUDERDALE

Once beautiful grove of coconut palms at Las Olas Inn (GIFT, MRS. LEAIRD RICKARD)

its mainmast snapped off at the crosstrees. Most of the boom-time yachts and speedboats were battered or sunk by the storm, and many expensive automobiles were destroyed. The Alexanders found their ride from the station was the only trip they would ever make in their new Chrysler. Completely buried in sand, it was later dug out and towed to the junk yard. The family yacht was also a total loss.

Franklin D. Roosevelt kept a log of the "Larooco" and gave this dramatic account:

In September 1926 a violent hurricane swept the east coast of Florida. The houseboat "Larooco" was laid up at the Pilkington Yacht Basin, about 2 miles up the Fort Lauderdale River. This was near the center of the hurricane area. Most of the yachts were in the big shed and were destroyed when the river rose and the shed collapsed. "Larooco" was moored outside along the bank and made fast to two palm trees. As the river rose above its banks, the two trees were pulled up by the roots and "Larooco" started inland on her last voyage. Driven by the hurricane, and disregarding river course or channel, she finally brought up in a pine forest four miles inland and as the waters receded she settled down comfortably on the pine needles, at least a mile from the nearest water. As the old strains to the hull were made worse, salvage was impracticable, and she was offered for sale as a hunting lodge—and finally sold for junk in 1927. So ended a good old craft with a personality. On the whole it was an end to be preferred to that of gasoline barge or lumber lighter.

The following is a copy of the official report of the September 14-20,

132

The 1926 Hurricane: 1926-1928

1926, hurricane as written and filed by R. W. Gray, Official in Charge of the Miami Office of the United States Weather Bureau at that time. In part it read:

There was a steady increase in wind velocity from that time to 5 A.M., when the anemometer recorded a maximum velocity of 80 miles, indicating a true velocity of at least 115 miles per hour. The top of the raingage blew off at 3:42 A.M., and was recovered and replaced by Mr. C. B. Moseley, Jr., the assistant at this station. It was again blown off a few minutes later and lost.

A Robinson anemometer on the roof of the Allison Hospital, Miami Beach, connected with a Weather Bureau type triple register, made by Julien P. Friez & Son, recorded a maximum velocity of 128 miles per hour from the east or southeast at 7:30 A.M. The extreme velocity cannot be determined from the record, but it was probably between 140 and 150 miles per hour. The anemometer blew away at 8:12 A.M., at which time it was recording 120 miles per hour.

The intensity of the storm and the wreckage that it left cannot adequately be described. The continuous roar of the wind; the crash of falling buildings, flying debris, and plate glass; the shriek of fire apparatus and ambulances that rendered assistance until the streets became impassable; the terrifically driven rain that came in sheets as dense as fog; the electric flashes from live wires have left the memory of a fearful night in the minds of the many thousands that were in the storm area.

The property loss in the greater Miami area has been estimated at $76,-000,000. This does not include damage to house, store and office furnishings. Approximately 4,725 homes were destroyed and 9,100 damaged in the area extending from Fort Lauderdale to Miami. There were 25,-000 persons without shelter after the storm.

August Burghard, a reporter for the *Fort Lauderdale Daily News*, was assigned to write a hurricane story for the September 27 issue, based on his observances made during a flight over the damaged area:

Build for yourself a toy city—a beautiful little city with tiny palm and pine trees for shade. Make the buildings of a gay color and put bright roofs on them. Stretch a winding ribbon of a river through it and put in miniature lakes and parks. Then—with an angry sweep of your hand—tear your little city to pieces, pour muddy water over the houses and into the fields, strew boats from the stream along the banks. Twist it and wrack it. Shake it like a terrier shakes a rat, and leave many of its citizens half dead and dying. Make the angry sweep of your hand very angry and then—stand up and view it. Resulting confusion and destruction will give you an excellent idea of how Fort Lauderdale,

133

FORT LAUDERDALE

Dania, Hollywood and Davie looked from the air after the devastating storm of last Friday night and Saturday morning.

Merle L. Fogg, former pilot for Tom M. Bryan's seaplane, arrived in Fort Lauderdale Friday afternoon from Troy, N.Y., in a 1,050-pound Waco land plane. Saturday morning he flew two *Fort Lauderdale Daily News* reporters over the storm struck territory of Broward County and for the first time a comprehensive idea of the totality of the destruction was gained. Rising from the temporary land field in Lauderdale Isles Fogg hovered over the wrecked Las Olas Beach section. Broken bits of sea wall, sections of sidewalk along Ocean Boulevard, giant pieces of timber along the beach and pieces of wrecked barges and boats which had been blown ashore looked like a pigmy playground wrecked by a petulant child.

Further south on the beach lay the three-masted Mills and Mills schooner "Richmond." The vessel was blown 50 feet on the shore above the high-water line and dragged eight tons of anchor and anchor chains and lines after her. She lies on her side with a "broken back."

Dredges which had been working in Bay Mabel building Port Everglades were floated to points high and dry back of the present water line. During the storm Lake Mabel and the ocean were one body of water. One or two bridges over the inland waterway were also floated away from their former positions.

The plane circled over the Hollywood Beach hotel and the casino section. From the air the big hotel showed only slight damage to the roof and to the several ornamental tower effects. In the body of water in front and to the right of the hotel facing Hollywood a two-story house with water up to the top of the first-story windows could be seen. Power craft which evidently had been tied up at docks along this body of water were sighted 20, 30 and 40 feet from water.

Dania presents one of the most completely wrecked views from the air of any community. Buildings were not only unroofed and blown down here, but a two-story house had actually turned upside down, the roof being on the ground and the first floor in the air.

Carrying out the idea of the wrecked toy village the large lumber mill in Hollywood on the Florida East Coast railway was a match box with the matches scattered all over the floor. Pieces of the roof could be seen far across the right-of-way.

Davie out-Venices Venice. She not only has canals for streets, but has water all round and in her scattered houses. A rowboat would be needed to get within 50 feet of the schoolhouse and fine orange groves have the appearance of having grown from a lake.

Houses and trees were blown in the wildest confusion in this section. Not only were the roofs gone, but the house bodies followed, leaving planks, window sashes and doors strewn behind. Circling over the almost completed $7,500,000 plant of the Florida Power and Light Co., in the extreme southwestern section of Fort Lauderdale on the Dania cutoff canal, the airplane passengers were surprised to see practically all of the big plant standing in water, in one vast lake, in fact.

None of the main buildings nor the water tower or fuel tanks were materially damaged, but the workingmen's cottages were flattened. From this position over Broward County the outlook was described as being especially desolate. To the west could be seen the waterlogged Davie section. Flying closer in, the completely demolished tent city of the beach bore mute testimony of strength behind the giant fist which smashed it.

Coming towards Fort Lauderdale from the west the first things to be marveled at are the yacht basin and various boat yards. How those heavy boats were lifted on top of one another and knocked about, and into pieces like eggshells is a puzzle to any one who did not actually see the fury of the storm in action. As the houses of Fort Lauderdale get closer and closer together the damage becomes more and more apparent. Roofless buildings, broken and dismantled telephone and power poles, caved-in schools and churches. Truly, Fort Lauderdale suffered as much as or more than any other section.

A final circling of the city brought out another most cheerful feature. On the bald roofless surface of houses tiny figures could be seen at work. Along telephone poles and even out on cables between poles were linemen. Everywhere the work of rehabilitation was going on as the city came back into its own. Hammers, picks, shovels were being swung. Four barracks for refugees had been completed at the hospital. Tiny trucks loaded with roofing and food were scurrying down the city streets and a busy crowd was hurrying in and out of the Realtor's building, established headquarters.

For years afterward, all time and all events were referred to as "before or after the storm," meaning, of course, the great September, 1926, hurricane. Hurricanes were an almost yearly occurrence after the great 1926 storm. In 1928 a severe one brushed through Broward County with comparatively little damage, but then hit the Lake Okeechobee area with results which made it by far the most tragic of south Florida tropical storms. An estimated three thousand persons were drowned when high winds forced the waters from the shallow lake out to engulf all of the towns on the eastern shores. Among the victims was Ed King, Fort Lauderdale's first contractor and first council president.

In 1928 President-elect Hoover made two appearances in Fort Lauder-

FORT LAUDERDALE

President-elect Herbert Hoover visits city in 1928 (VAIL COLLECTION)

dale. The first, through no fault of his own, proved completely disappointing. The second proved completely surprising and startling. Hoover planned a personal tour, leaving from Miami, over the devastated area around the big lake. When William H. Marshall and others close to the national administration learned of the tour they ascertained the route and time and arranged for school children to be released. Bearing flags, they lined East Las Olas Boulevard near its western terminus. But someone of the secret service or other presidential protectors switched the route and the motorcade zipped north on Andrews Avenue, completely by-passing the crowds on Las Olas. The town was considerably upset. Later, after vehement calls to the President-elect's party at the lake, he agreed that on the return trip he would not only stop at Fort Lauderdale, but would also go to the band shell in Stranahan Park and make a short talk.

That plan did not work either. When Hoover's car stopped and he stepped out, he was immediately surrounded by a friendly but excited crowd so dense that he never did make it to the curb, much less the park. Hoover, in the crush, was separated from his secret service men and pushed on down the middle of the street for more than a block before he could be rescued. He wore canvas shoes and a thick white collar, and both were pretty well wilted. His face was red and his protectors upset, but he took the local over-enthusiasm with good grace. The Hoover Dikes he helped design and promote have saved many lives over the years in the Lake Okeechobee region.

136

Mayor John Tidball (*right*) welcomes railway president S. Davies Warfield (*left*) and Governor John W. Martin on arrival of first Seaboard train

The Long, Hard Depression

The citizenry recovered gradually from the shock and tragedy of the hurricane. Full realization of its total impact was mercifully slow. It was easier for numbed minds to take up tasks immediately at hand than to contemplate, or even speculate, on future effects of the great storm. Business leaders knew the future outlook was bleak. The big clean-up job for the winter season of 1926-27 was accomplished despite heartbreak that accompanied removal of some of the wreckage.

On New Year's Eve, 1926, the San Carlos Opera Company presented *Rigoletto* at the Sunset Theater. On January 14, 1927, the county offered a new entertainment feature—thoroughbred horse racing at

Chapter 12
1926–1934

137

Pompano race track. Parimutuel betting was not legal, but subterfuges kept the tracks running despite Governor John Martin's objections.

The county commission on September 20 voted unanimously to sell the seven hundred thousand dollars' worth of road bonds remaining in the issue approved earlier that year. The money was needed. It also voted ten thousand dollars for emergency storm relief. The city commission took similar emergency relief action.

Dave Oliver and E. R. Heimburger, caught with a large stock of plumbing and building supplies, moved most of their inventory to Jacksonville, realizing that there would be no building here. They moved their main office back as soon as possible, however. Other firms with large inventories liquidated stock as the opportunity presented. Fort Lauderdale tightened its belt. Playdays were over. It was time to return to harsh reality. The program of public works continued. The Florida East Coast Railway went on with its double-tracking, the Seaboard Air Line was "a-building," and work on the port was accelerated. Although the city was forced to abandon the costly, recently started sanitary sewer system, the new water plant was operational, and the new golf course was ready for the 1926-27 season.

The 1926 storm ruined many people financially and might have been expected to cause a general exodus from southeastern Florida. Most fly-by-nighters did leave. Many who liked, or loved, the city remained. The idea of moving away did not even occur to them. If hurricanes were one of the things to be coped with, then they would learn how.

Among the local yachts reported in mid-November as repaired and in service after being damaged in the hurricane were W. C. Kyle's "Billy, Jr.," Reed Bryan's "Vincent VI," Tom Bryan's "Princess," A. G. Kuhn's "Victoria," and Hugh Sample's "Gadfly."

It is entirely possible that none fully realized the length and arduousness of the road back. Governing bodies were millions of dollars in debt. The supply of credit from northern banks had dried up. Many were rich on paper, but the paper was worth only what it would produce. Only too often this was nothing. Its holders ended up with the property—property encumbered by debts that mounted as values declined. As 1927 dawned, a great depression began here that was not to be felt in the North for another two years. It was an era of desperation, an era in which steadfast courage and high morale at first seemed to lead only to despair.

The great Florida land boom has been described in books and articles, many written by top authors. None were able fully to explain or to

Las Olas Boulevard renamed Memorial Drive in honor of World War I
dead (BURGHARD COLLECTION)

evaluate it. Certain it is that many were hurt, even ruined, in the fantastic course of events. Subsequent happenings, however, proved that even
the most fantastic dreams of the more responsible developers would
come true. They did, and many who were able to hold on to property
during the long, bitter depression prospered. Fort Lauderdale and Florida, as a whole, because of the boom, gained much in capital improvements that would otherwise have required many years. Among these
was the huge new power station opened July 10, 1926, by the Florida
Power and Light Company. The Fort Lauderdale Gas Company opened
for business the following month. A contract was signed with Tom
Bryan for the construction of a new post office at the corner of what is
now South West 4th Avenue and 2d Street.

But if the land boom had brought a "new world" to Fort Lauderdale,
there was another new world waiting just around the corner. At its
dawning, 1927 might have been called the "year of hope." Now the
town had most of what it lacked at the peak of the deader-than-dead
boom: a fine new eighteen-hole golf course to supplement the old nine-
hole course, ample water pressure, adequate schools, and a vast improvement in streets and traffic. Las Olas Boulevard was to be dedicated to
the soldiers of World War I as Memorial Boulevard, widened, and a new
two-lane bridge built to replace the original single-lane span. A causeway would replace the old wooden approach. The need for a commodi-
ous bath house at Las Olas Beach was recognized by all. Commodore

Brook had set his mind on securing this need and he received encouragement and cooperation.

The first Seaboard train rolled in majestically January 8, 1927, to be met at Fort Lauderdale by an enthusiastic welcoming delegation. The "Orange Blossom Special" brought tourists, but no speculators nor land buyers. The event was considered to be an historic one. It afforded satisfaction to businessmen that there was now an additional railroad to break the Florida East Coast Railway's monopoly. Double-tracking of the Florida East Coast, completed soon thereafter, gave additional comfort. There would be no transportation shortages nor freight embargoes now.

The Southern Bell Telephone Company moved into the modern new building completed at the corner of Valentine (3d) Avenue and North East 5th (2d) Street. The building was two stories high and cost eighty thousand dollars. Building, lot, and equipment represented an investment of three hundred and fifty thousand dollars.

Contract for construction of the eighteen-foot "Federal Aid" highway was let in 1927 to S. P. Snyder and Son, with the state paying fifty per cent of the cost and the federal government the remainder. The town paid for additional paving from North East 10th Street south to the city limits, where the contract called for a fifty-foot width. From 10th Street east to what is now Gateway was considered out in the wilds and was left at eighteen feet. This contract was the last to be completed by S. P. Snyder of S. P. Snyder & Son, builders of most of the city's streets. After his death, the company was continued under the same name by his son, Byron F. Snyder. Construction of the new highway helped the town spread out. Zoned for business, the new through route attracted several business places. One, Joe's Barbecue, run by Joe and Lucille Hudson, was a popular eating place which gained fame in a poem by Edgar A. Guest.

The population of Fort Lauderdale grew from three thousand in 1924 to an estimated thirteen thousand in 1926, but much of the new population proved temporary, in part made up of speculators and "get-rich-quick" real-estate operators. It leveled off quickly after the boom and hurricane to a permanent four thousand eight hundred, a figure it was never again to go below. Not only tax collections were down in 1927; mortgage payments also were drastically down. The season of 1926-27 brought some tourists, mostly "regulars" who had wintered here before. But in spite of the many improvements few new tourists came.

The city commission and its legal department found an inadvertent mistake made in checking the title to property the city had received. Land donated for the Westside Golf Course by Judge John P. Grace was found, after acceptance and construction of the course, to have an outstanding mortgage on it, a situation difficult to explain.

If merchants were disheartened, city officials were even more depressed. Huge payments were coming due on bonds now totaling nearly seven million dollars, and tax payments were seventy-five per cent delinquent, and getting worse. The money wells that had flowed so freely only a few short months before had suddenly gone dry. Water department collections were almost as bad. Although it had the power to cut off water service, the city found collections slow and only thirty-five per cent of its accounts paid. People simply did not have money to pay.

The city commission remained undaunted. Glowing experiences of the great boom had proved what could be done. It now had the City Plan and went to work to activate it, letting a contract for beautification, including construction of a concrete sea wall along both sides of New River, of the entire length of the city's riparian rights. The contract for this work was let to Powell Brothers at a cost of $91,720. Economists pointed out later that although the city was spending borrowed money (from bond issues) which would be difficult to repay, the projects were of utmost importance and were done at a cost far lower than in later, more prosperous days.

Banking troubles had disturbed the city for some time. Now there were rumblings and rumors concerning the First National Bank. No actual run took place, but withdrawals were heavy. Most simply moved across the street to the still powerful Fort Lauderdale Bank and Trust Company, the same one established in 1910 as the city's first under the name of Fort Lauderdale State Bank. The First National on November 2, 1927, announced its merger with its rival, and now became the town's only bank. The proud new skyscraper was sold to William L. Sweet, Jr., of New York, who renamed it the Sweet Building. The resources of the merged banks were listed as four and a half million.

The state legislature authorized the creation of the Port Everglades Port Authority in its 1927 session, and this body now took over the two million dollars in bonds Fort Lauderdale had issued for port construction, taking over at the same time a like amount from Hollywood. This reduced the city's bonded indebtedness to five million dollars but added a new taxing body with new burdens for property owners.

When the legislature created the Port District, the port was a "dream" under construction. Named by Governor John W. Martin to the first Port Commission were C. C. Freeman, Hollywood; Martin Frost, Dania; Samuel L. Drake, Fort Lauderdale. R. J. Blank was secretary and C. L. Chancey was attorney.

By 1928 rumors centered on the last remaining bank. Withdrawals this time went into postal savings, a last remaining shelter. Most citizens stoutly defended the bank, and many took pride in leaving money on deposit. Bank heads, however, were distressed. Collections were down and many of their borrowers did not pay taxes on property which served as security for loans. The vast depression in values of property hurt to a degree almost unbelievable. If 1927 had been the "year of hope," then 1928 bade fair to become the "year of despair."

Early in 1928 there were several small runs on the bank and withdrawals grew heavier. On February 15, 1928, the pressure became too much. The bank doors failed to open on the next morning, February 16. This was the telling final blow. Hundreds of citizens saw their last available cash swept away. There seemed nothing left in which to put faith. Taxes were already intolerable and destined to increase materially in view of bond interest and payments due. The city was one of the large losers in the closing, but the bitterest memories of all were those of at least two depositors who got into the bank after closing hours to make heavy deposits. One was Commodore Brook who had just received a check for eight thousand dollars. He, however, put half of this money in his safety deposit box in cash. R. G. Snow, former mayor, was not so fortunate. Snow had just returned from Kansas City where he had raised ten thousand dollars for the purchase of new farm machinery to be placed on sale in his seed, fertilizer, and equipment store. He put the entire amount on deposit, the last business transaction of the bank.

That the city could survive without a bank was doubtful. The specter of a ghost town was a real threat, but into this breach stepped John D. Lochrie. With help from friends, he immediately began negotiations to open a new bank. Among those who came forward was Hugh T. Birch, who made one of his rare visits downtown for the purpose. The new Broward Bank and Trust Company (now Broward National) opened its doors on March 5, 1928, with C. C. Freeman as president; J. D. Camp, cashier; R. N. West, assistant cashier; L. H. Dresbach, trust officer; and B. G. Johnson and Joseph Morris, tellers. Directors were John D. Lochrie; T. D. Scales, Indiana; W. P. Tanner, New York; W. L. Sweet, Jr., New York; Thomas Garrett, Jr., New York; and Hugh T. Birch, C. D. Kittredge, J. P. Young, C. C. Freeman, J. W. Tidball, A. L. Weiss, M. A. Hortt, C. N. McCune, J. S. Powell, D. T. Hart, and J. D. Camp.

The Las Olas Beach area in 1928 (PHOTO BY A. W. ERKINS FROM MERLE FOGG'S PLANE)

The new bank was receiver for the old, handled collections, and did well from the start though few local citizens had money to deposit.

The old Fort Lauderdale Bank and Trust Company board of directors was hard-hit, for each was required to pay a double assessment on stock owned. Among the directors were many of the town's founders and leading citizens, including Will Kyle, Frank Stranahan, C. P. Weidling, Tom M. Bryan, C. J. Joiner, H. G. Wheeler, C. G. Rodes, C. N. McCune, and H. D. Dichtenmueller. Many of these men felt disgraced, and the knowledge that the life savings of their friends had been swept away bore heavily on them. The fact that their own losses outweighed all others was of little comfort. Eventually, by April of 1940, depositors got back thirty-one and a half per cent of their money.

Elsewhere the nation rolled along on the great post-World War I boom, but southeast Florida was beaten to its knees. The 1927-28 tourist season was a replica of that for 1926-27. Many came, but few spent, and none invested. Only one thing was certain: things would get much worse before they got better. A proof was the failure of the Broward Building and Loan Company, which had been incorporated in 1922.

FORT LAUDERDALE

If dead, the city was not yet buried. That was to come, the wise ones said, when it defaulted on bond obligations. That it would do so was inevitable. The due dates marched inexorably through the calendar, and the city coffers remained empty. It was believed that a "default" would utterly ruin the credit of the city for all time and would black-list it in the books of every financial institution in the land. But even as this fate approached the populace, straws at which to grasp were given. For instance, President Calvin Coolidge stopped briefly in Fort Lauderdale. When the Coolidge Special whistled at 3:50 P.M. January 12, 1928, a crowd of seven to eight thousand people packed the station platforms and spaces along the Florida East Coast tracks. The President hardly spoke except to tell W. H. Marshall, Republican candidate for Congress, that he was glad to be able to stop. A number of girls were in the throng at the station. They stared at the President and he stared back.

"Say something to the Girl Scouts," their leader requested.

"Hello, Girl Scouts," responded the taciturn Coolidge.

Life in Fort Lauderdale was a far cry from boom-time. Chain stores were becoming popular and independent grocers took advantage of the situation to advertise: "Now that you're broke, go to the chain store and ask for credit." Getting groceries for their families was the major problem of most men. Hardest hit, perhaps, were construction workers. Construction work had gone to well-nigh absolute zero. Unions were forgotten. A journeyman carpenter might make as much as a dollar a day, and would consider himself lucky if he worked more than two days a week. The other trades were as bad. Such things as rent, taxes, utility bills, and luxuries were by-passed almost completely.

Good "imported whiskey" sold for four dollars a quart, and was far too expensive for the average man. He could, however, drink his troubles away on moonshine at two dollars a gallon. Bootleggers, who found increasingly efficient and ingenious ways to get alcoholic products to the thirsty North and Middle West, also got cash for their wares. Coast Guard Base Six, here to halt rum-running, provided another payroll that brought cash money into town.

One of the most served depression meals consisted of a nickel's worth of grits, a mess of grunts, and enough grease to fry them. "Grits and grunts" became commonplace. Grunts were small, easily caught fish on the close-in reefs. Outlying chicken farms offered fryers for thirty-five cents if you caught and cleaned your own. Hamburger cost a quarter for two pounds. Farmers who stuck to their growing through the boom continued to prosper on about the same basis as before the boom. Often they found it unprofitable to pick their entire crop and they gave the leftovers to the needy.

During the winter many of the town's leading citizens rented their homes to tourists who might pay them twelve hundred or even two thousand dollars for the season. Most of this money went to pay taxes. The families either doubled up with relatives or rented cheap apartments. Others did a day's labor in the city's parks or on the streets to pay their water bills. City employees worked part time when funds for full-time salaries ran out.

Then, in 1929, the stock market crashed in New York. Factories closed, and the rest of the nation joined Florida in the worst depression of recent history. Throughout the South one heard the wail: "Ten-cent cotton and forty-cent meat. How in the world's a man gonna eat?" N. B. Cheaney estimates that during the depression years twenty-five per cent of the homes in Fort Lauderdale were foreclosed and lost for taxes and other liens. He also estimates that eighty per cent of the vacant lots and eighty-five per cent of the nonfarm acreage in the city and its environs were similarly lost.

A welfare department was not badly needed in the very early days of Fort Lauderdale. The town's pioneers lived close to nature and food was abundant. Little clothing was required and the closely knit community took care of its own without any organization. But after the great storm of 1926 the charity picture changed. Fort Lauderdale's economy had fallen apart with the bursting of the boom, and a vast influx of new people made the former living-off-the-land impractical. In 1926 the city was forced to begin a welfare program and the Red Cross hurricane relief provided a pattern. In 1927 Mrs. Sandy Adams was employed as a welfare worker with headquarters in the police department. Before her time, the work had been carried on by Red Cross workers sent in after the storm.

The city had not completely recovered when a second hurricane struck in 1928 and a third followed in 1929. Although the economy of the community had supposedly leveled off after the 1926 storm, the succeeding ones removed any immediate hopes for real recovery. The only available employment, and that was spotty and seasonal, was on farms. Some of the fishing areas and a few of the shops continued to employ a minimum of people, and bootleggers were active. Many families were stranded without funds, means of livelihood, or a way of returning to former homes in other states. The city had lost money in the bank failures and was unable to collect taxes.

FORT LAUDERDALE

Miss Jane Moxley, a dedicated and efficient Red Cross worker who had come to Fort Lauderdale immediately after the 1926 hurricane, returned in 1928. She was asked to remain as a follow-up worker in charge of the Fort Lauderdale, Pompano, and Deerfield areas and assumed these duties in 1929. With aid from city and county the Red Cross carried on the welfare work through 1934. During this period, Miss Moxley became the wife of Ray Whyte, a prominent businessman. With the coming of the Roosevelt administration in 1933, employment increased as work was made available through various government agencies. In that year Mrs. Whyte resigned after performing services for which she was highly commended.

The city staged a crash program of cutting costs. Operating expenses for the first half of the 1928-29 fiscal year were $77,058.66 lower than for fiscal year 1926-27. This reduction in operating expenses was brought about by a strict economy system, by paring salaries and payrolls wherever possible, and by cutting down investment in equipment. The pinch was on at city hall. Revenues from all sources had totaled seven hundred thousand dollars in 1926, and were confidently expected to top a million dollars by the following year. By 1929 they were down to a hundred and forty-three thousand dollars. The major portion of the Schermerhorn City Master Plan was shelved in the lean years that followed.

Although 1928 was dismal financially and economically, it was not without some grisly divertisement. Chief Deputy Sheriff William A. Hicks was indicted for first degree murder on September 12, 1927. Gory details of the crime with which he was charged, together with the facts that Hicks held high office, was extremely popular, and was a leader in fraternal circles, made it a sensation.

Hicks was charged with the murder of Robert R. Barber, a trusty in the prison. He was alleged to have arranged to have the body buried after a fake examination. Barber's brothers, hearing rumors of foul play, demanded its exhumation and a certified examination. Dug up, the body plainly revealed a crushed head and bullet hole in the chest. Testimony developed that several persons actually witnessed the crime, but they were bootleggers beholden to Hicks for protection, or trusties in the jail. Their testimony was questionable. It was also alleged that Hicks, himself, was involved in bootlegging activities. The jury failed to reach an agreement and was discharged. The defense was handled by the firm of Farrington and Lockhart with G. H. Martin assisting. Prosecutor Louis Maire employed Thomas G. Farmer as special assistant. Circuit

Stranahan Park, a popular gathering place (KELCY PHOTO)

Judge Vincent C. Giblin, who had been appointed to the post created only a year before, disqualified himself, and the case was heard by Judge L. L. Parks of the 13th District.

Finally, after several convictions had been set aside, the State Supreme Court reversed the indictment on February 18, 1929, and Hicks was set free. Pale from his long incarceration at Raiford, Hicks created a sensation when he showed up at Easter Sunrise Services on Las Olas Beach. He was a large, paunchy man and wore a ten-gallon, cowboy hat. Later he was reported to have gone back to New York State, where he became police chief of a small city.

Although Fort Lauderdale was firmly in the grip of the great depression long before it was touched off nationally by the 1929 market crash, its people still managed to have good times. The specter of poverty hung heavily, but it could be forgotten when it was realized that everyone else was in the same boat. Saturday nights in Fort Lauderdale were typical of the times. People from neighboring communities came in to the county seat for the evening and attended the free band concert in Stranahan Park. If they had even a little small change it was enough to get an ice cream treat at Williams-McWilliams ice cream emporium just across the street. If they were really "flush" they could precede the concert with a fine dinner at Brown's restaurant, the "works" for fifty cents.

Logan T. Brown, a traveling salesman, had taken over the boom-time "Soda Smoke" shop on Andrews Avenue to run it for a friend. He finally took title and converted it to a restaurant, first moving into larger quarters near Wall Street. He later moved into still larger ones in the Bryan Arcade on the southeast corner of Andrews Avenue and 2d Street. "I remember all the bad meals I ate in restaurants on the road," said Brown. "I try to give people what I always hoped I might get when I went into a strange restaurant." His policy worked so well that, in winter seasons, lines several blocks long formed outside his restaurant waiting for room to sit and be served. Homer C. Stuckey managed the restaurant, a post he was to keep for thirty-four years.

Prohibition was still alive in the early part of the depression and the common meeting places in town were the drugstores. W. G. (Doc) Hardy's, opposite Brown's in the Bryan Arcade, was the first in town to establish a lunch counter. He also provided the citizenry with its first inspection of the wonderful new neon signs. On the morning Brown's opened in the Arcade, Hardy, his wife, and Curtis Byrd were the first customers.

Ballou (Blue) Maxwell ran the drugstore in the Sunset Theater building and catered largely to the high school crowd. A. J. (Doc) Beck had opened another, his second, on the corner of North West River Drive and Andrews Avenue. Bootleg booze and moonshine were readily available. One of the bootleggers drove a Cadillac coupé known to all drinking people. Each night it was parked on Andrews Avenue at the corner of Wall Street and it was from this "stand" that he peddled his wares. The downtown section of the city was thronged. The Salvation Army band played. Seminoles, in their colorful costumes, joined in the spirit of the multitude. Almost everyone was known to all others by name, including Indians and Negroes—and of each it was known that, though happy, he was broke.

With the help of government agencies the city was able to accomplish much needed street work and general construction. Also, working through the Salvation Army and the Red Cross, the city exchanged grocery orders and water bills for labor. Under this latter plan, additional worth-while projects were accomplished. In 1934 the average number of families on work relief was two hundred twenty-one, on direct relief thirty-three, and on supplemental aid one hundred seven. If these numbers are not impressive it must be remembered that the population of the town was less than ten thousand. The Salvation Army acted as the city's welfare agent from 1934 until 1956 and earned the gratitude of many citizens and officials.

(KELCY PHOTO)
Dredging of Port Everglades at Lake Mabel

Port Everglades

Violent acts of cold-blooded piracy and multiple murder exploded August 7, 1927, some miles off Fort Lauderdale and chilled the nation. It was a Sunday morning when Coast Guard Cutter 249 set out for Bimini with her six-man crew. Also aboard was Robert K. Webster, a Secret Service Agent en route to the Bahamas to investigate the passing of counterfeit money by bootleggers.

Chapter 13
1927–1929

The following is a contemporary account of the incident as written to his father by participant Hal M. Caudle.

Last Sunday afternoon, I came near being killed. The skipper [Sidney Sanderlin] and motor machinist and a secret service man were killed, and our cook wounded. I'll send a newspaper clipping, but first I'll tell it all word for word. We left the base about 10 A.M. Sunday and about 1:30 P.M. we picked up the boat. It only had a small load. The two men looked pretty old and gave a hard-luck story, so we took them aboard the boat and unloaded the "rummie." Johnny Robinson found some in the stern of the rum boat and I went to help him get it. I heard two shots and turned and saw the men standing on the deck of the patrol

149

U.S. Coast Guard Patrol Boat 249 (GIFT, HAROLD CAUDLE [*extreme right*])

boat, one with a 45. Johnny threw a wrench at him and dived into the engine room of the rum boat. The bootlegger held up the S. S. man and the cook [Jodie L. Hollingsworth] and made them get aboard the rum boat. We saw he had the drop, so we came out with our hands up. Johnny climbed aboard and he held us in the stern of the boat. He then told us that he had two of us (the Skipper and [Victor] Lamby) and that he was going to burn the patrol boat and take us out in the Gulf Stream and make us jump overboard and shoot us. He then made his partner burst all the gas lines in the engine room and set fire to it. Lamby was not dead, but wounded, and they were going to burn him alive.

They loaded the booze back on the rum boat. They procured our guns and tried them out in the deck. Then they got aboard the rum boat to get it started before setting fire to the patrol boat. The fellow [Robert] Weech held us up with two guns, while [James Horace] Alderman, the guy running it, started the motor. Alderman came out and took one of the guns, and sent Weech into the engine room to watch the motor. We all must have been looking for a chance because Alderman barely turned his head when we all rushed him. The Secret Serviceman was shot down right in front of me. Alderman raised the gun on me and I grabbed the barrel. He shot twice in my face and I don't see how he missed me. I think it was because Johnny's weight must have pulled me down, as he climbed over me with the ice pick. Frank Tuten had the other gun. As soon as I got the gun I hit him in the head a

150

couple of times and then went for Weech. He must have thrown his gun down because he had one when he went into the engine room. He was going out of the hatch when I got to him. I put the gun in his back and pulled the trigger, and it snapped. I pulled again and saw it was empty so I knocked him out with the butt. Johnny came and commenced clubbing him, and I told him to hold Weech until I got another gun and I would kill him. I found Weech's gun in the engine room. When I got back Johnny had thrown Weech overboard. He swam to the patrol boat and the two Franks took him aboard. Johnny went to the patrol boat. Somehow the rum boat got pushed into reverse and broke loose from the patrol. I threw it out of gear and helped the cook aboard. He had been knocked overboard by a 45 through his head. We got aboard the patrol boat and took the casualties.

The Skipper and the Secret Serviceman were dead and Lamby wounded (he died today), the cook wounded and the bootlegger with ice pick holes all in him and a busted head, and the other with a busted head. We called base for a fast boat and got one motor started for a little while. The Commander came and took in the wounded and our crew let a relief crew bring in the boat. The prisoners are to be taken to Jacksonville tonight. I will not be home on leave as must stay for trial.

Alderman was tried in federal court and after two years of retrials was convicted. The Alderman hanging was first set to take place at the Broward County Court House, but the county commission demurred. Maritime law provided that a pirate must be hanged at the port where he was brought in, so the execution was rescheduled for the federal property. Alderman finally was hanged August 17, 1929, in the seaplane hangar at Coast Guard Base Six on Fort Lauderdale Beach. Few civilians were allowed to witness the hanging. To Dr. Elliott M. Hendricks, prominent Fort Lauderdale physician, and surgeon in the Public Health Service and Quarantine Officer for Coast Guard Base Six, Port Everglades, fell the duty of witnessing the hanging and pronouncing Alderman dead. His daughter, Dr. Anne L. Hendricks, recalls that he lost sleep for two weeks before and suffered from nightmares for some time after the event. "Alderman," according to her father, "was the only calm one at the hanging."

Associated Press and other newspaper representatives were kept on the far side of the wire fence surrounding the hangar, but by prior arrangement, were signaled from inside by an enlisted seaman. He tipped his hat when the trap was sprung and when Alderman died. These exact times were flashed over the press wires. It was the only legal execution to take place in Broward County up to that time. Weech was given a year and a day.

During the trial it was brought out that Alderman had smuggled Chinese from Cuba and had murdered some of them after taking their money. The forty-one cases of whiskey may have been explained by the mysterious disappearance of a speedboat containing two men which had left Bimini with approximately that amount. Neither boat nor men were ever heard of again. The entire affair created a mighty diversion for the populace, but now politics was getting hot.

Al Smith opposed Herbert Hoover for President in the 1928 election. Broward County, like the rest of the solid South, was Democratic. This did not always hold true of nonpartisan city elections, when Fort Lauderdale had often elected Republicans. This time the voters responded to the cry, "Clean out the Courthouse!"

When the dust of the Democratic primary settled it revealed only a scant handful of incumbents left. In the ensuing general election Broward County voted Republican candidates into office for the first time. The county gave Republican Hoover a majority over Democrat Smith. Important posts going to local Republicans included the Broward school superintendency to John M. Gerren, and the county prosecutor's office to Robert J. Davis. This change was important only to the future hopes of the embryonic Republican party of Broward County. None were re-elected in immediately following years. Judge Vincent Giblin was defeated in the Democratic primary by George W. Tedder, who thereafter retained his post of judge, usually unopposed, until his official retirement July 1, 1954. Ten years later, still "sharp as a tack," Judge Tedder served on special circuit court cases by assignment from the Florida Supreme Court.

Another great excitement of the year was the oil well project. The Arpin brothers had shown a group of local businessmen where bubbles were rising from the water in front of Commodore A. H. Brook's home at the fork of New River. They trapped in jars gas which burned with a blue flame. Sent to a testing laboratory it was found to contain methane (swamp gas) and also ethane, which would indicate the presence of oil. In a great flurry of hope a company was formed to drill. Selling stock in an oil well was not easy in so hard-pressed a community, but rosy dreams of a great recouping of the entire economy provided great incentive. The "oil fever" became so intense that a picture of an oil rig appeared on 1929 Fort Lauderdale tax bills. The group obtained leases from city and state and the well was started on the spot now occupied

Left: Al Smith at Fort Lauderdale Golf and Country Club (KELCY PHOTO)

Right: The great "oil well" in Croissant Park (KELCY PHOTO)

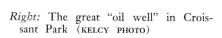

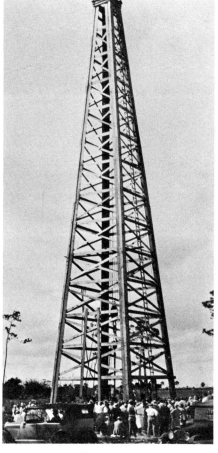

by the old Fort Lauderdale Spa at 500 South West 14th Court. At the three-thousand-foot level lack of financing and any sign of oil forced its abandonment. That the boring penetrated a vein of sulphur water instead of oil was the ultimate disappointment.

In World War II, with pipe in short supply, a Miami firm bought the lot occupied by the well to reclaim the pipe in the well shaft. It was necessary to use nitroglycerin and the explosion tapped an artesian well. The Miami firm took the pipe, capped the casing, and left after selling the lot to F. P. Medford, who lived near-by. Medford put a spigot on the casing and used the well water to irrigate his near-by garden, its natural pressure being sufficient to move the water. His gardens thrived. He later had the water tested and found it contained minerals believed to be healthful. Its mineral content was found to equal that of many of the famous spas in America. This led to the eventual establishment of the Fort Lauderdale Spa.

Meantime, Coast Guard officials expressed satisfaction with the success attending concentration of forces at the Fort Lauderdale base in the effort to mop up the stream of liquor flowing into Florida from the Bahamas and Cuba. Captain Harry G. Hamlet was the officer in charge of the Coast Guard destroyers. As the depression rolled along bootlegging, with its easy money, attracted more and more hard-pressed citizens. But the Coast Guard, stirred by the Alderman affair, was now equipped with faster, shallow-draft boats. These boats were armed with machine guns, and the guardsmen had orders to shoot. Hauling contraband liquor became more and more dangerous and difficult, and hijacking more and more common.

Bootleggers began using airplanes. A plane could not carry so heavy a load but it could make three or four trips daily. A boat often took as long as two days and in bad weather even longer. Seaplanes were first used. Then an enterprising pilot, who has told his story on tape to the authors and to the Fort Lauderdale Historical Society under the name of "Mr. X," bought a landing field at West End and started using a land plane. Where the seaplanes had been forced to land in inland lakes or canals, the land ships could use any golf course, cow pasture, or, in dry weather, even the Everglades. Any deserted road, and there were many, would suffice. "Mr. X" sold his landing field back to the original owner, but continued to use it. He had paid fifty dollars for it, and sold it back for the same amount. Thereafter he and other pilots paid a ten-dollar landing fee each time they used the field. As many as two hundred planes per day landed there. Soon hundreds of planes were in the business, and in the entire history of bootlegging "Mr. X" recalled only one incident of a pilot being caught. It was evident much of the law enforcement machinery had been corrupted by bribery.

This made it easier for a new illegal practice, gambling, to gain a foothold in the county. Until that time gambling had been on a petty scale at fraternal clubs and in a few scattered "rummy" rooms in the various towns. These were little different from games indulged in in private homes. Now, professionals began eyeing tourists, some of the comparatively well-off farmers, and the bootleggers. The first big operation was the "Plantation" on Hallandale Beach Road. There horse race betting complete with charts and calls, roulette, craps, and a giant nightly bingo game were soon under way. Locals had little money with which to play, but took a tolerant view. Their attitude was: "We don't begrudge anyone a living, any way they can make it."

Smaller operations were soon set up in various parts of the county. Most stayed out of Fort Lauderdale, avoiding the necessity of "dealing" with the local police. Along with gambling came houses of prostitution, the latter gaining impetus when Port Everglades brought occasional crews of seamen into town. These houses also stayed on the outskirts, but soon three or four, running wide open and known to most of the citizens, were located in various quiet suburbs of Fort Lauderdale. The people, for the same reason, took the same tolerant attitude as shown gambling.

In 1928 the old wooden casino, built in 1915 at the beach, was replaced by a new municipal casino and added an Olympic-size pool. It eliminated the upstairs dancing pavilion. Commodore Brook was a prime mover in the construction of this major municipal asset. Called Las Olas Beach Casino and Pool, it was erected by Fort Lauderdale to supply a convenience recognized by all coast resort towns as highly desirable. It was of Spanish design, neat, practical, and above all durable. It stood on heavy piling sunk deep in the beach formation.

The pool, sixty by a hundred sixty-five feet, graduated from a depth of three feet to twelve. A wading pool for children was eighteen inches deep. The pool was arranged that the salt water changed every ten hours. The cost of casino and pool complete was about seventy-five thousand dollars; site, fifty-five thousand; total, a hundred thirty thousand. F. L. Abreu was architect; John Olsson, contractor. An audience of three thousand people attended the formal opening and dedication in late January, 1928. City Commissioner W. J. Reed gave the introductory speech, dedicated the casino, and introduced the casino committee that

(VAIL COLLECTION)

American Legion Drum and Bugle Corps at Beach Casino

acted upon appointment of the city commission in selecting the site— A. H. Brook, A. M. Taylor, and J. P. Young. Clifford A. Root, Red Cross official and an engineer, was the pool's first manager.

* * *

Then Port Everglades became reality. A month later, in February, 1928, a grand celebration was held at the port when it was dedicated and opened to the sea. President Coolidge was to press a button in Washington that would set off the final charge of dynamite to blast a chan-

Almost entire populace attended official opening of Port Everglades in 1928

nel connecting the port to the ocean. The celebration was attended by virtually every resident of the area and was marred only when Coolidge either forgot to push the button or there was a power failure somewhere along the line. Local wags said that "Silent Cal" was unable to stand the thought of the noise of such a charge. Engineers finally touched off the blast locally and the port was dedicated as "Bay Mabel Harbor." Warren T. Eller, a post-land boom Chamber of Commerce manager, became the first secretary of the Port Authority, and Port Manager after Port Everglades opened for business. He founded the Port Everglades Terminal Company in 1933 and was a factor in the port's early growth.

It was at this juncture that a few people began to realize that southeast Florida was not dead. R. H. Gore had come here from Chicago in 1929 to try to sell an insurance program to the newspaper then owned by Thomas N. Stilwell. Stilwell turned down the insurance and offered instead to sell the newspaper, point-blank, setting a cash price of ninety thousand dollars. Gore thought it over briefly and then, through a distant relative, J. Rogers Gore, whom he had met in the newspaper office that day, offered Stilwell seventy-five thousand dollars. Stilwell took it. Gore went to the bank the next day and sold three hundred shares of stock in a Boston Bank at fourteen hundred dollars per share. A few weeks later, when the stock market crashed, these same shares had dropped to a maximum of three dollars each. With acquisition of the

Early Port Authority officials. (*Left to right*): Charles Perkins, George Kelly, John Clark, Attorney R. R. Saunders, and Manager R. T. Spangler (BURGHARD COLLECTION)

Port Everglades dredged to 35-foot depth

newspaper Gore spent more and more time in Fort Lauderdale and soon made it his permanent home. In him the city had gained an unusual convert in that he had money to invest. There were plenty of bargains.

Stilwell, for his part, had not lost faith in his community. He had sold the newspaper largely to allow him to retain and develop Stilwell Isles. This fine property immediately west of Idlewyld and Riviera was now among the city's choicest residential lands. He had to delay plans when the depression hit the North and deflated his holdings in Anderson, Indiana, where he owned gravel pits, a traction company, and the town's leading hotel.

City Hall complex on Andrews Avenue at site now occupied by Burdine's

While there were faint glimmerings of hope in the activities of a few individuals, the over-all corporate picture was gloomy indeed. In its tax struggle the city called upon its ablest and shrewdest businessmen to serve as commissioners and they, in turn, had employed an extremely capable young lawyer, George W. English, Jr., as city attorney. He took office in 1928. He was familiar with city problems, having been associated with M. Lewis Hall, his predecessor as city attorney. English had been trained at the University of Illinois and at Harvard Law School. He saw a chance to rid the town of one of its greatest eyesores, the gaunt old Wil-Mar hotel skeleton, that had stood for years a bleak reminder of failure and boom "bust." He persuaded Mr. Gore to buy it for thirty thousand dollars. Gore also bought the building across the street which had started out as the proud new Pioneer Department Store, long since gone broke and out of business. English had hoped that Gore would immediately complete the hotel, expecting that this would bring in new taxes. But this project was delayed for several years until the time was more "ripe."

FORT LAUDERDALE

Tenure of city managers was brief in this period. C. E. Fritz was appointed city manager November 8, 1927. On July 6, 1928, Glenn E. Turner, who was city auditor and clerk, was made city manager and served until October 19, 1931. A. J. (Bert) Merrill was city manager from November 4, 1931, until March 31, 1932. R. M. Kerr was appointed in November of 1933 and served until November of 1935. Mr. Merrill was back from 1935 to 1937. Bond refunding was not really set up and completed until Merrill was again made city manager in 1941. This time he served until November, 1945, bringing the city through the shortages and tensions of the war days.

The Pompano thoroughbred race track opened in a blaze of glory, but was in trouble almost immediately. Its slogan was, "Off They Go at Pompano." As stated earlier, parimutuel betting was contrary to law, and Governor John Martin had explicitly stated that he intended to uphold the law. When the sheriff's deputies did not move against the track Governor Martin threatened to send the state militia. This forced the track to close after a week. A long legal fight ensued which ended that summer with a final State Supreme Court decision that the gaming as conducted was illegal. The track must close. It was used thereafter for occasional automobile races before it finally gave way to weeds and decay.

If there was to be no horse racing, there was still fun to be had. On February 5, 1927, the Trianon, billed as the South's finest ballroom, opened with great fanfare. The huge room was on South Andrews Avenue between 14th and 15th streets and included a large, beautiful garden in front of the dance hall proper. It remained for years the most popular amusement place in Fort Lauderdale.

One form of gambling hitherto unmentioned was Bolita. From the beginning Bolita operated in several areas of the county but was confined to Negro sections. The major "house" in the Fort Lauderdale area was that of "Humpy." The name of the operator was never openly revealed in court, but it was generally believed to be named for a hunchbacked ex-printer named Montgomery.

In Bolita, "runners" sell tickets usually for ten cents a number or "piece." The number is drawn each night. A canvas bag containing a hundred numbered balls is passed around a circle of customers who toss it from one to another. At a signal one holds on to a single ball which is then cut from the bag. It is the winning number. Inasmuch as the house pays off usually at from sixty to seventy-five to one, it will be seen that the "take" of the operator is generous. The game has had great popularity throughout the years and the "take" is reputedly enormous. The best efforts of police and the sheriff's office have failed to stamp it out. In the middle 1930's the "house of Humpy" was rivaled by another, the "house of Piccolo." In later years the game, though continuing to operate, went under cover to the extent that no name is given the operating "houses."

The picture in Fort Lauderdale was already grim before the stock market crash in 1929 ushered in the so-called "Hoover depression." Bootlegging, gambling, and houses of ill-repute were tolerated. Law-abiding people, with the exception of successful farmers and a few tourists, were dead broke. Taxes were highly oppressive, if not completely confiscatory. The roaring 1920's departed in gloom. Fort Lauderdale was paying the fiddler for her dizzy dance.

Mounted fish placed on Andrews Avenue bridge by Commodore A. H. Brook

The Long Road Back

Chapter 14
1930–1935

Hard times smothered the land. By 1930 Fort Lauderdale's proud new golf course, like almost everything else, appeared to be at the end of the line. The city had leased the course to a Chicago syndicate headed by Joe Roseman, who had acted as pro and manager. Play fell off and revenues dropped to almost nothing. The Roseman syndicate gave up the course. It came back to the city in bad condition. Water and fertilizer are prime necessities for maintenance, and both cost money. The syndicate had spent an absolute minimum. The city put Norman Sommers back in charge for a time, then leased again to another Chicagoan, Roy Quayle. It had been thought that the latter was a wealthy bootlegger but it developed that he was almost as broke as the city itself. He allowed further deterioration of the course until the fairways were little more than sandy, weed-grown prairies. The clubhouse continued to serve as the center of social life in the hard-hit community, but the game of golf was for die-hards who did not mind battling sand and loose turf.

The Long Road Back: 1930–1935

The old Southside Golf Course was turned into an airfield and named Merle L. Fogg Field in honor of the aviator who had come to Fort Lauderdale to fly Tom Bryan's seaplane during the land boom. Fogg had remained to pioneer aviation in the community prior to his death at Palm Beach when, on May 1, 1928, he crashed with S. C. Nelson, a student pilot. Nelson survived the crash, but Fogg and Thomas Lochrie, son of the financier who had been mainly responsible for reopening the bank, were both killed. Fogg was locally loved as the operator of a flying service, a unique vocation, and because he was a personable, outgoing young man. Among his exploits were the flying of the first airplane from Maine to Florida, and setting down the first land plane on Andros Island and the island of New Providence (Nassau).

Little work or expense was involved in converting the old golf course to an airfield. Its few bunkers were leveled off and a monument was erected in memory of Fogg; but for many years thereafter the field was not even mowed. Runways were the unpaved former fairways of the golf course and soon grew high with weeds. Only bootleggers could

Right: Merle L. Fogg, Fort Lauderdale's first pilot, at hangar on East Las Olas Boulevard (GIFT, JANET W. KELCY)

Below: Dedication of Merle L. Fogg Field, now a part of Hollywood-Fort Lauderdale International Airport (BURGHARD COLLECTION)

First train into Port Everglades. Arthur N. Solee (*far left*), Samuel L. Drake (*far right*)

afford to fly airplanes during the depression, and bootleggers chose more remote spots. The city named H. Willard Langmead, a semiretired former Cincinnatian, as airport director. Langmead served without salary and without budgeted expense money, even for upkeep. Revenue from the field was nil. Landing fees would not have been sufficient to pay for their collection. The site is the present Fort Lauderdale-Hollywood International Airport.

Meantime, Boyd H. Anderson, well-known local businessman, was sworn into office as clerk of the county judge's court by County Judge Fred B. Shippey. Anderson was later to become county judge.

In 1931 Franklin D. Roosevelt, a candidate for President of the United States, came out flatly for repeal of prohibition. This stand was also adopted in southeastern Florida by J. Mark Wilcox, a candidate for Congress against the well-beloved, long-time Congresswoman, Ruth Bryan Owen. A daughter of William Jennings Bryan, Mrs. Owen, though she correctly read the temper of the times, said earnestly that she "couldn't vote for repeal." It was the death knell of her elective political career. Roosevelt stood for many innovations other than repeal, but it is doubtful if local citizens read much further in his platform. Repeal was enough to sway a populace fully fed up with national prohibition and its attendant evils.

164

The Long Road Back: 1930-1935

During the prohibition years Fort Lauderdale, which had been a dry town prior to the "noble experiment," had become widely known among wags as "Fort Liquordale." Drinking had become commonplace, practiced in almost all social gatherings. "Speak-easies," selling home-brewed beer, were numerous throughout the town and county. Imported liquor from the Bahamas was as easy to buy as ginger ale, and it was no more expensive than it is today. Every dance hall and night spot, including those in the big hotels, served "set-ups" and permitted bottles under the tables or, in some cases, on them. The effect on the young people was demoralizing. It had become "smart" to drink, and obedience to law was taking it on the chin. Both Roosevelt and Wilcox won.

The year 1931 was also to see other vastly significant political maneuvering. This was the year that the famed Hialeah Bill came before the state legislature, bringing with it a host of suspicion, accusations, and counteraccusations of crooked politics and hints at bribery. The bill, which permitted parimutuel betting in the state, passed after a torrid floor battle in the senate, culminating in a subterfuge that enabled passage by the narrowest possible margin after Governor Doyle Carlton vetoed the bill. To get the vote of the small northern counties which controlled the legislature, the Hialeah Bill provided that all revenue from racing be divided equally among the sixty-seven counties, regardless of size or population. This was manifestly unfair, inasmuch as some counties numbered the residents in the hundreds and others in the hundreds of thousands. This provision has since been carefully guarded by the smaller counties. The subterfuge used for final passage was a simple one. A two-thirds majority was needed over the veto. A number of senators favoring the bill were suddenly called home by illness but, before leaving, they "paired" their vote with senators known to be opposed. Since, under the circumstances, a "no" vote was equal to two "yes" votes the needed majority was thus obtained.

Another bill that came up in the 1931 session, under the sponsorship of Broward County's own representative, Dwight L. Rogers, was the controversial Homestead Exemption measure, which provides complete relief from ad valorem taxation for the first five thousand dollars of value assessed upon any resident's home. The exemption could not legally apply against already incurred bonded debts, but it did apply to all current and future ad valorem taxes for operating and maintaining city, county, state, or other political subdivisions. Under the system then in force most of the homes fell below the five-thousand-dollar assessment

165

and were thus exempt from current taxation. The legislature finally passed the Homestead Exemption Bill in 1933, and it was adopted at a general election held in 1934.

The parimutuel bill provided for local option. Any track granted a license must then pay for an election in which the proposed track must be approved. The first such election held here was on behalf of the Hollywood Kennel Club, proposed by a Chicago group headed by William Syms. The vote was overwhelmingly in favor of the track, to be built just off Federal Highway in Hallandale.

Still another bill (adopted in 1930 by a general election) related to bond issues. This provided that any such issue which pledged revenue from ad valorem taxation must be approved in an election by a vote of fifty per cent plus one of the freeholders. A simple majority would be sufficient to pass the issue but more than half of those owning property must participate in the election. Thus far no bond election held since in Broward County has ever come close to drawing the participation of the required percentage of property owners. The law drew little attention at the time, for no governing body in this area had good enough credit to consider selling a bond issue; but in the future the law, admirable as it seemed in theory, was to further hamstring the hard-hit school system by making borrowing for capital improvements almost impossible.

Representative Rogers, rapidly pushing forward to the prestige that was to send him to Washington as Broward congressman, also pushed hard for the construction of State Road 26. This road, which was to connect Fort Lauderdale with South Bay on Lake Okeechobee, utilizing the banks of the north New River Canal for roadbed, had been established as a project in 1923 by Representative Carl P. Weidling. Though getting the road adopted along the already existing right-of-way, he never got an appropriation for construction. Rogers' efforts failed in their purpose but did serve to alert the members of the Dade County delegation. If there was to be a road from southeastern Florida to Lake Okeechobee, they wanted it for Dade County. The legislature took no serious thought of the matter in that depression-ridden year, but it was filed for future reference.

If the state legislature neglected State Road 26 there were other agencies that did not. These were depression times and Franklin D. Roosevelt and his advisors were looking for any sort of "make work" project. Many local people, struggling to hold their claims to homes or other property, remember working on this project under one of the various government agencies which adopted it as an experimental program.

First ship of foreign registry docks at Port Everglades (BURGHARD COLLECTION)

Rogers' efforts to get an appropriation were eventually successful, and the road, thirty-feet wide, was started in 1937 and completed in 1938 by the Florida State Road Department at a cost of $449,330.60. By 1940 the road was completed from 20-Mile Bend to Dade County, giving that county equal access to the lake region. This road was renamed State Road 25 and later U.S. 27, while the cutoff from 20-Mile Bend (Andytown) to Fort Lauderdale was renamed State Road 84. Road Department records show that portions of the project were classified NRH, which would indicate a federal grant. The road was retreaded several times after its original construction.

An advertisement of Table Supply Store at South West 2d Street between 2d and 3d Avenues in the *Fort Lauderdale Shopper*, August 26, 1932, showed the current prices of food:

Potatoes	10 lbs.	14¢
Steaks, round, club, or Porterhouse		19¢ lb.
Hamburger	2 lbs.	21¢
Stew beef		10¢ lb.
Onions		3¢ lb.
Coffee		19¢ lb.
Milk—5 tall cans	@	18¢
Pillsbury's Best Flour	12 lbs. bag	44¢
Lettuce—2 large heads		9¢

FORT LAUDERDALE

Port Everglades struggled with an occasional foreign cruise ship. or freighter. There was almost nothing to export and little money to purchase imports. The area was not yet inviting to shippers.

With Hoover's defeat in 1931 one thing was plainly in sight, the end of prohibition. Congress repealed it in February, 1933, but the repeal by a special amendment to the Constitution had to be ratified by the states. The end came in December of that year. This put many bootleggers out of work, but it cleared the way for new opportunities in legitimate fields. Many opened legal saloons. Of the four major bars that were established along New River three were owned by former bootleggers. The river front immediately became headquarters for those who liked a nip. It was already headquarters for one of the finest charter fishing fleets the nation had thus far seen. Part of the city's boom-time bond money had gone into the modernization and beautification of the docks on both sides of the river. The charter fleet occupied the space from South East 1st Avenue east of the Andrews Avenue Bridge and west to the old vegetable dock at Brickell Avenue (South West 1st Avenue).

One exception among the charter boats docked along the river front was the double-decked sight-seeing boat "Abeona," which made daily trips up New River and into the unique jungle that bordered its western reaches. The "Abeona" was owned by Harry Kestner, and the magnificent oft-time mayor, Will J. Reed, served as its "spieler" with real knowledge and talent. In all there were twenty charter craft, most of which sailed daily during the winter season. Fish display racks were on each side of the Andrews Avenue Bridge. Every evening these racks were decorated with huge deep-sea specimens hung for display and picture-taking, and to stimulate future charters. The spectacle never failed to attract throngs of tourists. An evening on the riverfront soon became one of the most colorful features of life in Fort Lauderdale.

Fort Lauderdale was deep in the financial woods, but progress was being made and hope was beginning to show. During the 1930's many people of varying kinds and degrees of importance visited the city. A large number were attracted by the fame of the charter boat fleet. Among those who fished with the fleet during this period were Cardinal Spellman; baseball greats Babe Ruth and Harry Heilmann; radio singer Kate Smith; radio priest Father Coughlin; football great Tommy Harmon; financiers Owen Young and R. K. LeBlond.

The town merchants through the Chamber of Commerce held an annual fishing tournament, and at one of the award presentation dinners A. B. (Happy) Chandler of Kentucky served as toastmaster. Habitués

The Amphitrite floating hotel moored beside causeway on East Las Olas
(GIFT, JANET W. KELCY)

of the docks were Labor leader John L. Lewis, writer Octavus Roy Cohen, and blues singer Helen Morgan. Other fishing enthusiasts of notoriety were "Machine Gun" Jack McGurn and Al Capone, mobster accused of the Valentine's Day massacre in Chicago, and his "blond alibi." An astute young naturalist, Joseph T. Reese from Oklahoma, founded what was to become one of the world's largest taxidermy establishments.

The "Amphitrite," a floating hotel now often referred to as an eyesore and a menace to sanitation, had been opened here amid great rejoicing and fanfare in 1931 with John Needham in charge. The ship was originally a United States monitor, started in 1870 but not completed for many years thereafter. In the Spanish-American War she had assisted in the bombardment of San Juan and Cárdenas and had put ashore a landing party which occupied and held the lighthouse at San Juan. It was the second ship of that name built by the Navy. During World War I the "Amphitrite" was located in New York harbor in charge of the torpedo nets and general defenses. In January of 1920 the ship was sold to A. L. D. Bucksten of Elizabeth, New Jersey, for thirty-five thousand dollars. The ship was later converted into a floating hotel at a cost of half a million dollars by the Amphitrite Corporation, headed by Henry G. Bulkley of Cleveland, Ohio. Before being moved to Fort Lauderdale it had been operated at Beaufort, South Carolina, and Sea Island, Georgia.

FORT LAUDERDALE

First docked in the bay at the east end of the city-owned beach casino property, the ship became a popular social gathering place. On November 4, 1935, however, a violent hurricane bounced the cumbersome craft across the shallow bay and beached her on the shore of Idlewyld at the cove at South East 26th Avenue. Attempts were made to reopen at this location, but residents of the neighborhood objected; the Board of Health also advised against it. Finally, arrangements were made to berth the ship alongside the then-existing Las Olas causeway mole, which included a city park beside the road. Here the "Amphitrite" stayed and remained in business until July of 1942, despite growing objections from residents who claimed it a nuisance. The ship was forced to move after several years of hot negotiations between the owners and the city commissioners. Because of the veil of secrecy maintained during wartime over all shipments, she was moved at night with no formal farewells from the citizenry.

By 1934 Fort Lauderdale had its first marina at the beach. Al Huss was granted permission by the city to build a dock system on the north side of the causeway just west of the Intracoastal Waterway above East Las Olas Boulevard. The venture was successful from the start, though his wooden docks were considered another eyesore by many residents.

It was in this period also that Commodore A. H. Brook and others began a campaign to add to the city's public beaches. The land in front of Las Olas-by-the-Sea was already owned by the public, but during the boom Birch had sold much of the property to the north to permit the creation of Lauder-Del-Mar, another subdivision. Birch had originally owned the rights to the beach. Now it was a question of eminent domain since the public had been using the strip east of Atlantic Boulevard. In selling the land Birch had excepted all lands east of the boulevard from his warranty as to the deed. In turn, John Lochrie, who had sold the land to the Charellen Corporation, owners of the Lauderdale Beach Hotel, had given a warranty deed only to the land west of the boulevard, though he had given a quitclaim deed to the beach itself.

Brook wanted the beach for the public, all of it, including all the land still owned by Birch and that to the north which had been platted and sold during the boom. When aroused over a city project Brook would gnaw at the heels of the elected officials with such persistence that action was sure to follow. And it did. In this he had help from many farseeing citizens, including Mayor Lewis E. Moore. The struggle to obtain title to the beach was neither simple nor easy and it went on for a number of years. That it was ultimately successful is a tribute to many civic-

Pilkington Yacht Basin explosion and fire, 1935 (GIFT, MRS. PAUL RODE)

minded citizens and officials. A deed for the right-of-way for North Atlantic Boulevard was conveyed to the county, dated July 13, 1923. Easement deeds from Birch and his son-in-law, Frederick Clay Bartlett, granting use of the ocean front to the city of Fort Lauderdale were dated November 24, 1940, covering all of Section 31 except a four-hundred-foot strip of beach. The deed to the beach was granted in the years 1935 to 1939 by the Lauder-Del-Mar developers, headed by J. W. Tidball. These were recorded as a "sale" with tax certificates used in lieu of money. Other portions of the beach were acquired by the city in 1940 through condemnation or purchase. In 1945 the city was deeded the beach in front of Birch Estates and Birch Ocean Front subdivisions (original and number two).

As hard-hit financially as any by the depression, Brook was the least despondent. His ebullient and enthusiastic predictions for the future were farfetched to many, but the commodore yielded to no doubt or pessimism. Any who ventured objections were immediately overcome by the powerful force of his logic. When he had the time Brook reverted to his former profession and painted large signs advertising the city of his adoption.

As things began to look better, more thought was given to the city's golf course, now in disgraceful condition. The city took it back from Roy Quayle and appointed a golf commission composed of Tom B. Manuel, Luther Remsberg, Dr. H. J. Peavy, Joel M. Taul, Don D. Freeman, and Tom F. Fleming. One of its first acts was to employ Norman Sommers as pro-manager.

President Roosevelt had the Works Progress Administration under way and Sommers applied for help. He got it, and he and Remsberg scoured the country for suitable marl with which to cover the fairways and rid them of sand. Although a losing proposition since the death of the boom, the golf course soon went into the "black" and stayed there until it was sold to the Men's Golf Association, the present owners. By that time the clubhouse had been completed, the entire course rebuilt, and eighteen holes added.

During this period nothing had grown so rapidly as the gambling profession. Horse books operated in most of the bars in the county, and full-fledged "joints" with wheels and crap tables were operating without interference at many spots. Most blatant was the Plantation where the nightly "come-on" Bingo game was attracting more than a thousand players per night. Even the big, barnlike building could not hold them all, and the Bingo numbers were called out over loud-speakers while the players sat in their cars in the huge parking lot beside the joint. Naturally the progress of the game could be heard for miles about. The main prize contended for with a two-dollar card sometimes ran to fifteen hundred dollars or more, a veritable fortune in those times. Gambling operations hitherto had been conducted under local operators, who were regarded with a certain amount of sympathy by the public in the same manner that bootleggers had been condoned.

Now gambling was big business. Elaborate clubs featuring "games" were springing up both here and in Miami to operate only for the lush winter months. The operators were members of national syndicates and pieces of these clubs were owned by names familiar to law enforcement authorities in northern cities. The syndicates did not bother with small Horse books. In most cases, however, they handled "layoff" money and often in larger operations furnished initial capital for a piece of the operation. The syndicates also controlled the service. This was the means by which the bookies got their lines of odds, running descriptions of races, final results, and pay-offs. Fees for this service ran to fifty dollars a day, plus the cost of the telephone.

The syndicates controlled the gambling business and were able to say who could and could not operate. It was openly apparent that local law enforcement officers were aware of what was going on and that some sort of arrangement had to be in effect between them and the gamblers. Such arrangement, if any, had to be handled locally. None of the big name gamblers appeared openly on the scene, though some had homes in the county and were known to visit the area often. According to contemporary newspaper reports, one syndicate operated in the eastern part of the county. The other, controlled by the Chicago gangsters, operated in the midwest. At the outset Broward County gambling was operated mostly by the Chicago group but later, after the two groups had a "meeting," Dade County was "given" to the Chicagoans and Broward to the New Yorkers. This New York mob was the syndicate headed by Frank Costello. It held a tight grip on Broward County for many years.

In 1933 when President Roosevelt was giving his fireside chats about "priming the pump" the Florida legislature decided to help a bit. It passed a law legalizing slot machines, setting a license fee of fifty dollars per machine. If the pump did not get primed it was not because the handle was not worked enough in and about Fort Lauderdale. Winter visitors in the 1933-34 season found the machines entirely irresistible and plentiful. Every bar in the county prospered greatly during that era, together with most drug stores, grocery stores, and even filling stations. The so-called one-armed bandits drained away a goodly proportion of local cash. The fact that the slot machine law was decisively defeated in a referendum vote held in the next general election was of importance, historically, because it marked the first act of revulsion of the people against open, flagrant gambling. Since the benefits, to southeast Florida at least, probably outweighed local objections from a purely economic standpoint, it was significant and a tribute to their characters that the people chose the more ethical path. The cynicism that had gained such deep root during the worst of the depression had given way to a modicum of civic pride. That slot machines remained illegally was not due to any public expression of the people's wishes.

In 1935, by a lucky coincidence and some resourceful work on the part of the citizenry, Fort Lauderdale obtained a unique winter attraction which had far-reaching effects. It was the Collegiate Aquatic Forum. The forum began with a visit to Fort Lauderdale by Sam W. Ingram, swimming coach at Colgate University in Hamilton, New York. Two members of his squad from Fort Lauderdale persuaded him to come here for the Christmas vacation. He met Al Gordon, pool man-

Mayor Thomas B. Manuel pays tribute to Katherine Rawls, famed aquatic
star. Governor R. H. Gore (*left*)

ager and swimming instructor at the beach casino. Sitting in the warm
sun beside the pool the two got into discussions with Chamber of Commerce Manager August Burghard about winter training for collegiate
swimmers. Until that time the swimming coaches met in winter with the
National Collegiate Athletic Association. Ingram conceived the idea of
holding a forum here and inviting the swimming coaches to hold their
annual meeting during the Christmas holidays.

Gordon made a trip to the North at his own expense to help sell the
idea. Burghard persuaded members of his organization to provide special
rental accommodations, sight-seeing tours, and boat trips for the coaches
and athletes. In this he got enthusiastic support from A. J. Beck, J. B.
Fannin, G. H. Martin, and other professional men, merchants, and
Chamber of Commerce officials. The forum became an excellent me-
dium to build the city's Christmas business, then at low ebb. The National Collegiate Aquatic Forum has been an annual event ever since.

174

Not only did the forum provide a spectacle in itself, but it was a shot in the arm for what had been slow holiday tourist seasons. It also provided the original impetus for the annual spring invasion of college students, and many present residents trace their introduction to Fort Lauderdale to the Aquatic Forum.

A local son received a signal honor in 1935. D. Marston Bates was elected by the Rockefeller Institute to do research work in Italy and France. Marston was a local high school graduate and the son of the late Glenn F. Bates.

During this period Commodore Brook started one of the few campaigns in which he failed. New River, in its earlier days, had been crystalline clear and, though narrow, very deep. The digging of canals through to the lake had brought in muck and debris which clouded and choked the water. The later construction, during the boom, of miles of canals emptying into the river caused it to silt badly. Keeled sailboats had difficulty negotiating it, and wreckage of the storms lined its banks.

Brook wanted the river dredged "while spoil areas are still available for use." Being a navigable stream, New River was controlled by the War Department and was the responsibility of the United States Corps of Engineers. Time after time Brook went to Washington to present his case to the engineers and to Congress. Several times appropriations were made for the job, but the division office at Jacksonville found other more pressing needs for the money. When State Representative Dwight L. Rogers was elected to Congress, Brook acquired an able and enthusiastic ally. On one occasion the engineers sent a hopper dredge to clear out the lower reaches of the river. The complete job was never done and the river remains distressingly shallow in many places—"belly-deep on a high-hipped Indian," was the salty way Tom Bryan put it.

Charter boats, normally drawing three feet or less, had little trouble with the shallow depth, but they did have trouble from a different direction. Almost all big game fishing boats now used outriggers—long cane poles attached to the side of the boat which fold out when in use but jut straight up otherwise. Outriggers caused innumerable openings of the drawbridges. The Federal Highway bridge, which carried a tremendous traffic load, was a major bone of contention. The distressing part was that peak traffic loads came at the same time the boats set out or returned. Long delays at the bridges, followed by the sight of the tops of outriggers gliding past, infuriated motorists. The truth was that most of the boats, including those without outriggers, could not clear the unopened bridges even at low tide. The protests came not only from locals but also from Miami and Palm Beach. Their newspapers commented unfavorably and complained of the "deplorable situation" on United States Highway Number 1 at New River in Fort Lauderdale. The situation at the Las Olas bridge across the Intracoastal Waterway was little better. Federal law governing traffic on the navigable stream plainly gave the right-of-way to the boats.

A former *Fort Lauderdale News* reporter, Price Day, of Fort Lauderdale, had a story in the December 14 issue of the *Saturday Evening Post*. It was the sixth story the local writer had published in the *Post*.

Harry Davis, a tennis enthusiast, saw what Norman Sommers and Luther Remsberg had accomplished at the golf course and got busy on his own. Until then the city's only tennis courts had been two asphalt-paved courts in Stranahan Park. Harry wanted good clay courts for the city. He could use the same source of marl as that used by the golf course and the same WPA labor. He got himself appointed, at no pay, as an assistant to the city and sweated out the construction of the municipal tennis courts at Davis Field (named for County Engineer H. C. Davis, no relation to Harry). These courts, models for their time, soon attracted tournaments of some importance. They are still in daily use in the old Southside Park just west of the Southside School on South West 9th Street. (The park was renamed in 1963 in honor of Florence C. Hardy, long-time city clerk.)

All this activity meant little to the average citizen to whom poverty had now become an accepted way of life. Taxes were still high, and construction work was almost nonexistent. Property values were depressed. The winter seasons brought big increases in tourists, many financially able, who patronized the hotels, the gambling houses, the charter boats, and occasionally the bars. Some of the cash they left trickled into general circulation, but the season's "take" was not great enough to spread over the full twelve-month year.

Many of the town's leading citizens wielded shovels for the WPA. Among these was Charles G. Rodes, developer of Venice and a boom-time millionaire. Although broke, Rodes was trying to save what property he had left from the "tax sharks." His son, C. G. Rodes, Jr., worked beside him on the job. Rodes was to become a multimillionaire again, and remains so to this time.

On December 19, 1935, the United States Treasury Department awarded a contract of ninety-seven thousand dollars to A. C. Atherton & Co., Chicago, for the new post office building for South East 1st Avenue and 2d Street.

Financial Readjustment

In one more year I hear,
We'll have light wines and beer,
If we have beer in one more year
Everything's gonna' be all right,
All right, everything's gonna' be all right.
PARODY SUNG IN TRAVELING TENT SHOW

Everything was far from all right on Fort Lauderdale's fiscal horizon; and its condition reflected exactly that of all other governing bodies, including the county, school board, Port Authority, and all of the various drainage and subdrainage districts. Taxes were not being paid. The reason was simple enough. People did not have the wherewithal; the money well had dried up completely.

Chapter 15
1932

Bond payments had been defaulted by virtually all these agencies despite the dire predictions of the bankers that the city's credit and its financial resources would be forever impugned. The city had struggled. It had cut personnel and salaries, neglected nearly all public works. Work on the new sewer system was abandoned and much of what had been spent became completely wasted. There was no way, however, to save what the city did not have, and what it did not have was enough money to meet its obligations.

The first big blow fell on the day following New Year's Day in 1932 in the form of a suit for an alternative writ of mandamus filed by and on behalf of Annette Causey and Francis F. Causey against the city commissioners. It demanded that taxes be raised to pay interest on bonds held by the litigants. It was only the first of a flood of such suits. By April of 1937 the city was to see no fewer than twenty-eight actually filed and many more threatened. There was no way to pay these demands. Raising the tax millage would not materially increase collections. Since it was ordered by the courts it was done; but tax assessors found an escape. They simply lowered valuations by a corresponding amount. The first default came in the second half of 1930. Defaults continued, and were to continue. Some of the suits took slightly different form. They sought to segregate choice property, on which the taxes would go to one specific bondholder, with foreclosure power. Such suits were battled in a spirit of desperation by the hard-pressed commissioners. In the meantime downtown businessmen wryly referred to city hall as "Mandamus Manor." If they wondered where it would all end they nevertheless kept their spirits up as best they might.

At the outset, in 1928, tax millage had been six mills, or six dollars per thousand dollars of valuation. At the height of the mandamus operation this rate reached a staggering forty-eight mills, or forty-eight dollars per thousand, without increasing the dollar inflow of taxes to any material degree. To illustrate what happened to tax valuation, the city had been appraised in 1924 at $11,021,359, in 1925 at $51,208,417. By 1935 this figure had decreased to an almost unbelievable $5,600,000. These operations, of course, also affected the value of the outstanding bonds. Their appraised value dropped to about ten cents on the dollar though there were, of course, variations. The lowest known quotation was eight and one-half cents. There were few takers.

In this situation vacant lots in the city were almost all dead on the tax roll and considered worthless. Taxes on most residences were delinquent to some extent, and the owners of downtown buildings, apartment houses, and other highly improved property adopted a practice of paying taxes every other year. This allowed tax sharks to buy tax certificates, paying a high rate of interest, but did not permit the purchase of a tax deed on which foreclosure could be sought. Tax deeds were sold only when tax certificates were issued for the second consecutive year. As a stopgap, or holding action, this worked; but time was certain to run out eventually. The city appeared to be merely getting deeper into the mire.

Perhaps the worst phase of the situation was its effect on prospective new buyers of property. There were still people coming to southeastern Florida and liking it there. But when the question of buying property arose, a good look at the tax situation and the city's status with regard to the bondholders was sufficient to scare away all but the boldest. The state legislature passed a law designed to help. It provided that by paying current property taxes in cash one could pay back taxes with defaulted bonds. The bill was designed to bring property back on the active tax roll and, at the same time, retire at least some of the outstanding bonds. The bonds, selling at ten cents on the dollar, would be accepted at face value for back taxes. This offered a golden opportunity to many who were badly, if not hopelessly, in arrears, but it had a drawback. The bonds were in one thousand dollar denominations, and one had to buy a bond issued by each of the taxing bodies in order to pay.

The situation gave rise to the Fort Lauderdale Bond and Tax Adjustment Bureau, a private firm which would pay off one's taxes at a discount. Then was seen the spectacle of citizens paying their taxes at the Tax Adjustment office in the Sweet Building instead of at the courthouse. The head of this bureau was Ralph A. Horton, and Fred Hixson and Leaird Rickard were administrators. There were those, even then, who foresaw that the difficulties would some day be overcome, and many fortunes were founded by the buying up of tax deeds on Fort Lauderdale property.

Horton, who headed the tax adjustment firm, was an early citizen, a large landowner, and builder. His bureau was making money, but he wanted an end to the situation and he envisaged a refunding agreement that would make it possible for the taxing body to continue to operate as a means of working this out. The great drawback to such a plan was that of getting all the bondholders to agree. If only a few stayed out they would be in a position to take enormous advantage in future suits. Franklin D. Roosevelt had become President in 1932 and, true to his pre-election promise, had light wine and beer legalized, to be followed by repeal of prohibition. He also had passed other new laws affecting finances, among them the Federal Municipal Bankruptcy Act. Under it if two-thirds of the bondholders of a taxing body in default agreed to a refunding, then the other one-third was forced to go along. Horton's problem was simplified greatly. He now had to get not all, but only two-thirds of the bondholders to agree.

When Horton located a large block of bonds controlled by Spitzer-Rorick and Company of Toledo, Ohio, Commissioners M. A. Hortt and John Needham went to Toledo to confer with them. They demonstrated that if all current mandamus suits were upheld taxes in Fort Lauderdale would go to an impossible four hundred mills and as a result the city must simply collapse. They showed members of the firm that city operating expenses had been cut from six hundred eighty-five thousand dollars per year to one hundred forty-two thousand. Even then the city continued to go into the red. Finally an agreement was won, and the needed two-thirds of the bondholders accepted.

Although agreed upon in 1937, the entire bond-refunding campaign was not set up and put into actual operation until 1941; but in the meantime action had been taken along other lines to clarify property status. The 1937 session of the state legislature passed what is still commonly known as the Murphy Act. This provided that at the expiration of two years from the date the chapter (18296) became a law, the fee simple title to all lands in this state, against which there were outstanding tax sale certificates which, on the date the law went into effect, were more than two years old, became absolutely vested in the State of Florida, and provided for the sale of said lands by the Trustees of the Internal Improvement Fund of Florida. Former owners were given preference in the sale of the lands. Subsequent legislation confirmed these titles.

The effect of this law can hardly be understood today. It is significant, however, that not less than sixty thousand parcels of property in Broward County changed hands under the terms of this act. This brought the land back onto the active tax roll. It cleared away litigation that might have continued for years, or even scores of years, over titles. It put real estate back on a firm and buyable foundation and it created a burst of activity which has never stopped. It also created heartbreak and real suffering. Many had clung desperately to their homes for years, struggling by every means just to "hold on." Many failed to make it, and lost their property. The tax sharks got rich. All the other taxing agencies in the county went through similar maneuvers, the last to reach final agreement with bondholders being one of the special school districts, late in 1938. Some, including Fort Lauderdale, had further refundings where it was found advantageous from a fiscal standpoint.

It is significant that during these trying years the city had consistently elected its ablest men to office. This was no time for sentiment, or even for "glad-handers." Tightfisted, blunt-talking Republican (in a sea of Democrats) John Needham was in there, as was, usually, equally tightfisted M. A. Hortt. The city attorney, throughout this trying period, was George W. English.

The financial wringer through which the city was going has been presented as a backdrop to the long, lean depression years. In telling the story of these years references may be made to the various phases of the great refinancing program explained in this brief chapter.

Above: Ralph A. Horton, whose foresight and business acumen guided the city out of its financial doldrums (GIFT, MRS. FRED HIXSON)

Top right: J. Fred Hixson, associate of Horton in Bond and Tax Bureau

Right: F. Leaird Rickard, prominent in civic affairs and associate of Horton in Bond and Tax Bureau (HYDE PHOTO)

Governors' Club Hotel (old Wil-Mar skeleton) completed by R. H. Gore in 1937

Hope Blooms Reluctantly

Chapter 16
1930–1943

The sun shone brightly in southeast Florida almost every day after the 1926 hurricane, but ten long and desperate years were to pass before the inhabitants really noticed and enjoyed it. Whether President Roosevelt's extensive "pump-priming" and relief programs were responsible, or whether the natural vigor of the nation was reasserting itself remains a matter for argument, but whatever the cause the nation was emerging from the depression. Normal prosperity was rounding the corner. Optimism was felt and hope bloomed anew. Around city hall Fort Lauderdale officials breathed more easily. There were bond refundings ahead, the debt was still massive, but no longer completely insurmountable. The cost had been and would remain heavy but the way out was at least in view. Bonds were actually selling at near par again. The Chicago bondholders group, through Julian E. Ross, local attorney, filed writs seeking judgments totaling a million two hundred and seventy thousand dollars against the City of Fort Lauderdale and the Broward County School Board, in a gesture typical of the times.

Hope Blooms Reluctantly: 1930–1943

These early 1930's, henceforth to be known as the "Depression Years," had been times to try men's souls. They had seen the citizenry behave at its worst with open gambling, prostitution, and bootlegging tolerated; yet these years also revealed many stalwart citizens in what may have been their finest hours. Much had been accomplished that marked the town for future greatness. These feats included acquisition of additional beach front for public use, development of Port Everglades, renovation of the golf course, and construction of the Town and Tennis Club. There was also a notably sad loss: Clarence Elliott Rickard, 65, pioneer citizen and builder, who came here in 1912, died at his home at 505 North West River Drive on February 5, 1936. Mr. Rickard had served as the first city manager, without pay, and headed a large lumber company.

Perhaps the first sign of the "new spring" was the reblossoming of Las Olas Boulevard. In 1934 Thomas N. Stilwell, one of the original developers of Idlewyld, began clearing the first of a series of "finger islands" he had purchased during the boom and partially developed. These islands lay between Venice and Riviera and extended from the Boulevard on its south side to New River. The work progressed slowly and was under way when he died in 1936. His widow, Grace, working with Dr. Sahler Hornbeck, J. S. Powell, and Bryon F. Snyder, carried the work to completion. Almost at once, beautiful homes sprang up in what is still known as "Stilwell Isles."

In May of 1936 a permit was issued to the Coast Guard Development Company, a Chicago firm headed by Preston A. Wells, for construction of an eighty-room hotel in the six hundred block on East Las Olas to be named Champ Carr, after the man chosen to manage it. The hotel, now known as the Riverside, opened that same year. Early in 1937 R. H. Gore opened the one-hundred-ten-room Governors' Club Hotel. Its completion erased from the Fort Lauderdale scene the Wil-Mar skeleton that had marred the landscape since the failure of the 1925 boom. Frank Parsons, Jr., completed the Boulevard Hotel in the four hundred block of the same thoroughfare in 1939. Meantime, the Charellen Corporation, headed by James S. Knight, former Chicagoan, finished the Lauderdale Beach Hotel in time for the 1937 winter season. An addition, contracted for during the following summer, enlarged it to one hundred ten rooms.

By 1936 many of the boom-time developers had returned to Fort Lauderdale. Among them were W. F. Morang, whose Lauderdale Isles development north of Las Olas Boulevard was still incomplete and in litigation; A. G. Kuhn, Victoria Park, back from Mexico City; and G. Frank Croissant, former sales and promotion manager for Croissant Park, which included most of the southern portion of the city. Morang failed in efforts to find financing and did not resume operations, leaving shortly thereafter. Croissant and Kuhn remained until their deaths. None of the three became active in development again, but the excellence of their early planning has been demonstrated. Most of their promises, made in 1925, were fulfilled.

Other boom-time developments that showed signs of reawakening included Harrison McCready's Chateau Park, in the northwest corner of the city, and E. J. Willingham's Wilton Manors, due north of the city. Chain stores began taking an interest in the city. In September of 1936 Sears, Roebuck and Company took over a three-story building on North Andrews Avenue; McCrory's announced a new Five and Ten Cent Store; and Walgreen's Drugs opened in the newly completed Governors' Club Hotel.

Illegal gambling still ran wide open in the county. The newest thing in this line was the building of the palatial Colonial Inn on South Federal Highway just north of the Dade County line within the limits of Hallandale. Virgil W. Peterson, Operating Director, Chicago Crime Commission, representing the American Municipal Association, testified in Washington, D.C., on July 7, 1950, that "just recently records were uncovered by the district attorney's office in New York which definitely established that the Colonial Inn in Hallandale, Fla., has been owned by Joe Adonis, alias Joe Doto, one of the most powerful gangsters in this country; Frank Erickson, Meyer Lansky, Jake Lansky, Vincent Alo, alias Jimmy Blue Eyes, from the New York mob; and Mert Wertheimer, head of the powerful Chesterfield syndicate in Michigan. Notes found in the amount of $50,000 in favor of Frank Costello would indicate the possibility of his connection with the place as well. The gambling racket in Broward County has attracted the gangster element to settle there."

* * *

In 1936 President Roosevelt visited the city. He came to Port Everglades by train where he was greeted by tremendous crowds. There he boarded the U.S.S. "Potomac." The following facts are taken from the typescript of the log of President Roosevelt's cruise, March 23 to April 8, 1936:

[On Monday, March 23, 1936], the train was taken onto the dock at

President Franklin D. Roosevelt on vacation at Fort Lauderdale (GIFT, MRS. PAUL RODE)

Port Everglades alongside the destroyers "Monaghan" and "Dale." The President, accompanied by his uncle, Mr. Delano, his son James, and several others of the party, embarked on the "Monaghan." Colonel Watson, Captain Ross McIntire and other members of the party embarked on the "Dale." Both vessels started immediately and layed a course through Northwest Providence Channel for Cat Island.

The U.S.S. "Potomac" had left Miami early on the morning of the 23d to proceed to a rendezvous for the morning of the 25th at Tortuga Island. The "Potomac" and "Monaghan" got underway from Great Isaac at 0530 and stood toward Fort Lauderdale at twelve knots. The sea was perfectly calm during the early forenoon but the wind freshened from the southeast in the early afternoon.

When eight miles off the entrance buoy to Fort Lauderdale the "Monaghan" lay-to and the "Potomac" stood to the northward in the Gulf Stream at five knots for a final trolling. Several strikes were made almost immediately and the President hooked a large sailfish. When this fish appeared to be well in hand and almost a sure catch, the hook (a Japanese feather lure) straightened out and the "sail" escaped. The President shortly thereafter caught a bonita after which it became necessary to increase speed to ten knots in order to arrive at the dock at Fort Lauderdale as scheduled at 1300.

FORT LAUDERDALE

A rather large crowd were assembled at the dock to receive the President. The transfer from the "Potomac" to the train was effected with great convenience as the train was drawn up directly opposite the "Potomac."

The log of President Roosevelt's cruise was kept by his Naval Aide, Captain Wilson Brown, U.S.N. This was President Roosevelt's first cruise on the presidential yacht "Potomac," which had been converted from the Coast Guard Offshore Patrol Vessel "Electra" late in 1935.

* * *

The McKillop-Hutton Lion Farm at the north city limits (now the Gateway Shopping Center) was rated one of the "Five-Star" attractions of the state. Fort Lauderdale was being noticed.

Charles L. Swaggerty, who had held the sole city taxi franchise for many years and had taken over the beach bus service from Fred Ormsby after the land-boom collapse, now gave the city its first general bus line. Swaggerty applied for and obtained a franchise for a "belt line." The bus he used was an ancient Pierce Arrow sedan. The fare for any and all trips was ten cents, and Swaggerty had a standing offer to any prospective driver which would allow him to retain all fares collected in return for his services. He seldom found any takers and seldom had riders, so he drove the bus himself. Like many others Swaggerty saw big things in the future. In spite of the dearth of business he stoutly maintained his route to keep his franchise alive. For company on his lonely trips he was often accompanied by his two dogs, Piggy and Brownie. However, the beach bus, particularly during the winter, did much to make up losses on the belt line. Operation of these buses, when Swaggerty himself was at the wheel, was strictly informal. When a fire engine, its siren screeching, turned off to a side street in front of the bus, Swaggerty stopped and asked, "Anyone in a hurry?" If not, he and his passengers attended the fire.

* * *

Fort Lauderdale was given world-wide fame by the phenomenal exploits of a colorful, sprightly, girl athlete. She was modest, almost bashful, Katherine (Katy) Rawls. Her feats in diving and swimming won her many national championships, a 1936 trip to the Olympic Games in Hitler's Germany, and recognition of sportswriters as the "Greatest Woman Athlete of the Year." Katherine Rawls began swimming almost as soon as she could walk. In the 1920's her father worked on road construction in the center of the state. Most of his locations were near fresh-water lakes and provided Katy with her opportunities to swim.

186

Governor Fred Cone is saluted by *(left to right)* Col. John D. Kennedy, Katherine Rawls, and Col. Walter R. Clark (BURGHARD COLLECTION)

Later the family moved to Hollywood and then to Coral Gables. While in Coral Gables she often watched the great natator and later movie Tarzan, Johnnie Weissmuller, and Pete Des Jardins, a champion diver. In 1931 Katy began diving under the tutelage and encouragement of Georgia Coleman. Her swimming coach was Willis Cooling, aquatic director of the Bath and Tennis Club in Miami.

In 1934 the Rawls family moved to Fort Lauderdale and she received further training and encouragement from Las Olas Casino Coach Al Gordon and his son, Bob. She became one of the few, if not the only athlete, who competed successfully in both swimming and diving. According to Katy the high point of her career was reached in a tournament sponsored by the *New York Daily News* when Jones Beach was opened. This was a decathlon. She won first place in each of the ten events competing against the best swimmers and divers of the nation. During her career she won hundreds of medals, trophies, and ribbons, as

187

well as twenty-six national and international championships, and set a number of world records.

Katherine met Tony Piper, son of W. T. Piper, producer of the Piper airplanes, and soon she became adept at flying. She often spent her total allowance on flying lessons. She married her instructor, Ted Thompson. As World War II threatened, the United States Army Air Force set up a program for women aviators to ferry planes. Katy was one of twenty-five women, each with a commercial pilot's license and at least five hundred hours' flying time, selected to initiate the plan. They became known as the WASPS. Partially because of the inspiration of the outstanding achievements of Katherine Rawls, Fort Lauderdale developed many outstanding swimmers and divers.

There were less idealistic developments. The British freighter "Welcome" left Port Everglades laden with six thousand tons of scrap iron for Japan on February 1, 1936. On April 1, 1937, the freighter "Clarissa Radcliffe" embarked from Port Everglades with sixty-five hundred tons of scrap iron, also for Japan.

Rumblings from abroad were becoming more sinister. Adolf Hitler had turned Germany's vast industrial resources and manpower into a great war machine. The comforting thought "that surely no one as unbalanced as that could possibly carry out such wild schemes" faded. He perfected his plans and took his countrymen down the road with him. British Premier Sir Neville Chamberlain remained calm and in making concessions to the arrogant German dictator he spoke reassuringly of "peace in our time." The war threat grew. In July, 1937, Japan invaded China and in the following year Hitler took over Austria. Mussolini completed his conquest of Ethiopia.

Vaguely uneasy, Fort Lauderdale citizens continued their struggle toward recovery. The end of the depression came quietly, unmarked by any actual realization on the part of the people. In 1937 the Barnett banking chain, headquartered in Jacksonville, opened a new bank in the Sweet Building in the quarters formerly occupied by the boom-time First National of Fort Lauderdale. This Barnett bank, with E. M. Barnett as chairman of the board and W. T. Coates, president, was later to become the present First National Bank in Fort Lauderdale.

Mid-1937 saw the end of activities by the tax sharks and also the end of the practice of paying back taxes with bonds. The city and other governing agencies were once more solvent, going concerns and the still heavy tax burden was less burdensome. The return to fiscal stability saw the climate change in the construction field. Home building again became an important industry. Jobs were available at last in many fields.

On to center stage now stepped Joseph M. Smoot. Smoot was the gaudily dressed promoter of thoroughbred horse race tracks. He had previously promoted Hialeah in Florida and Santa Anita in California. In both he had lost all his financial interest, but he was recognized as responsible for their creation. Smoot set up headquarters in the Sweet Building and announced that he would build a new track at Hallandale, to be known as Gulfstream Park. He engaged Robinson Reese Saunders, a popular young Virginian who had established his practice in Fort Lauderdale, as his attorney. He got his promotion under way, mean-time treating Fort Lauderdale to a display of lurid haberdashery never before seen in these parts. He would combine the wearing of vivid red trousers with a flamboyant yellow jacket and accouterments to match. He said, "I want people to know when Joe Smoot is around."

He was an able salesman and promoter. A referendum election authorizing the track was necessary and Smoot found the money to pay for it. It passed by a big majority. Realizing that a construction project of such proportions would bring in substantial payrolls the citizens gladly supported it though few had money to invest. Smoot obtained an option on the needed land and had preliminary plans prepared. Hialeah Park had done well in recent years, and the Hollywood Kennel Club near-by made money. Hialeah's biggest day's handle that year had been a half-million dollars and under prevailing economic conditions that was considered a veritable "gold mine." This was the bait needed by Smoot to lure prospective investors. The largest of these was John C. (Jack) Horning, Jr., son of a prosperous Miami contractor, who could provide money, building equipment, and "know-how." The construction of Gulfstream Park gave incentive to other Broward building programs and Fort Lauderdale got its share.

Gulfstream's big opening day came in 1939 and it ran concurrently with Hialeah's. The first day was a magnificent success, with Sonja Henie, famed ice skating movie queen, cutting the ribbon. Mutuels play dropped sharply in the next three days, and on the fourth day the "bank-roll" money needed to make change and pay off the winners of the first race failed to appear. Its supplier, a Miamian, gave no reason but the track was thrown into bankruptcy shortly thereafter. For several years during feverish refinancing efforts, it remained a "ghost track."

Night clubs were popular during the lush days of the land boom in the mid-twenties but thereafter hit the doldrums. The roof garden had been blown down in the 1926 hurricane. With the depression, night club investments were not regarded as financially productive. Trianon Gardens, the large dance hall on South Andrews, was a crowded Saturday night attraction at a dollar per couple. The next attempt at a night club was Kenneth Mendel's Victoria Park Gardens on what is now North East 18th Avenue. The building, later known as the Alamo Apartments, was a residence when Mendel took it over in 1934. The next year he made his restaurant into a night club and renamed it the Rendezvous. The following year he sold out to Alfred Parker Crooks, owner and operator of the downtown Deck Bar. Crooks renamed it the Alamo (Crooks' last stand) and as such it achieved a degree of notoriety. Entertainment usually featured an orchestra and a few strip-tease artists. The night club business continued spotty. By 1938 prosperity was returning and that year the famed entertainers Chick Endor and Charlie Farrell opened the Coral Club.

Endor and Farrell were internationally known as a singing team, but they were not businessmen. The Coral Club was located on East Las Olas at 9th Avenue in a specially built building owned by M. A. Hortt. It was a lavish production from the start and was in trouble almost immediately. Its location was near many private homes, and not only was the club noisy but it operated all night. The city at the time had no bar closing hours but the police could close any place adjudged a nuisance. They became almost nightly visitors as a storm of neighborhood protests arose. The ebullient Endor and Farrell greeted the police jovially as they did their other guests, plying them with hospitality of every kind. Quiet was achieved briefly but never lasted long after the officers departed. The entertainers soon began writing songs about their neighbors, serenading them by name. They were called before the city commission of which Hortt, their landlord, was a member, and here again they proved their mettle as entertainers and made promises. But still the neighbors found room for complaint.

In the meantime lack of business acumen on the part of the partners also caused trouble. Every guest was a friend and every friend had credit privileges. Moreover, both liked to gamble and frequently "tapped" the till to visit race track or bookmaker. The clammy hands of creditors began to close on the carefree Coral Club. Finally the place "folded." The city had never before seen such a club and probably never will see another like it. As entertainers the two owners were "tops" and their jovial openhanded friendliness was something to experience. They attracted many famous people, among them Chicagoan Fred Snite, the courageous "Iron Lung Kid." He was brought here in the lung by trailer from Miami Beach. When it was discovered that the lung was too large to get through the Coral Club doorway, Endor and Farrell pushed their little piano out onto the sidewalk and gave him open-air concerts. Needless to say, passersby stopped to enjoy the free entertainment.

Fort Lauderdale was on the way back. People who had sweated profusely in past years to hold onto property now found a ready market, though prices remained low. All but unregenerate loafers were back at work but at salaries based on depression scales. The tourists who packed the town each winter strained the facilities. Most residents were still deep in depression-time obligations and were forced to go to great lengths to obtain money. But the outlook was brightening. True, prohibition had left scars, drinking was now commonplace even among women, unheard of in prior days, and social functions were frequent and wet. Newfangled iceless refrigerators had doomed the "friendly iceman" and given rise to a new item of importance, the ice cube. But the radio—a tremendous development—was now commonplace and had a telling effect upon the world outlook as Hitler continued his rise to power.

Locally, once each week in summer months the police had to close a large section of downtown Andrews Avenue to all traffic. This was "Bank Night" when almost the entire population gathered at the theater for the awarding of prizes. Meantime, a substantial factor, home building, which had started on a modest and rather timid scale, continued to feel its way. The long depression left a number of the older homes with new owners. Many had foreclosed mortgages on homes they did not need. At first these homes were rented for whatever they would bring, but the demand was beginning to catch up. Most of them were now for sale and the market continued to strengthen. The depression was far from forgotten, and caution rather than confidence was the watchword. Many bargains in real estate continued to go begging. Confidence during this period stemmed more from the newcomers than from the depression-scarred citizens.

The black clouds had only started to clear when citizens began to think of a new road to the beach. It was agreed that it should be north of the now badly overcrowded East Las Olas Boulevard. The city fathers first considered a route extending North East 6th Street to the beach. Engineering investigation by J. H. Philpott of the Solomon & Keis Company revealed that this route was impractical. The Florida State Road Department finally turned its attention to North East 10th Street, a large portion of which comprised the North Federal Highway, already a state-maintained road. Much of the needed right-of-way was ready for use. If such a project was to be undertaken it would have to be accomplished without the use of municipal money, for there was none available. The problem was tossed into the lap of City Attorney George W. English, Jr., and he was given immediate help and encouragement by Mayor Thomas B. Manuel, other city officials, and leading citizens.

Details of the forthcoming sleight-of-hand performance which produced the causeway, now known as Sunrise Boulevard, take us far ahead in time in the story but must be told in sequence. The plan for building the causeway was first endorsed by citizens in a referendum election held October 1, 1938. This election formally approved the 10th Street location. The election was the result of lengthy negotiations on the part of Mr. English, the mayor, Commodore A. H. Brook, and many others. English had powerful connections in Washington. He made many trips to the Capitol, often accompanied by Sheriff Walter R. Clark and Commodore Brook. He finally succeeded in getting federal approval for the purchase of revenue bonds for construction. The revenue, however, was to come from tolls and the city of course wanted no part of a toll road.

The next step was to approach the Florida State Road Department, which could readily justify the new road inasmuch as it connected two existing state roads, Federal Highway (U.S. 1) and State Road A1A along the beach. The road department, spurred by one of its local agents, Guy W. Stovall, agreed to pay off the bonds through use of the county's share of a portion of the state gasoline tax. Thus the need for actual collection of tolls was removed. The agreement did provide, however, that the city furnish the rights-of-way and maintain the road. M. A. Hortt and Ralph Horton donated the part they owned, but most of the land needed was the property of Hugh T. Birch, the aged recluse who had no reason, after the city's intrusions on his cherished privacy, to love it. He also felt that city and county taxes were not designed to benefit him. The new road would pass through the heart of his treasured estate, cutting it in two.

An effort had to be made to acquire his land and a city delegation arranged to call upon Mr. Birch. The group went prepared to offer Birch fifteen thousand dollars which was but a fraction of its worth, but the maximum available. Representing the city were Mayor Thomas B. Manuel, Commissioners J. H. Durham, John W. Needham, M. A. Hortt, and Mrs. Genevieve Pynchon, City Attorney George W. English, City

Clerk Florence C. Hardy, and City Manager John K. Huey. Present also were Birch's attorney, Curtis Byrd, Commodore A. H. Brook, and J. B. Fraser. Birch was awaiting them and his manner was disheartening. He listened patiently to the request and then remarked that he understood they came prepared to pay fifteen thousand dollars for the land. He then related in detail his grievances against the city. When he had concluded and the delegation was completely crestfallen, he reached into a drawer of his desk and pulled out a deed to the desired property which he presented as an outright gift. This should have provided the happy ending, but not quite. For the Florida State Road Department refused to go ahead on the basis of the one-hundred-foot right-of-way thus obtained. They demanded the addition of much more extremely valuable land directly on the ocean front to make possible a Y-shaped entrance from the causeway to State Road A1A. The need was for three hundred feet, not one hundred.

The job of again approaching Mr. Birch with this added request fell to Commodore A. H. Brook, who remarked that it was "the hardest job I ever undertook." It was indicative of the character of Birch, the old philanthropist, that he was gracious and understanding. He agreed to the further donation. Work on the new causeway, which was sixty-five hundred feet long with two bascule bridges, began on December 29, 1938, and was formally opened to the public February 25, 1940.

In the late 1930's, with the great depression on the run, America was looking toward improved living conditions among its people. In spite of a waxing economy the long dreary years had left deplorable housing conditions in many areas, conditions that had been ignored or overlooked in the common hardship. The "chicken in every pot" promised by President Hoover in the early days of the depression had finally become a reality; but housing conditions, which had seen little effort at improvement for ten long years, were deplorable. In Fort Lauderdale this was particularly true in the Negro sections of the city. Among President Roosevelt's newly created agencies was the Public Housing Authority, devoted to rectifying this situation. In a survey of the city's Negro area it was determined, in 1938, that there were 950 families. Of the 875 who were questioned, a total of 621 were renting, and a survey revealed that 94.7 per cent of such accommodations were definitely substandard.

A concerted effort on the part of the city, which included many trips to Washington, was made by various officials. Under some of the regulations which governed the Authority Fort Lauderdale was not eligible;

but these objections were overcome and, finally, on May 28, 1938, definite approval for a public housing program was won. Appointed to the local branch of the Authority were Luther Remsberg, William G. Hardy, R. E. Dye, George E. Haskins, and Floyd Miller, and under their stewardship two great projects were completed. These were the 150-unit Dixie Court for Negroes; and the 108-unit Doctor Kennedy Homes project for whites. Byron F. Snyder was the first new member of the board, appointed in 1943 after the death of George E. Haskins. He has served as chairman for many years. Both projects were built within the estimated budget costs, with the total well under a million dollars. Once again it was City Attorney George W. English, Jr., who did much of the behind-the-scenes maneuvering, with genuine help from Mayor Lewis E. Moore.

Rents in these units are based upon the tenant's ability to pay, with the provision that those with higher incomes are ineligible for tenancy. Because it is tax-exempt the Authority makes money, but it refunds to governmental agencies ten per cent of all income above the cost of utilities. The projects afford suitable housing for families who would not be able to pay the rents commanded by similar private facilities, thus creating no handicap to private industry while serving their purpose. The Authority was to be of great help in the housing crises of World War II.

Birch Estate. Bonnet House, foreground; Birch State Park at right

War Clouds Dim Progress

I n 1939 Hitler invaded Poland and England, and France declared war against Germany. World War II was under way by that September. For several months thereafter there was little active warfare and the term "Cold War" was born in the American press. President Roosevelt inaugurated the Civilian Conservation Corps which, he carefully explained, was not a military organization. Later he resorted to a franker approach and drafted men into the Army. Although the dangers of Fascism and Nazism were recognized, the United States was determined not to become involved. It was only twenty-three years since the boys had come home from World War I. The memory was still fresh.

Chapter 17
1939–1941

Despite war clouds construction had zoomed upward. Local taxes were reasonably low and Fort Lauderdale's overpowering public debt was melting. Trade-unions, which had disappeared during the depression, were re-formed. New automobiles, long a rarity, reappeared. Homes were modernized and worn equipment replaced.

Fort Lauderdale had seen literally dozens of weekly newspapers come and go, but the *Daily News* had remained the only daily publication since its founding by Colonel George Mathews in 1924. One of the perennial publishers of weeklies was J. Walter Day, a transplanted Texan with a strong newspaper bent. In 1939 Day was able to interest a number of local businessmen in a new daily paper, the *Fort Lauderdale Times*, which was launched as a morning daily. The principal backer was Ralph A. Horton. The plant was located in a building on South West 1st Avenue owned by Horton. Most of the equipment was secondhand. Many of the printers and pressmen came from the old Hearst *Atlanta Georgian*, which had ceased publication. In the last few weeks of its approximately three-year existence, the *Times* changed to the afternoon field. Day was a jovial, aggressive man, well liked in the community. But the newspaper battled stern competition from the *Miami Herald*, which had a strong hold on morning readers and offered much more complete service. In advertising, its chief competitor was the well-established *Daily News*. In its closing issue the *Times* was to announce itself a war casualty.

Because of the war in Europe, Port Everglades assumed new importance. The port had attracted many of the big oil companies and a large tank farm had been created. Tankers came into the port on regular schedules. A car ferry line which took on loaded railroad cars at the port and discharged them in Cuba was established. The cars were returned loaded with sugar, pineapples, and other products of the island. This trade immediately became of significance in the growing problem of supplying nations at war. From the start the United States sympathized with the allies, but among the most important shipments from the port were huge cargoes of scrap iron destined for Japan. The United States got a lot of it back shortly afterward—at Pearl Harbor.

* * *

In April of 1940 the division offices of the Florida State Road Department were removed from Miami to Fort Lauderdale. Meanwhile, with activity sprouting in every direction, developers began looking for more land. The Morang development of Rio Vista Isles was far enough along to be livable and lots, by then no longer owned by

Morang, sold. Some of Morang's bridges had to be repaired and roads rebuilt, but the major portion of the work was complete.

This was not true, however, of the beach property south of the old Coast Guard Base Six. Morang's bridge to the land had rusted and decayed and was now useless. Once again it was George English who stepped in. He organized a firm which included Harlow N. Davock, Lyn Pierson, George E. Haskins, M. R. McTigue, Byron Snyder, and others, to develop Harbor Beach. The land was duly purchased from Tom M. Bryan at the seemingly cheap price of a thousand dollars per acre for two hundred acres. But the problem was access. The cost of a bridge from the mainland would be fantastic. Needed was access through the Coast Guard Base, the only land touching theirs.

Much political maneuvering went into gaining permission for this road. But it was finally granted with provisions requiring an overpass from Base Six to the ocean, and a bond to guarantee all maintenance of the road. The Coast Guard also permitted a guarded gatehouse at the juncture of the road with the base on its south end.

This was the first really big, all-new post-boom development. It was successful from the time it was opened in 1940. The city's dream of a new route to the beach, the 10th Street Causeway, eventually to be renamed Sunrise Boulevard, was realized. It spurred the northward trend of growth to an even faster pace. The east-west stretch of the Federal Highway on 10th Street between North East 6th Avenue and North East 19th Avenue, which had remained at two lanes when the road was built, now began sprouting new business in earnest. A number of tourist cabin colonies had already been erected, together with a few hamburger stands and beer joints. The residential section pressed from the south. As a through street to the beach as well as to points north, it was obviously too narrow.

Another feature of the road annoyed near-by residents. In 1936 a lion farm had been built to utilize a huge and deep rock pit where the Gateway shopping center now stands. The rock pit served as a natural cage or closed area. At first, although lions were displayed, they were raised for the circus and zoo trade by a firm known as McKillop-Hutton. This firm was sold to Clyde Beatty, famed animal trainer, and in 1940 he established Clyde Beatty's Jungle Zoo on the site. The facility was located on Middle River and could be reached either by car or boat. It proved highly popular, and Beatty and his wife, Harriet, "fell" for Fort Lauderdale and built a home here.

Neighbors began to complain. The lions roared at night, or for that matter, whenever the spirit moved them. Monkeys escaped and even entered neighborhood houses to do mischief. The blare of the loud-speakers during the evening show was irritating. These complaints were duly taken before the city commission and argued long and heatedly. Lawsuits were threatened. City officials argued in vain that the zoo had been there first, and had indeed been there when the current owners bought their property. They argued also that the circus and the Beatty name were important advertisements. But the clamor continued in an effort to force Beatty to close. The beleaguered city commission finally gave in and ordered it closed. Beatty and his wife sold their home and departed in bitter disgust. As a footnote it might be added that when Harriet Beatty died, Clyde, pursuant to her wishes, brought the body to Fort Lauderdale for burial.

* * *

Fort Lauderdale got a brief look at actual combat on December 19, 1939, when the British cruiser "Orion" chased the German freighter "Arauca" into refuge at Port Everglades, where it was interned. The "Arauca," a new diesel-motored ship on its maiden voyage, was return-ing from Brazil en route to Germany when intercepted. When the "Orion" put a shot across her bow, the "Arauca" ran for the Florida coast. The "Orion," unwilling to fire shells that might go astray onto the beaches, held her fire and stood guard off Port Everglades, grimly lying offshore for several days until certain the ship had been interned.

On March 20, 1941, President Franklin D. Roosevelt visited Fort Lauderdale for the last time. Just as it was getting dark, the President's train arrived at the pier at Port Everglades for an inspection trip and cruise. While at Port Everglades President Roosevelt broadcast on March 29, 1941, the last of his Jackson Day speeches. He said in part:

I am sitting in the little cabin of the little ship "Potomac," in the har-bor of Fort Lauderdale, Florida, after a day of sunshine out in the Gulf Stream. That I cannot in person attend one of the many Jackson Day Dinners I regret; but it is good that you are again celebrating the mem-ory of a great American leader who believed fanatically almost in the principles of a democracy based on the freedom of the ballot box.

I try to get away a couple of times a year on these short trips on salt water. In Washington as you know the working day of the Presidency in these days averages about 15 hours. Even when I go to Hyde Park and to Warm Springs, the White House office, the callers and the tele-phone all follow me. But at sea the radio messages and the occasional pouch of mail reduce official work to not more than two or three hours a day.

So there is a chance for a bit of sunshine or a wetted line, or a biography or a detective story or a nap after lunch. Above all these is the opportunity for thinking.

On March 30 President Roosevelt gave his approval for the seizure of Italian, Danish, and German ships in American ports. Under the date of March 30, the ship's log of the President's cruise mentions the seizure of the "Arauca" only four hours after his train had left Port Everglades.

On April 1, fifty-two men, including Captain Frederick Stengler, were taken off the "Arauca" and held at the Coast Guard Base. On the following day they were moved to Broward County jail where they were held by United States Immigration officials on a technical charge regarding the length of their stay in the United States. After spending a week in the Broward County jail, they were moved to Dade County jail and eventually to Ellis Island.

* * *

Fort Lauderdale was experiencing something new in the housing field —project housing. Smart new houses, usually two bedrooms with one bath, cost around $2,500, with $250 down and $25 a month. Many areas of the city, notably the northeast portion, saw hundreds of these houses go up. Among the builders were Lester Preu, Hook Construction Company, and Earl Folsom. The houses were usually built on identical floor plans, but the builders overcame sameness by facing them in different directions and painting them a variety of colors. Such housing did not extend much beyond the city limits.

* * *

Lauderdale Memorial Hospital had been under intermittent criticism for many years as Mrs. Juanita G. Clay, owner and operator, strove to keep it on a paying basis. Finally, in May of 1937 she sold the property to a local insurance company called Medical Services, Inc., owned by Dr. F. A. Brunson and M. L. Monger. The Broward County Medical Society refused its support to the proposed method of operation of the new institution and, instead, leased the old Battle Creek Sanitarium on Federal Highway at South East 17th street and opened a temporary hospital.

On May 26, 1937, the society adopted a resolution calling for an appointed committee to "explore the general feeling toward a community drive for a publicly supported hospital." On June 14, society members met with prominent citizens from all communities in the county and formed the Broward Hospital Association. Chairman of the new group was James D. Camp, and Ernest Bratzel was secretary. It included members from Pompano, Oakland Park, Deerfield, Dania, Hollywood, Hallandale, and Davie. This group appointed a financial committee, also headed by Camp, which was assigned to raise funds for a building and equipment. It was quickly decided that in order to acquire a hospital in a reasonable length of time an existing building should be bought and remodeled. The building selected was the Granada apartments, on the present site of Broward General Hospital. The three-story buildings could be made into a sixty-five-bed hospital with all facilities needed. Purchase price was twenty-six thousand dollars. The Fort Lauderdale city commission, under Mayor Lewis E. Moore, agreed to take title if the purchase could be financed. Camp had already arranged for a loan of fifteen thousand dollars from the Broward Bank and Trust Company, of which he was president. The Medical Society underwrote the balance of eleven thousand dollars for the purchase.

The city took title September 18, 1937, and appointed a five-man Hospital Commission consisting of J. D. Camp, William J. Kelley, Logan T. Brown, William T. Coates, and E. Gex Williams (later Howard C. Jelks replaced Coates who left the city when the Barnett Bank was sold), once again by public subscription, with Camp as chairman. The commission was authorized to proceed and to raise money needed to remodel and equip the institution. Robert Jahelka was the architect who drew remodeling plans and George Young, Sr., was contractor, doing the work at cost. The total cost of the project came to fifty-seven thousand, five hundred dollars, and the first patient (Bill Miller) in the new hospital was accepted January 2, 1938, with Doctor R. L. Elliston as physician.

During the process of conversion several additional lots were acquired, and soon the entire block was secured at low cost through the purchase of tax certificates and deeds and the transfer of city-owned land. The neighboring Obispo apartments were also purchased for nurses' quarters. The group which had purchased the old hospital found during the fund drive little response to their medical insurance plan and agreed to change their policy to conform to Medical Society practices, but it was too late. In 1938 they sold the institution to Carl Wismeyer, who renovated it and operated it as Pine Crest Sanitarium until 1939, when he leased it to Mrs. Mae McMillan who converted it to Pine Crest school.

War Clouds Dim Progress: 1939–1941

Less than two years after Broward General Hospital opened, it was found that an expansion program was necessary. Fort Lauderdale was growing. Its population had jumped from just under ten thousand in 1935 to approximately twenty thousand in 1940. Chairman Camp took the matter before the city commission and received favorable response for a new wing. A Reconstruction Finance Corporation commitment for one hundred fifty thousand dollars was made available for the purpose. The city issued the needed revenue certificates in that amount, and the new wing was started in 1941 and completed in early 1942. It was just in the nick of time. The nation was at war and building materials were frozen. Had the matter been delayed the city would have been woefully short of hospital space during the crucial and trying period to come, for the new wing brought the capacity of the hospital to one hundred twenty beds. It has since been further enlarged and improved, with the capacity now approximately four hundred beds.

* * *

World affairs were becoming desperate. Hitler, with the most powerful war machine the world had ever seen, completely overran all of Europe and was driving deep into Russia. He extended his domination from the edge of the Arctic down into North Africa, only excluding Spain, where Franco was an ally, and tight little England, now holding out almost alone (though with help from the United States).

On the other side of the world Japan was making warlike noises. China had been gobbled up, and now the British and Dutch colonies of the far East and the Philippines attracted covetous glances. Japan, too, had built a mighty war machine. When this machine started after Siam and French Indo-China, President Roosevelt cut off oil shipments and froze Japanese assets in the United States. New tension developed. In November, 1941, Saburo Kurusu, a Japanese diplomat, came to the United States ostensibly seeking a formula for reducing tension. He was joined in the talks by Japanese Ambassador Kichisaburo Nomura. By late November, Secretary of State Cordell Hull warned the cabinet of this nation that matters had "gone beyond diplomacy and were now military in nature."

In the midst of these ominous forebodings, however, came a pleasant burst of good will on the local scene. Hugh T. Birch announced his intention of donating a strip of his choicest ocean front land for use as a state park. Senator Spessard L. Holland, in a letter to August Burghard, dated August 16, 1961, wrote of the circumstances surrounding Birch's gift, and the eventual presentation of the deed.

FORT LAUDERDALE

Entrance to Birch State Park and Glenn F. Bates Memorial Garden Center

My first information about the Birch property was received from John Lloyd, Esq., who told me of Mr. J. B. Fraser, Sr.'s closeness to Mr. Birch and of Mr. Birch's desire to do something for the Florida public because of his enjoyment of life at Fort Lauderdale and his belief that his life had been prolonged many years by living there several months each year. I was invited by Mr. Fraser and Mr. Lloyd, acting for Mr. Birch, to come to Fort Lauderdale to discuss the situation. I arrived there some time during the day of December 6, 1941, and had a long talk with Mr. Birch that afternoon and that night, as I recall, and during the next morning, after which I caught a train for Jacksonville about noon and arrived in Jacksonville in time to hear the report of the bombing of Pearl Harbor.

Mr. Birch told me that he had had some friction with the city and county and wanted to find out about the State park system of Florida. I told him about the park system and that a grant to it could be made in perpetuity for the use of his property as a public park. He took me over the property the morning of December 7, and I was impressed with his vigor and quick mind. At that time he was well over ninety.

At the end of the conference, he told me that he had decided to deed the property, comprising his home and nearly a mile on the intracoastal waterway, and something like one-third of a mile on the Atlantic Ocean, to the State for use as a State park [valued at a million dollars]. He also said that he would continue, at his expense, the bulkheading of the property on the west side and the filling of a certain portion thereof, which work I believe was being handled by Mr. Fraser. His wife had passed away long before and he had also lost his only daughter, and had made generous provision for his daughter's family, who lived just south of the property in question. He advised me, in general, that he was well-to-do and was making generous bequests to Antioch College, and perhaps other causes. Mr. Birch, who was most gracious, wanted me to draw the deed, or have it drawn by the Attorney General.

I advised Mr. Birch that because of his great age and the fact that others might claim undue influence or lack of competence, I felt that the necessary papers should be drawn by his own personal attorney. He told me that he had a long trusted friend and attorney in Chicago whom he would have come down to handle the matter for him. Later that attorney came down and we had several conferences over the telephone, following which the papers were drawn, submitted to the Attorney General, and approved in advance of delivery.

At Mr. Birch's invitation, Mary [Mrs. Holland] and I came down to Fort Lauderdale to receive the deed [March 4, 1942]. Mr. Birch delivered it to me for our State in his living room, which fronts through a large picture window on the Atlantic Ocean and, as he said, on the Gulf Stream. He had a radio hook-up and in his own words stated his gratitude to Florida, his decision to make the gift, as well as my insistence that the matter be handled as he had handled it. I have rarely heard a more appealing statement than his, which attributed to our State and its beneficent climate the fact that he had lived so long, and that his last years had been so happily spent. He said some extremely generous things about Mary and me, but the burden of his statement was that he wanted through that gift to express in a permanent way his appreciation to the people of Florida.

. . . Mr. Birch retained the right to live in the home for the rest of his days and he also completed the bulkhead and filling work as per his earlier statement to me.

Following his death, an attorney for some remote relatives came down to check on the validity of his Will, and also on the validity of his grant to the State. This attorney came to see me in Tallahassee and I opened my file to him. After checking it in detail, he told me that there was no possible way to upset the grant to the State and that he would not be a party to making any such attempt.

* * *

December 7, 1941, was a sunny Sunday in Fort Lauderdale. Despite the ominous signs in world events, both Fort Lauderdale and seemingly, the nation, remained complacent. A golf tournament, won by Byron Nelson, was in progress at Hollywood. The ocean was calm. A good run of mackerel and bluefish enticed many fishermen to the sea. The beaches were crowded. Neither the *Fort Lauderdale Daily News* nor the *Times* published on Sunday, but the *Times* was a morning paper and Price Day went down to the office early that afternoon to turn on the teletype machines carrying United Press and International News Service material. He was still there, sitting at his desk, when the alarm bells on the machines started clanging madly.

"What now?" he mused, as he strode over to see what the special bulletin was about.

The "Orion" chased the German "Arauca" into port

Fort Lauderdale Goes to War

Chapter 18
1941–1945

World War I had been as remote from Fort Lauderdale as was the little town of Sarajevo where the flame was kindled. To be sure many local young men had gone, as service flags in windows testified, but aside from that the first world conflict had not come close.

World War II was in sharp contrast. This time the city was to hear shots fired in anger, to care for the wounded and shipwrecked, and to witness harsh conflict and its inescapable results. It was to see its economy turned topsy-turvy, and the whole way of life undergo vast change. Radio, now, could bring hour-by-hour and almost minute-by-minute accounts of the action. This time Fort Lauderdale as a whole, not just its young men, was to participate in war.

204

This superficial excitement was but the prelude to another period when it appeared that Fort Lauderdale was once again doomed. In World War I the town had had no tourist-based economy. Now it was almost entirely dependent on tourists, and tourism was among the first of the war casualties. Not only were there gasoline rationing and numerous travel restrictions, but even taking a winter vacation was considered unpatriotic. The city had no industry, and another rumor that started almost with Pearl Harbor was that no war industries would be permitted within one hundred miles of any coastal area. A further rumor was that the southeast portion of the peninsula was "beyond the defense line" set up by the armed forces. In seeming conflict was an equally strong rumor that machine guns and other artillery had been mounted on the roofs of the Florida seacoast hotels. Stagnation for the duration seemed initially to be the prospect for this part of the country.

To be sure Florida, and the area surrounding Fort Lauderdale, would still produce winter vegetables, much needed by the armed forces; and there were acres of producing citrus land in the county. But these provided no source of income for the city dweller. The outlook was bleak. But Fort Lauderdale was far from beaten. Chamber of Commerce officials began an immediate survey of assets in the community and its environs and entered wholeheartedly into the war effort. It was brought out that the terrain here was almost entirely flat and that flying weather encompassed nearly the full 365 days of the year. It would be easy to build air training fields; and there were plenty of now-vacant hotels to house personnel. Port Everglades was strategically close to many suppliers of raw materials for war use. The port's huge oil storage capacity provided an ample source of power for industries which could be housed here in buildings in a climate requiring little artificial heat and a minimum of artificial lighting. It was an ideal place for health and rehabilitation. The Chamber of Commerce voted to send its secretary, August Burghard, to Washington for several months to explore possibilities and to represent the city and county in gearing the area into the war effort.

Even as it rather timidly advanced these theories, the Chamber, under the presidency of Attorney Curtis Byrd, pondered other matters. Typical questions were: "Did the enemy have the capability of attacking this coast?" "Was our defensive system adequate?" "How strategic, actually, was Port Everglades?"

The city had not swung into the war effort in dead earnest before the first of these questions was dramatically answered. On January 15, 1942, the first vessel, an unidentified merchantman, was sunk by torpedo off the southeast coast. On May 4 of that year the British tanker "Eclipse" was torpedoed within sight of the Florida coast and towed into Port Everglades. For that story we refer to the account of Arthur Inwood, radio officer on the ship at the time, as related in a manuscript in the Fort Lauderdale Historical Society's archives:

The convoy of some two dozen ships and their meager escorts proceeded westerly across the north Atlantic without incident when, believing things to be safe from submarine attack, the convoy was dispersed north of the Bahama Islands on May 3rd, 1942. The sailing orders for the "Eclipse" were to proceed to Beaumont, Texas, to load a cargo of aviation gasoline. Being in ballast and riding high we were soon out of sight of our companion ships.

The morning of May 4th dawned bright and clear and the course we had set the night before brought us across the Gulf Stream in the vicinity of Fort Pierce. Heading south, and parallel with the Florida east coast, it felt good to have the deep, merciless Atlantic and, what is more, the war, behind us for awhile. From a mile and a half to two miles offshore Florida, land at arm's length looked wonderful, and we felt safe.

A few minutes before noon I remember remarking to the Third Officer on watch on the bridge, "That's Florida, where it costs a dollar a minute just to breathe the air!"

We were now off Boynton Beach, watching through the telescope automobiles moving north and south on a beach road. One mile ahead of us was a cargo boat heading south too, and we were just about a mile and a half off shore. About 11:55 A.M. a reconnaissance patrol plane with pilot and observer aboard passed us low on the starboard side, the observer indicating with his hand motions that we should hoist our signal, or call letters by flag. We ignored him, and I went down to my cabin just before the Second Officer took over the watch at noon.

At precisely three minutes past the hour I heard the officer on the bridge give an urgent command to the helmsman: "*Hard-a-starboard! Hard-a-starboard!*" His words, in a fraction of a second were lost in the damned awfullest explosion one's ears ever cared to hear, while simultaneously our ten-thousand ton tanker appeared to lurch some six feet out of the water! The war had come to the western limits of the Atlantic Ocean—a German submarine had torpedoed a British ship inside American territorial waters in broad daylight. And, the submarine was between the ship and the shore!

Stunned, all aboard at first wondered what had happened, except that the bridge was quick to inform all hands of our predicament. The submarine was not observed by the deck officers, but the rapidly approaching torpedo was as it raced straight for the ship's boiler-room where two men succumbed to the death-dealing weapon. Stopped in our tracks, an anchor was dropped immediately to the ocean floor some thirty fathoms down, and so we waited aboard while the ship started to settle by the stern.

With the ship dead the emergency radio transmitter very soon crackled over the air-waves with the SSSS SSSS SSSS—submarine alarm signal, warning all other shipping of our distress and our position. Reaction was immediate. U.S. Coast Guard radio station NOL, and the British coast station in the Bahamas wanted to know whether or not we were mistaken—hadn't we struck a mine instead? An enemy submarine off the Florida Coast? Impossible! The next morning the American tanker "Java Arrow" was torpedoed—and we knew the war at sea had really crossed the Western Ocean. . . .

On May 6 two naval tugs arrived on the scene and towed our crippled ship into Port Everglades. . . .

So, from Britisher and Radio Officer, to American and Architect, and in due course with the most wonderful wife by my side, only because the Battle of the Atlantic came to the Gold Coast of Florida on May 4, 1942, I became an American and a Fort Lauderdale citizen.

The "Java Arrow" was not, like the "Eclipse," in bunker. She was loaded with gasoline additive, a cargo worth millions of dollars, but with a strategic value of incalculable worth. The cargo was saved despite the fact that five men were killed aboard and two torpedo holes blown clear through both sides of the ship. The following is the summary of statements by survivors of S.S. "Java Arrow," American tanker, owned by the Socony Vacuum Oil Company, from the Office of the Chief of Naval Operations of the Navy Department, Washington, D.C., dated June 5, 1942:

At 2347 EWT, May 5, 1942, the first torpedo struck the port side at #5 tank, just off the bridge, about 15 ft. above keel. Approximately one minute later, the second torpedo struck the starboard side about 10 ft. above keel, penetrating the engine room. Vessel made a 180° turn after explosion. A distress call was sent, but doubt was expressed as to the actual transmission inasmuch as both the regular and emergency antennae were down. No defensive action was taken since submarine did not surface until approximately 15 minutes after torpedoing. Confidential codes were thrown overboard in a steel box by the Master. Judging by the brief lapse of time between the two explosions and from the opinions of the survivors, it is apparent that two submarines were involved in the attack on the "Java Arrow." Past experience proves that enemy submarines do not surface when vessel is armed. Need for camouflage of guns or false partitions to lure submarine to the surface is apparent. All lights were out at the time of attack but several crew members stated that the Captain's cabin light burned all night May 4.

The five months of war that had preceded the torpedoing of the "Eclipse" and "Java Arrow" had seen many such incidents along the coast. They had also seen the city gird itself for war. The submarine menace, in itself, served to inspire a bright page in the history of the city.

Neither the Navy nor the Coast Guard was equipped at the start of the war to battle this menace, and on December 13, 1941, just six days after Pearl Harbor, Flotilla No. 2 of the Coast Guard Auxiliary was organized upon the request of Lieutenant Commander G. A. Littlefield of Jacksonville. The Flotilla was made up of a group of men who volunteered both their own services and their boats for patrol duty both offshore and in inland waters along the coast. Fort Lauderdale boatmen were ready for the challenge. Under the able leadership of J. H. (Jack) McVey they held a later organizational meeting on March 18 at which a total of sixty-one members were accepted out of a hundred thirty applicants. This number varied from time to time, largely because the owners of some of the larger and more capable boats simply donated them to the Coast Guard for the duration of the war. The Flotilla received praise in articles in such nationally circulated magazines as the *Saturday Evening Post* and *Motor Boating*.

Most of the boats of the Flotilla were not big enough nor fast enough to use depth charges, and none of them carried other than side arms. They were, however, used for day and night patrol duty in the area they covered—Dumfoundling Bay (just south of Hallandale) to Boynton Inlet in Palm Beach County. Their duties included the reporting of all submarine sightings, warning small craft away, spotting any attempt at landing of saboteurs from submarines or other craft, and rescue work. The most spectacular of these jobs was the latter. During the war the Flotilla was officially credited with bringing in two hundred fifty-three survivors of torpedoed ships, many of whom had been wounded. In later stages of the war the submarine menace to shipping was overcome as Coast Guard and Navy began receiving equipment. Flotilla No. 2 of Division 10 was thereupon reorganized under the Coast Guard Reserve Act and was made responsible for the security of the waters in and around Port Everglades. McVey had a total of approximately four hundred fifty volunteer citizens under his command in this work.

Perhaps the most exciting incident in the experiences of Flotilla No. 2 was one concerning Captain Willard Lewis. He came across a sub surfaced close to shore and under the deep shadow cast by the Hillsboro Lighthouse light. Believing the sub was attempting to land saboteurs, Lewis gunned the "Diane," a powerful forty-five-footer, in an effort to ram the sub's conning tower. He missed by a narrow margin and the sub quickly sped away.

Just as the Navy and Coast Guard had no available boats for patrol duty at the outset of the war, so they likewise lacked any sufficient number of airplanes for similar duty, and again civilians were called upon to form a Civilian Air Patrol. It was pointed out that while submerged objects are difficult to spot from the surface, they can readily be seen from the air in the clear waters that border our coast. A unit of the Civilian Air Patrol was consequently formed with local pilots, many of them women, using their own planes to fly over the sub-infested waters. These planes were also unarmed. They could only advise of the presence and location of the enemy; and the Navy and Coast Guard were almost equally helpless. Every ship capable of carrying adequate arms was on duty either in the Pacific or on North Atlantic convoy duty. Although many local fliers were members, the squadron was operated out of Miami headquarters.

Submarines lying offshore just beyond the shipping lanes were able to outline their quarry against the lights of the coastal towns, so a complete blackout was ordered and enforced. Automobiles driving along the beaches did so without lights. One thing, however, remained disstressingly clear—the submarines were winning this fight. The sight of crippled ships, sometimes with torpedo holes blown through both sides, being towed along the beach toward the nearest harbor, was commonplace; and even the boom of striking torpedoes was heard by many.

The city had plenty of other reasons to know that we were at war. Many of the young single men had already been drafted into the armed service when we entered the conflict. Most of the remainder either were drafted or enlisted. Some of the older men were in the reserve and were called back. Meantime the "battle" off our coast raged on through 1942, but by 1943 the nation's mighty production capacity was geared up; and fast, well-armed boats were coming off the production lines. New warplanes were becoming more plentiful, and an even greater menace to the submarine, the blimp, was showing up along the coast. Able to hover over a submarine, the blimps became real sub killers. The battle for the coastal shipping lanes was ended. The advantage now was definitely with the defenders of the Atlantic coast.

Now the armed services suddenly realized the value of southeast Florida's mild, equable climate for accelerated training of combat personnel. Nearly all the big hotels along the "Gold Coast" were taken over for training and housing of men of all branches of the service. The Navy bought the old Merle L. Fogg airport from the city, with much other adjoining land, and began construction of a naval air station. The Army, meantime, was establishing a huge air training base at nearby Boca Raton. Soon city streets were swarming with servicemen. The city had been forewarned of this condition by the military, and the preparations made for it supply a proud chapter in the history of the high civic pride and community consciousness that has been a Fort Lauderdale trademark.

Most active throughout the entire war period was H. L. McCann, former Chamber of Commerce president, Fort Lauderdale mayor, and city, regional, and state rationing official. The first steps were taken at a joint meeting of the Chamber of Commerce and the City Commission, when a military affairs council was organized. As recorded in the Fort Lauderdale Chamber of Commerce minutes of June 19, 1942, the original members were: Julian E. Ross, chairman; H. C. Jelks, housing; W. C. Ruffin, transportation; John L. Trout, supplies; H. O. Pierce, entertainment; and Commodore J. E. Bartlett, hospitality. Early efforts to enlist the aid of the Florida branch of the USO were unsuccessful, but the council went ahead. The first, and perhaps the greatest, contribution made was the use of a huge building on the corner of East Las Olas Boulevard and South East 1st Avenue, the old Pioneer Department Store building. The structure had recently been purchased by R. H. Gore, who donated it rent free, provided the council would pay the taxes. These the council paid, and the money was promptly refunded by both county and city.

The building was ideal. The ground floor had a twenty-foot ceiling and ten thousand feet of completely unpartitioned floor space. Now the council needed money and three of its members, Sadie (Mrs. Mack) Katz, Jack B. Fannin, and Martin R. McTigue, raised five thousand dollars in five days.

The minutes of a meeting of the Board of Directors of the Chamber of Commerce, Thursday, August 27, 1942, recorded the following:

Right: Herbert L. McCann, World War II mayor (BURGHARD COLLECTION)

Julian Ross, Chairman of the Military Affairs Council; W. J. Kelley, Treasurer and Howard O. Pierce, Chairman of the Entertainment Committee of M.A.C. were guests. Mr. Pierce reported on the Recreation Center. He said that the subscription had been started off for the Military Affairs Council by the Business and Professional Women's Club. Six large fans had been contributed or had been purchased. Plumbing is now being set. Partitions, store rooms, toilets, shower room on the second floor, office space, a 2,400-foot dance floor on second floor, soft drink bars, installation of each flooring, library tables, reed furniture and other improvements are being made as rapidly as possible. He said that $7,500 had been collected to date and $1,600 has been spent. He announced that Ray Spencer was forming an orchestra, and that the Coast Guard would furnish its own orchestra once a month. He said that National and State recreation department officials had inspected and were highly pleased with the setup. He particularly commended Harry Hickson, Ray Meullier, and W. J. Kelley.

Maple flooring for the second-story dance floor was donated. Labor unions supplied men for remodeling work. Books, furniture of all kinds,

FORT LAUDERDALE

Members of the famed Service Men's Club. W. J. Eastman (*extreme right*) was unpaid manager of the Center, which catered to countless thousands of service men and women, many of whom returned and settled in Fort Lauderdale after the war (BURGHARD COLLECTION)

and carpeting were donated by the citizens, who were one hundred per cent cooperative. Hundreds of volunteer workers, mostly women, managed the new servicemen's center which remained open every day, seven days a week, until 11:30 at night for the duration. It was described as "the busiest and happiest place in South Florida" and "the most beautiful Service Center in the United States." Records of the organization indicate that more than two million servicemen and women were served there, and to this day, board members receive letters of appreciation. William J. Eastman, manager of the center, records that its Saturday dances drew as many as three thousand persons. To provide continued maintenance of the center sixty local people agreed to provide twenty-five dollars each per month for a period of six months. Said Eastman: "The Fort Lauderdale Service Men's Center was one of the great cooperative successes of our people back in the days when we did not look to the government to furnish us with facilities which we considered it our patriotic duty to provide and operate."

In the meantime things were happening in other fields. The armed services took over the huge Miami Biltmore Hotel in Coral Gables and made it into a hospital. Wounded were beginning to arrive from overseas. Ambulance transportation was desperately needed and into this gap came the American Red Cross, which sent out an urgent call for volunteer drivers. There were no able-bodied men available, but here again the women stepped in, many putting in long and arduous hours transporting the disabled at any hour of day or night. Many of the casualties at first were injured seamen rescued from ships torpedoed in the continuous struggle that raged off our coast.

According to the minutes of the Chamber of Commerce for September 9, 1942, "Lt. Hogue announced that 30 officers had been assigned to man the seven air stations which were being built in Florida and the South and of the 30, that 25 asked to be sent to Fort Lauderdale. He said the new station would be commissioned about October 1."

New plans were being put into effect. On April 27, 1942, contractor Fred Howland of Miami was notified to begin work on the new naval air station, and actual construction on the main station began on June 3. Though far from completed, the base was formally commissioned October 1, after only four months of feverish activity, rendered more difficult by the rapidly developing shortage of manpower. The commanding officer was Captain Donald E. Wilcox, and the first training officer assigned was Commander Joe Taylor, who had already won fame in action in the Pacific. The field was designed to train pilots of carrier-based torpedo-attack planes of the type that was eventually to sweep the Japanese Navy off the seas. Most of the pilots who trained here saw duty in its most daring and dangerous form. Actual training in 17 TBF-1's began October 12, 1942. With a constant program of construction and adding facilities to the field and its allied installations at Port Everglades, and with two satellite fields at West Prospect and North Pompano, this was to continue until deactivation on October 1, 1946.

The base occupied roughly a thousand acres extending from the Federal Highway and Florida East Coast tracks on the east to the Seaboard Air Line tracks on the west, and from the Dania cut-off canal on the south to South West 32d Street on the north. On this ground were two hundred seventeen buildings, some of which were, and are, elaborate. Most, however, were temporary structures to facilitate speed in erection and, except for the hangars, were designed to last for a minimum of five years. The Navy is unable to supply an exact record of the number of pilots trained nor of the total of men stationed here in connection with this facility. The greatest number actually at the base at a given time was just under three thousand.

With most of Broward an armed camp, new rules were put into effect. Until the arrival of the military, houses of ill repute were tolerated in the county and a number of them were in operation on the outskirts of Fort Lauderdale. They were closed immediately and have never been allowed to reopen. Another of the new rules concerned bar closing hours. In prior days there had been no law in this respect and bar and liquor operators used their own discretion. In Fort Lauderdale the bars had closed voluntarily during church hours. Otherwise they remained open at will unless neighbors complained; then police closed them under the nuisance laws. The military, however, felt that a curfew was necessary and the 12 midnight curfew was adopted and strictly enforced, largely by military police and the Navy Shore Patrol.

Gambling, which operated on an open basis in many parts of the county, continued but on a highly curtailed basis. Gasoline and travel restrictions made it difficult to maintain the more elaborate clubs and they closed. Smaller "bookies" and a few downtown joints continued to operate. The downtown bars reaped a vast harvest, being crowded from opening to closing with gay throngs consisting mostly of men in uniform.

Also doing a capacity business for the first time in his long career was Charles L. Swaggerty, who had doggedly kept his "belt line" buses in service though operating at a loss for many years. The war found him with his bus and taxi franchises still alive, with access to precious gasoline and with more customers than he could hope to haul. Swaggerty ordered more and better equipment and was able to get it. Though he sold out following the war, this marked the birth of modern bus service for the city.

The *Fort Lauderdale Daily News* of March 1, 1943, said that advancement of recreational facilities held the spotlight as the city commission met in city hall. G. Harold Martin, of the parks advisory committee, appeared to urge speedy action on the Holiday Park acquisition. Meanwhile the general business outlook, so bleak at the outset of the war, brightened. To be sure the tourists were not coming, but members of the armed services, some with wives and children, were here and had taken over most of the available housing. The proud and comparatively new Lauderdale Beach Hotel and a smaller counterpart just up the beach, the Tradewinds, had become a United States Navy school for radar and range finding. Security on these top secret operations was tight. All traffic on the beach was routed around and away from these locations, and wire fences blocked off the beach itself. Equipment used was on top of the hotels and on a concrete structure along the beach. A class was graduated every sixty days and the Navy reported that a total of five thousand completed the course. The men were housed and fed at the Lauderdale Beach with the Tradewinds furnishing additional housing and classrooms. Only a few downtown hotels remained open for business for overnight guests and they were always packed.

William G. Hardy, Fort Lauderdale druggist, received on April 15, 1944, an official commendation from Frank Knox, the Secretary of the Navy, for work he had done while serving with the Seventh Naval District (Key West to Stuart), as part of the nationwide survey of manpower in Navy, Marine Corps, and Coast Guard shore establishments.

The Chamber of Commerce drive to locate war industries in the area bore fruit. War material of every type was needed and even small plants could help to provide it. The most spectacular, if not the largest, plant to go into war contracting locally was Dooley's Basin and Dry Dock, a boat works on New River at South West 15th Avenue, owned by Paul G. Dooley. This company, which had marine railways and a large amount of covered storage, began building boats for war use. During the period of the war the plant constantly expanded. Its production record included seven 144-foot nonmagnetic mine sweepers, four 172-footers of the same type, twenty-one 110-foot sub chasers, eighteen 104-feet long, and twenty-eight of 85-foot length. Also built were a number of 65-foot air-rescue boats. The biggest problem faced by the firm was maneuvering the boats down the badly silted river and negotiating the turn at Tarpon Bend. Dooley's Basin employed approximately three hundred men and had as its head Naval architect Charles Roach, the excellence of whose work led him to high posts in Naval architecture.

Another among the biggest producers was Fort Lauderdale's oldest industry, Gate City Sash and Door Company, started by Jack Williams in 1912. This company was already engaged in making prefabricated wood windows and doors, and it evolved the still famed, and still-in-use, Gate City type of awning window. These windows were sold to the armed forces for use throughout the world. M. D. Ebert, company vice-president, was a member of the Chamber of Commerce industrial committee and rendered valuable service guiding other firms in procuring orders.

By contrast a brand new plant, the H. A. K., was started by Dr. Elliott M. Hendricks, Rollin Abel, and Dwight A. Krause. This company, which began in 1939, obtained the necessary lathes and other equipment and secured a contract for the manufacture of 37-millimeter shells. The plant was located on the Seaboard Airline railroad at Davie

Boulevard, and here the firm manufactured approximately 1,637,000 shells, hundreds of thousands of which were used in the African campaign. The shells were placed on planes daily and shipped to Ravenna, Ohio, where they were loaded. The firm also made projectiles and 50-millimeter shells.

Rex Bassett, Inc. had moved a portion of its plant here from Niles, Michigan, in 1940. Bassett had originally invented the washing machine which he sold to Bendix for production. Now he was interested in electronics and was the first to manufacture two-way radios for the use of police and fire departments. When the war started, his plant was devoted almost one hundred per cent to military production. It made quartz crystals and a wide variety of electronic equipment mostly for military aircraft and acquired a top rating for the excellence of its products. At its peak, the firm had a hundred seventy-five employees, mostly women. In 1959 the name of the firm was changed to Savoy Electronics, Inc., but it remains under the same management and is still active in manufacture of all types of components for this rapidly growing field. Still another manufacturer of radio parts for aircraft was the Florida Aircraft Radio Corporation, headed by Daniel K. Foster. The firm—on North East 1st Avenue—hired about seventy-five persons.

But these were the larger operations. The smallest of plants capable of producing useful material was not overlooked. Dale Redman, among the first to volunteer in World War I, was now physically unable to return to fighting. He operated a fishing tackle shop on New River and in his back room had a small metal lathe. Redman got subcontracts from producers of war material and stood in front of his lathe for endless hours turning out the goods. There were many other small plants in the city working as subcontractors.

Selective service was biting deeper and deeper into the city's available manpower. The few "professional" soldiers along with members of the Army and Navy reserves went into service early. It was becoming harder and harder to fill the ranks of the ordinary soldier and sailor and to supply industry with workers. The services had also called upon the fittest of our young women for various services. Katherine Rawls, the great girl athlete of the mid-thirties, was now ferrying military aircraft from factory to base, a highly exacting job. These were no cumbersome training planes, but were the "hottest" of the war craft. Almost every trained nurse was in service and the pitifully few left were augmented by the volunteer "gray ladies" who, though not graduate nurses, performed many of the same services adequately. The WACS and WAVES and all the other branches of the service were taking women for desk work and schools and draining them from the community life. Soon it seemed that any remaining civilian was old, blind, or crippled. But still they carried on, many doing humdrum, stodgy jobs and dreaming enviously of those younger ones who were actually at grips with the conflict.

Throughout this trying period the "hottest spot" had been Port Everglades. The port was under the tightest of security with Coast Guardsmen stationed around its perimeter on twenty-four-hour patrol. When war was declared, Port Everglades and the defense of all of its approaches came under the jurisdiction of the Coast Guard which, of course, was taken over by the Navy on the same day. Lieutenant Richard Stinson was Commander of the Coast Guard Base Six here and he at once became Captain of the Port of Everglades. This office is not to be confused with the Navy's Port Captain, who controls the movement of ships. Stinson was charged not only with the security of all facilities and installations at the port, but also with the patrolling of all beaches and other approaches from St. Lucie inlet south to Baker's Haulover. He was forced to transport men from the base, where Bahia Mar is now located, to the port by bus, and since then there was no 17th Street causeway, they had to go by way of Las Olas Boulevard and the Federal Highway.

Ever since repeal of prohibition, Coast Guard Base Six had been primarily a training station, and the opening of Port Everglades, which led to the eventual closing of the base's own inlet, had practically landlocked it. A Coast Guard cutter was usually kept at the port for lifesaving and salvage purposes, but the base itself had few serviceable boats and even these were immediately called upon for service elsewhere as was, of course, the cutter.

Also called elsewhere almost immediately was Stinson, whose place as Captain of the Port was taken over by Jack T. Nelson. Nelson, a local man, had served as ensign in World War I. He applied for a commission with the outbreak of the second war and, though over-age, was given a lieutenancy and put in charge of the port. Starting with almost no equipment the unit was built up as men and material became available. It was eventually moved from Base Six to a large houseboat, or Coast Guard barrack boat, towed here from Miami.

The first patrol of the beaches was undertaken on foot, an extremely irksome duty. Later, horses were used and the old saw "sailor on horseback" became reality. The horses were stabled at the Gulfstream polo

Left: Lt. Jack T. Nelson, local citizen who commanded Port Everglades during World War II

Right: Hunley Abbott, prominent civic leader and chairman of the Postwar Planning Committee

Below: Tank farms under construction at Port Everglades (BURGHARD COLLECTION)

barns, Delray Beach, Hallandale, and at the Silver Thatch Inn at Pompano Beach. Watchtowers were built along the beach. Nelson noted with amusement that many of his recruits had come from Oklahoma and Texas and had joined the Navy to see the world (from a porthole) but had wound up in the familiar saddle. Happily, during the war there were no successful landings by saboteurs. No significant fires nor trouble with dock workers at the port were reported. The port worked to capacity throughout.

One of the highly strategic materials handled at the port was molasses. Imported from Cuba by a British firm, the Pacific Molasses Company, it was stored in large tanks here until it could be transshipped to England. There it was made into industrial alcohol and later into explosives. But sugar, South American ores and chemicals, and, above all, gasoline were the important imports and exports. Port Everglades even then had extensive tank farms for the storage of petroleum products, along with modern loading and unloading equipment. Fuel for the defense of the entire Caribbean was stored there. Much of it was high octane aviation gasoline used by the planes at the Naval Air Station. Perhaps the most closely guarded secret of all was the movement of ships to and from the port, usually at night.

At the outset of the war the Peninsular and Occidental Steamship line had operated three car ferries between the port and Cuba. These ships, the "Estrada Palma," "Joseph R. Parrott," and "Henry M. Flagler," were ideally suited for mine laying operations inasmuch as the entire stern was in the form of a gate which could be lowered. All three were taken over by the Navy for this purpose, and although the event is still shrouded by secrecy, at least one of them, the "Estrada Palma," was sunk by enemy action. A number of the crew members, who volunteered to stay aboard as merchant seamen, were local men. It might be said here that although a complete list of those entering the armed services from Fort Lauderdale and those killed therein is available, no such statistics are available in the case of merchant seamen, many of whom were from Fort Lauderdale.

Among the other installations at the port was an undersea warfare experiment station, which still continues operations. The Navy also established a boat service for recovery of torpedoes dropped in training by planes from the Air Station.

Most of the charter boat fleet was immobilized at the beginning of the war, and nearly all its units volunteered for Coast Guard auxiliary work. As events wore on it became evident that some relaxation was desirable, and some of the boats, equipped with bottled gas converters to supply fuel, sailed out on fishing trips from the downtown docks.

With all due humility, the Chamber of Commerce began to turn its eyes toward post-war planning, as recorded in the Chamber's minutes of May 5, 1943.

Pres. Freeman advised the Board that Hunley Abbott, an engineer with wide experience, who had served on the Board of Review for the former Works Progress Administration, had accepted the chairmanship of the new Post War Planning Committee. Other members of the committee already selected, or to be invited, include George Haskins, J. H. Philpott, A. J. (Andy) Musselman, Paul Dooley, Roy Wilson, Alfred Jacobson, Ted Cabot, president of the Junior Chamber of Commerce, J. S. Powell, Byron Snyder, Ben Fraser, George Simons and the secretary [August Burghard]. Tom Berryhill, city attorney, and the city manager would act as ex-officio members of the committee.

What the war's onset would mean to the city had been confidently but erroneously predicted. The question now was whether the Chamber could successfully gauge the effects of a return to peace and plan properly for this eventuality. Fully recognized was the critical shortage of housing but under war priorities any large-scale increase was impossible at the present time. The Chamber was already receiving letters from servicemen asking for literature and information concerning the city as a place to establish a home after the war. Many of these letters recalled the Service Men's Center and the fine treatment they had received there. There was not one unrented or unoccupied place suitable for living quarters in the entire city. "If they come, where will we put them?" This question had the Chamber members nonplused.

In the *Report to the People of Fort Lauderdale, Florida, by the Post War Planning Committee of the Chamber of Commerce*, by Hunley Abbott, chairman, in the spring, 1945, it was stated that "the purpose of Post War Planning is two fold: First to help returning service men and war workers to find satisfactory peace time employment and to create jobs for them. Second to present a program for the general improvement and orderly growth of our city."

In other fields the city was busy pulling all possible strings to win a state senator to represent Broward County, which had hitherto shared its senator with Palm Beach County. The result had been that the man elected invariably was from Palm Beach County, then considerably larger than Broward. An amendment to the State Constitution was needed. State Representative John S. Burwell was dispatched to a legislative meeting at Pensacola to set up the necessary machinery, and he worked diligently for a new senatorial district. At the same time, a movement was also under way to set up a juvenile court in Broward. Until now juvenile cases had been handled by the county judge on a strictly part-time basis. There were no special provisions for detention or corrective measures.

The same Price Day who had been so disgusted when the bell on his teletype machine had begun ringing on December 7, 1941, had become a war correspondent for the *Baltimore Sun* and was the reporter chosen by lot to be the one to receive the news of Germany's surrender. He had relayed the news to his fellows but "not for release." The Russians were supposed to make the announcement. An Associated Press correspondent cabled the news anyhow, touching off a controversy. Day then returned to Baltimore to become editor-in-chief of the *Sun* papers.

With the war in Europe ended it became evident that, though a long and costly operation might be in prospect, Japan was certain to fall. Activities along the Atlantic seaboard were gradually easing, though all facilities here remained under tight military control.

More and more evidence of the return of the ex-service men as job seeking civilians was piling up, and the serious questions of providing enough jobs concerned the Chamber. Among the steps taken, in conjunction with the city and county, was the setting up of a veteran's service council. This council would undertake, among other things, to advise returning soldiers and sailors of rights and privileges under the flood of special legislation now being passed by Congress in their behalf. As for civilians, Fort Lauderdale had maintained a sketchy sort of tourist economy throughout the war. Many of our "regulars," tourists who never missed a season, either owned homes or had reservations in hotels or apartment houses not taken over by the military. They kept on coming, entering into the spirit of the wartime world of Florida along with their friends and winter neighbors. Gasoline rationing, crowded public transportation, and the closing of many of the larger amusement establishments had not affected the climate, and travel hardships could be overcome with patience and forbearance.

Then came the fateful day, August 6, 1945, when a United States plane dropped an atomic bomb on Hiroshima. The awesome results chilled the entire world. The largest bombs hitherto used in the war had been block-busters containing eleven tons of TNT. The single and comparatively small atomic bomb was two thousand times stronger.

FORT LAUDERDALE

The total destruction of mankind was now a distinct possibility. Another such bomb was dropped a few days later on Nagasaki, and the Japanese hastily gave up the fight. Hostilities ended with Japan's surrender on August 14, and the formal surrender was signed on board the U.S.S. "Missouri" in Tokyo Bay, September 2, 1945. The "Great War" ended as it had begun, in shock, horror, and disbelief! In all, Broward County supplied 5,536 persons to the armed services, a majority of them from Fort Lauderdale. The total who died or were killed in action stands at 76.

After the war, but directly concerned with military activities here, there occurred the greatest peacetime mystery on record. This concerned a flight of five TBM Avenger airplanes from the Fort Lauderdale Naval Air Station on a routine training mission over the Atlantic. The flight was led by Lietuenant Charles Taylor, an experienced navigator. A total of fourteen men was on the five planes, four of which were piloted by student fliers. The flight was last heard from by radio from the vicinity of the Florida Keys, reporting no trouble. It then disappeared over the ocean and was never heard from again. One of the most extensive air and sea searches ever attempted failed to turn up any trace whatever of the missing planes or men. The last contact was at 4 P.M., December 5, 1945.

Speculation as to what might have occurred has been the subject of many stories in newspapers and magazines. Records of the Office of Naval History and of the Judge Advocate General's office contain no further documents. Lieutenant Taylor was cleared of all blame by a Naval Board for the correction of records.

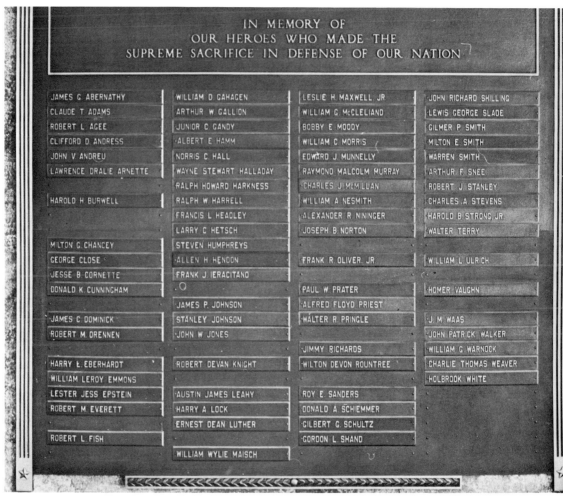

IN MEMORY OF
OUR HEROES WHO MADE THE
SUPREME SACRIFICE IN DEFENSE OF OUR NATION

JAMES G. ABERNATHY	WILLIAM D. GAHAGEN	LESLIE H. MAXWELL, JR.	JOHN RICHARD SHILLING
CLAUDE T. ADAMS	ARTHUR W. GALLION	WILLIAM G. McCLELLAND	LEWIS GEORGE SLADE
ROBERT L. AGEE	JUNIOR C. GANDY	BOBBY E. MOODY	GILMER P. SMITH
CLIFFORD D. ANDRESS	ALBERT E. HAMM	WILLIAM C. MORRIS	MILTON E. SMITH
JOHN V. ANDREU	NORRIS C. HALL	EDWARD J. MUNNELLY	WARREN SMITH
LAWRENCE DRALIE ARNETTE	WAYNE STEWART HALLADAY	RAYMOND MALCOLM MURRAY	ARTHUR F. SNEE
	RALPH HOWARD HARKNESS	CHARLES J. McMILLAN	ROBERT J. STANLEY
HAROLD H. BURWELL	RALPH W. HARRELL	WILLIAM A. NESMITH	CHARLES A. STEVENS
	FRANCIS L. HEADLEY	ALEXANDER R. NININGER	HAROLD B. STRONG, JR.
	LARRY C. HETSCH	JOSEPH B. NORTON	WALTER TERRY
MILTON G. CHANCEY	STEVEN HUMPHREYS		
GEORGE CLOSE	ALLEN H. HENDON	FRANK R. OLIVER, JR.	WILLIAM L. ULRICH
JESSE B. CORNETTE	FRANK J. IERACITANO		
DONALD K. CUNNINGHAM	O	PAUL W. PRATER	HOMER VAUGHN
	JAMES P. JOHNSON	ALFRED FLOYD PRIEST	
JAMES C. DOMINICK	STANLEY JOHNSON	WALTER R. PRINGLE	J. M. WAAS
ROBERT M. DRENNEN	JOHN W. JONES		JOHN PATRICK WALKER
		JIMMY RICHARDS	WILLIAM G. WARNOCK
HARRY L. EBERHARDT	ROBERT DEVAN KNIGHT	WILTON DEVON ROUNTREE	CHARLIE THOMAS WEAVER
WILLIAM LEROY EMMONS			HOLBROOK WHITE
LESTER JESS EPSTEIN	AUSTIN JAMES LEAHY	ROY E. SANDERS	
ROBERT M. EVERETT	HARRY A. LOCK	DONALD A. SCHIEMMER	
	ERNEST DEAN LUTHER	GILBERT G. SCHULTZ	
ROBERT L. FISH		GORDON L. SHAND	
	WILLIAM WYLIE MAISCH		

World War II dead—Bronze plaque in War Memorial Auditorium

Alexander (Sandy) R. Nininger, Jr.

In the vast crucible of World War II many Fort Lauderdale men distinguished themselves in desperate situations and many lost their lives, both in the armed services and in the merchant marine. The latter service, perhaps because of Port Everglades, drew heavily for recruits here. No actual statistics on how many lost their lives in this service are available. Since it is impossible, here, to describe all these heroic actions, your historians have elected to tell the details of only one, the first, and to let this tribute apply to all of our gallant young men.

Chapter 19
1942

FORT LAUDERDALE

Lt. Alexander (Sandy) Nininger, Jr.,
first soldier of World War II awarded
the Congressional Medal of Honor

In his peacetime pursuits Alexander R. Nininger, Jr., was as typical
as a boy could be. In war he became an inspiring legend. Pearl Harbor
was hardly a month past when the people of Fort Lauderdale were
shocked by the news of the first battle casualty among its local servicemen. Young Lieutenant Nininger, known to almost the entire population as "Sandy," was killed in action on January 12, 1942. Close upon
the heels of this announcement came the word that he had become the
first soldier of World War II to win the Congressional Medal of Honor.
People of the town were grimly proud. Sandy had been one of the
most popular of the younger citizens, a friendly unassuming youth,
polite almost to the point of seeming shy. As an usher in the Sunset
Theater, managed by his father, he was known to many. Sandy's gradu-
ation from West Point the preceding June had been the source of satisfaction for a host of well-wishers. Now he was dead and Fort Lauderdale, for its part, was at war with an earnest determination that would
never flag. His exploits, in the opinion of capable officers on the scene,
may have had a telling effect upon the entire tide of the war.

Sandy Nininger was born in Atlanta, Georgia, just after the close of
World War I. He was sickly in his early youth and spent some time in
the Catskill Mountains, near West Point, where he was inspired by the
activities of the cadets. Even then he may have determined upon a

224

military career. During high school days in Fort Lauderdale, Sandy lived with his parents in a home on the bank of New River. A next-door neighbor was Major C. W. Cole, retired from the Army after long service with the Philippine Scouts. Cole's stories further fascinated the earnest young man with the idea of becoming a soldier, with service in the areas described by Cole. Sandy compiled a fine record in high school, and his father, through the friendly intervention of City Attorney George W. English, Jr., persuaded Congressman J. Mark Wilcox to appoint the boy as one of his alternates to West Point. Sandy, still a skinny kid, was not tops in ensuing tests, but the others were prevented by circumstance from accepting, and Nininger got his chance. He finished twenty-third in the class. This gave him a choice of service, and he chose the Philippine Scouts. Events from this point on are best told by contemporary accounts and official testimonials.

A description of the action was given on February 20, 1944, to Sandy's father by Colonel George S. Clarke, in command of the forces on Bataan:

The date he was killed, January 12, 1942, was the day of a continuing series of attacks made by the Japanese on the 57th combat team sector under my command on the right of the line at Abucai on Bataan. The two battalions of the 57th Infantry were on the main line of resistance. The first attacks made by the Japanese on Bataan were made against this sector. Eleven Japanese attacks were made. The Japanese attacked in a series of suicidal frontal attacks.

. . . The Japanese constantly attacking at night, succeeded on the second night in throwing wave after wave of men onto the barbwire in front of our position, thereby forming a human bridge of dead Japanese over the wire for use by their men in their 3d suicidal attempt to take the position.

I have given the above sketched outline to show you why "Sandy's" actions followed. It must be remembered that officers and men, though well trained, were actually green troops under battle conditions.

The bizarre and extraordinary tactics of the Japs confused and amazed us all. Fire-crackers and drums—wild attacks seemingly going nowhere—whole companies of Japanese showing themselves in front of fields of cane, merely to draw our fire to establish our machine gun installations.

The lack of flares to light up "No-Man's Land," combined with the weird and unearthly screams in the native Philippino language by the snipers, established in trees inside of our position, makes it in retrospect seemingly almost impossible that the troops held on as they did.

FORT LAUDERDALE

Your son was in the first Battalion, 57th Infantry and therefore, to justify his death in the area of Company K., 3d Battalion, 57th Infantry, I must explain the situation of the 1st Battalion. In order that the Japanese forces be stopped from attempting to go around the right flank of the sector by swimming, or in boats, companies A and B, 1st Battalion, took up positions along a two-mile fish pond dike which extended through the mangrove swamps to the edge of Manila Bay.

Your son and the troops labored for days and nights in water up to their waists, cutting down the mangrove trees to establish fields of fire in front of the position.

As it turned out, these two companies on the dikes were never attacked except by a constant strafing by Japanese planes. The dikes were about six feet high and about three feet wide. Individual standing foxholes were built for the men the length of the dikes.

At this point I might tell you that I visited this position nightly during the construction, and I saw no one as happy as your son Sandy during this particular time. The difficulties of supplies, food, water and ammunition, and lack of sleep, apparently agreed with him. His enthusiasm and delight in my praise of his efforts were contagious. . . . His attitude struck me as the attitude of a soldier who at last was doing the job he had been trained to do.

Sandy received permission to go sniper hunting on the 10th and 11th of January. Please picture the situation again in his organization. No sleep for nights on end—only a standing foxhole in which to rest during the day. . . .

You have, of course, read of the marvelous ability of the Japanese to construct sniper nests in trees. I have personally walked up to a bole of a tree, looked up into the branches, and seen absolutely nothing, yet in that same tree, six Japs were killed while I was still in that vicinity. Three members of the 57th Infantry, also sniper hunting, walked into and stepped upon a group of fifty Japanese soldiers, magnificently camouflaged, lying prone upon the ground. They killed all fifty without one moving a muscle while still alive.

"Sandy" received my permission to go forward in the 3d Battalion Sector with two of his men. He was loaded down with grenades and with a Garand rifle slung over his shoulders. He carried under his arm a Japanese "Tommy-Gun." Instead of concentrating on snipers in his own area, he decided that there were more Japs in the area behind Company K. Many reports of his action, and the action for which I recommended him for the Congressional Medal of Honor, were reported to me by the company commanders of L and M companies, as well as other corroborating reports from men in Company K.

"Sandy" shot his first Jap out of a tree and as the Jap's body fell at his feet, he was so excited he stood up in the face of terrific rifle fire and yelled. He apparently was wounded at that time, since his leg was apparently bandaged. From then on, "Sandy" apparently went berserk. He threw grenade after grenade.

Men of Company K counted some twenty Japs killed by his grenades. Our counter attack was succeeding and their artillery laid down a fearful barrage. Many reports of further action by "Sandy" were then made by the 2nd in command of the 2nd Battalion, 57th Infantry, making the counter attack to regain Company K's position.

"Sandy" apparently had used up all of his Jap ammunition, and was now using his bayonet and leaping from one shell hole to another. At this time he was wounded a second time, since a first aid man crawled to his assistance. "Sandy" must have had a premonition that he was going to die, because the first aid man could not hold him in that shell hole.

His final action, as described by this same officer, was when he saw "Sandy" wounded again in the shoulder; and when he seemed to be staggering from loss of blood, three Japs charged toward him with bayonets. He killed all three of them, and apparently fell from exhaustion and weakness. From the reports of the first aid men, when they crawled to him, he was dead, and a dead Jap officer lay across his legs.

I cannot tell you how many of the enemy Sandy accounted for, but this I will say: his personal actions at this particular time cannot possibly be evaluated. Suffice it to say that his action acted like a tonic on the men around him, and added greatly to the success of our counterattack.

"Sandy's" remains were carefully brought to the church in the town of Abucai, Province of Bataan, the Philippines.

Captain Cecina, chaplain 57th Infantry, held a reverent and beautiful service for him. He is buried in grave No. 9, behind the South wall of the Abucai church, beside many of my fine brave young officers who also died in that same action. Men of his company carefully placed the exotic flowers of the Philippines upon the wooden cross that marks his last resting place. I was present personally for your son's funeral service. It was beautiful and reverent, honoring a man whom I loved—one of my fine young officers, and a brave man.

I may say that his men loved him too, and his memory will live with them as long as they live.

The significance of Nininger's action is explained by another contemporary in a story printed in the *Kiwanis Magazine*, July, 1962, written by Hal Higdon: "Colonel Frederick Yeager spent three and a half years in a Japanese prison camp following his capture on Bataan. He explained to me the significance of Alex Nininger's action:

"There was this hole in the line. Just by establishing where this hole was we were able to fill it. We held at Abucay for several days. Then we dropped back to another position. Our line refused to cave in. This delayed the Japs somewhat—and it surprised them. We weren't push-overs, as they had been led to believe. So instead of continuing their attack they stopped and waited until they could obtain more troops and bring up artillery and more supplies. This was the twelfth of January. They never really started to get serious again until early April. If they had met with some initial success, they might have pushed us over with sheer force. But they got cautious. They didn't know how many troops we had. There was an element of doubt, and this stopped them. The Japanese high command at this time was considering the invasion of Australia. But we had too many of their forces tied down. Had they been free, the whole nature of the Pacific campaign might have been changed. Alexander Nininger, Jr., was a soldier who gave his life at a moment in battle when the balance of victory teetered on a slender point. Measured against the entire War in which hundreds of battles occurred and in which thousands of men on both sides died, his contribution may seem almost insignificant. But measured by Ben Franklin's standard of a nail to a horse to a rider to a battle to a war, his contribution looms very large indeed. The quiet hero has done his job."

His official citation is contained in the following letter:

Upon the recommendation of General Douglas MacArthur, the President on January 29, 1942, made the award, posthumously, in the name of Congress, of the Congressional Medal of Honor, the highest decoration which can be awarded to a member of the nation's armed forces for bravery in action to SECOND LIEUTENANT ALEXANDER RAMSEY NININGER, JR., Class of 1941, United States Military Academy, with the following citation:

ALEXANDER R. NININGER, JR., SECOND LIEUTENANT, Fifty Seventh Infantry (Philippine Scouts), United States Army. For conspicuous gallantry and intrepidity above and beyond the call of duty in action with the enemy near Abucay, Bataan, Philippine Islands, on January 12, 1942. This officer, although assigned to another company not then engaged in combat, vountarily attached himself to Company K same regiment, while that unit was being attacked by enemy forces superior in fire power.

Enemy snipers in trees and foxholes had stopped counter attack to regain part of position. In hand-to-hand fighting which followed, Lieutenant Nininger repeatedly forced his way to and into the hostile position. Though exposed to heavy enemy fire, he continued to attack with rifle and hand grenades and succeeded in destroying several enemy groups in foxholes and enemy snipers.

Although wounded three times, he continued his attacks until he was killed after pushing alone far within the enemy position. When his body was found after recapture of the position one enemy officer and two enemy soldiers lay dead around him.

The Military Academy is justly proud that the first award in this war of the Nation's highest honor should be to one of its most recent graduates. All those who knew him will remember him as a man who adds lustre to the finest traditions of West Point and of the United States Army. By his supreme sacrifice above and beyond the call of duty he exemplified his devotion to the ideals to which he here dedicated himself.

By Command of Major General WILBY:

(Signed) ARTHUR C. PURVIS
Colonel, A. G. D.
Adjutant General
General Orders No. 6, Headquarters United States Military Academy, February 2, 1942.

The dead hero's name has been perpetuated in many ways. The main street at Fort McPherson was named Nininger Street. And on July 26, 1942, Nininger Park at Fort Knox, Kentucky, was dedicated.

The city of Fort Lauderdale adopted an ordinance designating the driveway or area leading from North East 6th Avenue (U.S. No. 1) to the War Memorial Auditorium as "Sandy Nininger Drive."

Sandy had been a charter member of the Kiwanis sponsored Key Club when it was organized in 1936 at Fort Lauderdale High School. In the spring of 1942, at a convention of Florida Key Clubs, Kiwanian Harold Martin of Fort Lauderdale proposed the Sandy Nininger Medal as an award in his memory. The medal was "to be awarded to high school students who distinguished themselves by making the most of their opportunities." The Sandy Nininger Medal was adopted in 1946 and since then hundreds have been awarded to outstanding high school students throughout the country.

His valor drew praise from high places. Among those who wrote testimonials were Generals Dwight D. Eisenhower and Douglas MacArthur. When Sandy died a long and bitter war still lay ahead of the nation, but the manner of his death added its share of courage to those who remained to fight on.

(BURGHARD COLLECTION)

Andrews Avenue during flood of 1947

Aftermath of Victory

Fort Lauderdale greeted V-J day with subdued, but deep relief. The war's outcome had been a foregone conclusion for weeks, even months. The horror of the atom bomb was bewildering, even terrifying to many. The boisterous high jinks of 1918 were missing. World War I ended at a time when the German army, though falling back and overpowered, was still a formidable, superbly trained, and disciplined force. A long, bitter fight was still possible even though that end also was inevitable. The Kaiser before his fall had not been willing, as had Hitler, to sacrifice hundreds of thousands of his soldiers for a few added weeks of grandeur.

It had long been a Chamber of Commerce ambition to acquire a Burdine's Department Store. During war years Burdine officials made a survey and determined upon the northwest corner of South Andrews Avenue and 2d Street, the site of the City Hall. The city commission agreed to sell for two hundred fifty thousand dollars. Shortly before war's end the deal was closed and construction of Burdine's began. Abbott, Merckt & Company was the engineer; Caldwell, Scott Company, the contractor.

Thus the commission found itself without a home. A new city hall was projected. Property on North Andrews Avenue, selected by a referendum of the voters, was purchased but plans had yet to be approved when the city was evicted. Temporary quarters were established upstairs in a building on the southeast corner of South West 1st Avenue and Broward Boulevard, above Dowdy's grocery store. The police station was moved into a two-story building on North Andrews Avenue at 6th Street which formerly housed Ray Whyte's Tarpon Lumber Company.

Rationing of gasoline and foods did not end at once and whiskey was scarce. Many employees of government emergency services, foreseeing the end, had been switching to private work for months. Now the big change-over to peacetime economy was upon the community. Its leaders had tried to plan for it well in advance. One of their chief concerns was to find jobs for the returning soldiers. They wondered, secondarily, what would happen to the tourist industry and whether or not newly founded war industries would be idled. Some predicted an influx of new residents and considered what might be done to find work for them. For a few months little happened. Servicemen returned in a slow trickle and were duly feted. Newspaper headlines did change, but other significant activities were slow to start.

* * *

Gulfstream Park, after its first big failure, had gone through bankruptcy with one plan for reorganization after another placed before the court. With the nation at war, interest had dropped. Then, James Donn, Miami florist and owner of a landscaping firm called Exotic Gardens, headed a group which acquired title. On December 1, 1944, with the war fading, the track reopened for a twenty-day meet. In 1945 it was opened on the same day of the month for a full forty days. Thereafter, with the exception of a late fall meet in 1948, it has run in the spring. In 1947 the track inaugurated the Fort Lauderdale Handicap,

231

a feature since. Donn made Gulfstream Park a garden show place and its accessibility and location made for success.

* * *

As the weeks wore on, speculation as to the forthcoming tourist season became a major conversation topic. Travel restrictions were lifted. Most rationing had been cancelled or forgotten. Many items, such as choice cuts of meat, were difficult to get, or only to be found in the "black market." But most consumer goods and supplies other than building materials, automobiles, and major appliances were more plentiful. The war had reduced unemployment to an absolute minimum. Money was far more plentiful than were attractive ways to spend it.

For all the careful planning and expert predicting, events did not take the turns expected. The dam burst. The winter season of 1945-46 was one of new and bewildering prosperity. Never had so many people, with so much money, descended upon Fort Lauderdale. Much of the money may have been black market earnings and undeclared for income tax purposes. Whatever it was, it was money, and people were anxious to spend it. The hitherto unsuccessful Colonial Inn was opened with a flurry of grandeur. Its winnings at the gambling tables that year were so fantastic that even the gamblers who ran it had trouble believing it. Gas and other rationing was ended. People wanted fun, and the pent-up floods were loosed. They could not buy new cars or new homes. There were none. The prices of existing homes in Florida skyrocketed. They doubled and then tripled and even quadrupled. One who had any sort of room in Fort Lauderdale could rent it during that hectic season for almost any price asked. Many visitors were forced to sleep in their cars.

Only a scattered few of the servicemen had returned to civilian life, but civilians—most of whom had made good money during the long war years—were in Fort Lauderdale as tourists and ready for anything. The returning servicemen, both former Fort Lauderdale residents and men who had trained in the area, knew what they wanted. They wanted the homes they had dreamed of during bitter years overseas. They wanted them in Fort Lauderdale. But homes were hard to get. The G.I. Bill of Rights offered them financing, and local lending institutions were well prepared to help; but building material was scarce and a black market soon was active. Into this situation came project builders. They bought every large available tract of land in Fort Lauderdale and its environs. The market was there. Materials, they knew, would eventually become available. They established a new price range for vacant lots (which had been selling for as little as two hundred fifty dollars) upward from a thousand dollar minimum.

Among the new builders were Gill Construction Company, Tolly Vinik, Keats Construction Company, Gus Nichols, Nasrullah Brothers, and many others. Houses were sold long before they were built, under long-term mortgages guaranteed by either the Veterans Administration or the Federal Housing Authority. Soon available land in Fort Lauderdale proper was used up and builders began looking westward. Now new problems arose. The city water plant had been built during the boom of the 1920's with a top-rated capacity of ten million gallons per day. This was surpassed daily in the unnaturally dry year. The plant ran at top speed but the demand continued to grow. Investigations revealed that the fresh-water supply under the well fields on the municipal golf course was dangerously near the underlying salt water. The threat of salt infiltration was imminent. Emergency measures, including the banning of lawn sprinkling, were taken. The city cast about for new well fields. Plant additions were planned.

Another public body which went into emergency sessions was the school board. No new schools had been needed since the big boom, but now the population was exploding and classroom space was at a premium. There were not enough classrooms to take care of the children, and there was not enough money in the till for more new schools. Split sessions and temporary, portable schoolrooms purchased as surplus from Army camps supplied only a partial and an unsatisfactory answer. The board reluctantly eyed the possibility of a bond issue.

In the first spring after the war, Fort Lauderdale had its first experience as a training center for a big league baseball team. The Boston Braves, managed by Billy Southworth, came and made the Broward Hotel their headquarters. West Side ball yard on West Broward Boulevard was small in size and in seating capacity. Before the war, Fort Lauderdale's entry in the class D Florida East Coast League used it and, prior to that, it was used by semipro league baseball and football teams. The Syracuse Chiefs of the International League were here for spring training several years prior to the war. In exhibition games against big league clubs, the Braves filled the park far beyond its capacity. Among immortals who visited the park that year were Cornelius McGillicuddy (Connie Mack), Honus Wagner, Hank Greenberg (playing his last year), and a rookie pitcher, Warren Spahn. The Braves did not return, blaming this officially on lack of accommodations, along with too much distraction for players. Actually, someone in the town had

233

incurred the displeasure of Bill Cunningham, Boston newspaperman, and Southworth had been arrested and fined for a minor traffic accident. Both were said to have resented what happened. In ensuing years minor league teams used the field.

* * *

Florida was not the only beneficiary under the will of Hugh T. Birch. The park land it received was only a small portion of his holdings in this area. Most of the remainder was willed to Antioch College of Yellow Springs, Ohio. This included land between the ocean and the Intracoastal Waterway from Granada Street north to the property occupied by "Bonnet House," a few hundred feet south of Sunrise Boulevard. The college board of trustees began development of this land shortly after the end of the war, cutting it into large hotel and apartment house sites. It was ready to be offered for public sale in 1946. Attorney Curtis J. Byrd was their local representative.

Also owned by the college was the tract bounded by Middle River on the west, the Intracoastal Waterway on the east, and Sunrise Boulevard on the north. This land was a mangrove swamp, but its location made it highly desirable. The trustees held it for later development. When Birch Ocean Front Estates was opened up, apartment house sites sold almost like ice-cream cones. Fort Lauderdale was vastly underbuilt and property on the ocean was in tremendous demand.

Unlike the boom in 1925, the post-World War II boom was not one of speculation. Property was bought primarily for the purpose of building. There were speculators, but they speculated with real money, not binders. Home loans were in tremendous demand and the First Federal Savings and Loan Association became one of the most potent organizations in the state.

Harry P. Greep, a young ex-serviceman with a banking and savings and loan background, came to Fort Lauderdale to live. He went into business arranging loans for ex-servicemen; but he found a need for new lending institutions. He interested a local group and founded the Atlantic Federal Savings and Loan Company, which experienced sensational growth. Another development saw the Broward National Bank, the city's oldest, solve a pressing need for expansion. State laws prevent branch banking, but officials of the older bank obtained a charter for a new, independent bank, the Fort Lauderdale National Bank, which was opened at South East 2d Street and South Federal Highway, with Joseph N. Morris as executive vice president and J. D. Camp as president.

Fort Lauderdale was achieving state-wide recognition. G. Harold Martin was elected governor of the Florida Kiwanis District.

The sixty-nine-piece Fort Lauderdale High School band, under the direction of Harry McComb, won highest honors in the Southeast Florida Music Festival. Dr. Anna A. Darrow won a thousand dollar second prize in the American Medical Art Exhibition in Atlantic City.

The winter of 1946-47 was another "Block Buster" and the seasonal peak in water consumption found the hard-pressed water department receiving much needed relief from Mother Nature. It rained unseasonably early—and it kept on raining. By midsummer the water table throughout southeastern Florida was high. Farmers began to worry about getting water off their fields in time for planting.

*   *   *

Then came the first of the 1947 hurricanes. The winds did little damage but the hurricane brought more water. Entire areas of the city were flooded. The extreme tides, driven higher by turbulence in the South Atlantic, held back normal flow-off of water down the river. Water stood in fields used to graze beef and dairy cattle.

And then came the second hurricane. It too was mild as to wind, but it deposited eleven inches of rain in less than three hours. Fort Lauderdale was flooded. Downtown streets were two feet under water. New River was out of its banks in many places and outlying sections were inundated, with water above the ground floor of homes. In sections to the west the situation was even worse. Cattle and horses sought shelter on canal banks, sharing their refuge with rattlesnakes, wildcats, deer, and other game. Where possible, farmers used boats to take food to their stock. A health hazard was immediately apparent, for ninety per cent of the city used septic tanks, which were now flooded and for the most part inoperative. In most cases the water was polluted.

In Davie and other farming sections where no city drinking water was available, the situation was crucial. The federal government declared it an emergency area and units of the Army came to set up portable water purification plants. Some units brought amphibious equipment to move cattle to what little high ground remained. Seed beds were drowned out and winter vegetables were threatened with extinction. And still the rain kept falling. Water sloshed from the streets into many downtown stores. Thoroughly soaked, softened streets pitted under their paving and large segments were washed away.

Old-time residents said that it had been thirty-six years since the city

FORT LAUDERDALE

had been as flooded as it was after the October 16 record downpour. M. O. Decker said that in that year (1912) twenty-two inches of rain fell in a twenty-four-hour period. In island sections fine homes saw lawns inundated and grass and shrubbery destroyed. In most cases floor elevations kept water from flowing through the house. Water in the citrus groves threatened the trees themselves, particularly when the sun heated the water. Government and local engineers could provide no suggestions for immediate relief. Runoff was slowed by the unnaturally high tides. Even so, an air view of Port Everglades showed a black line of sediment leading from the port far out to sea. The sediment was composed of rich loam and muck; the land that early pioneers referred to as "the richest this side of the Nile delta."

The United States Army Corps of Engineers, working day and night, came up with a plan and sent a civilian employee, Harold Scott, to Fort Lauderdale to explain it. The plan was large. It envisioned a huge, hurricane-proof dike to encircle one thousand square miles of Everglades lowland. The area would become a vast reservoir which would protect fresh-water supplies for populous coastal areas. Powerful pumps would backfill it in time of flood, thus draining the coastal ridge in both directions, east to the sea and west to the reservoirs. In periods of drought the reservoir could be tapped for water to irrigate fields.

The engineers also envisioned this vast area as a wildlife refuge. The cost, they declared, would be about $208,000,000. The plan sealed off, forever, any hope of draining the vast areas of the Everglades. Drainage was a project which the engineers labeled "impractical, if not impossible." Scott pointed out that for several miles the marginal land outside the reservoir could be made safe and tillable by the use of subdrainage systems. He estimated ten years as required to put the plan into full effect. Then, he said, facilities would be ready, but several good seasons of rain would be needed to build the water reserve. When this was complete, destructive Everglades fires would end and irrigation and drainage would be matters for local systems. Asked how he justified such a huge expenditure by the government (which was to foot eighty-five per cent of the bill), Scott said the flood had cost the government many millions in lost income taxes. "Every bit of this damage will be written off by returns," he pointed out, "and farmers and citrus men will have much greater taxable incomes than the preflood control amounts." The plan was adopted, and work was begun before the year was out on "Phase One"—the building of levees to protect the coastal areas from floods.

If individuals could write off their losses on their income tax, the city and county could not. Their losses were staggering in the many miles of streets and roads that required repaving. Fort Lauderdale instituted a "temporary" tax of ten per cent on public utility bills. The tax remains.

Coastal cities finally dried out after six weeks of the floods and quickly began big cleanup campaigns for the forthcoming winter season. The farming areas to the west were harder hit. Thousands of acres of citrus were killed. Many head of livestock were lost. Crops were either impossible to plant or badly delayed. People driven from homes were forced to live, well into the winter, in the special shelters provided by the Red Cross and other agencies. Floods recurred in 1948, but to a lesser degree.

Among the places hard hit by the first flood was a new development, Plantation, which lay directly west of Fort Lauderdale. Plantation was a project of Frederick C. Peters, who had migrated to Miami from St. Louis. Peters had built up large farming interests south of Miami and, during the war, had won special commendation from the armed services for food production. He determined to increase it and surveyed much of south Florida before settling on a ten-thousand-acre tract west of Fort Lauderdale. Here Peters established a model subdrainage district. The war ended before he could get into production. He then rented lands to tenant farmers. Later he determined to establish a new city which he named Plantation. His first housing project was largely flooded when dikes failed to hold in 1947. Peters rebuilt the dikes bigger and stronger and now had the added protection of the Army Engineers' plan. Plantation stayed dry in 1948. He built a golf course and engaged

an architect to design a model city and began selling acreage to developers. Russell T. Pancoast, noted south Florida architect, was the
planner. Chauncey R. Clark, also from Miami, built the first homes.

* * *

Fort Lauderdale was no stranger to boom-time conditions and the
big spree and resulting depression of the 1920's were well remembered.
The times of palmy days and easy money, and the memories of the
harrowing years that followed, were undimmed. If "boom" meant a
resulting "bust," then the older heads wanted none of it. Whether
wanted or not, the new postwar boom was here and all that could be
done was to try to keep up with the new course of events—and be
wary. Keeping up became difficult, then more difficult, and then impossible.

The first crisis appeared in the schools. The end of the 1926 boom
had seen Broward County oversupplied with schools. Now, overnight,
the county was critically short. New schools were expensive and their
construction required time. The school board had neither money nor
time. When the school year of 1948-49 began, School Superintendent
Ulric J. Bennett found that his approximately seven thousand peak en-
rollment at the close of the year the June before had now grown to
ten thousand, a gain of approximately forty-two per cent. This meant
that a hundred new classrooms were immediately needed. The schools
were jammed to capacity even before the 1948-49 year registration.

The school board went into special sessions. The cause of the vast
increase was evident: new arrivals in town, and a bumper crop of "war
babies" reaching school age. These factors added not at all to the tax
money immediately available. Despite school priorities, building materials were in short supply. The harassed board received an unexpected
blessing. The Navy decommissioned its Naval Air Station and leased it
to the county for a dollar a year plus maintenance. County commissioners were agreeable to the use of whatever was available for school
purposes. Though they were far from ideal, the school board took over
several buildings on a temporary basis. Seventeen years later they were
still in use.

Another emergency measure was the purchase of war surplus portable frame buildings from the old Florida army camps. Entire new
elementary schools were thus established. Despite these desperate measures, the press of new population vastly overtaxed facilities.

The school board projected a bond issue of six million dollars which
would have been sufficient to "catch up." Ad valorem bond issues,

238

Plantation Golf Club opens. (*Left to right*): Frederick C. and Frederick T. Peters, builders, and John Ring and Robert Hess, Chamber of Commerce officials

according to law, must be voted by at least fifty per cent plus one of the freeholders, a monumental accomplishment. Achieving it became even more difficult because the powerful *Fort Lauderdale Daily News* vigorously opposed it. The actual vote was strongly favorable, but the number voting was insufficient and it failed. The school board then asked the voters for the maximum 10 mills and got it; but collections were too far in the future to provide early relief. Schools were forced into double sessions, classrooms handling one group of students mornings and another afternoons. This was unsatisfactory to parents, pupils, and teachers—but it was the only way. The school board was then forced to take the long road of pay-as-you-go. Adding to its woes was the absolute necessity of raising teacher pay. Gradually through the years the board bought new sites and built new schools, and the Broward County schools remained fully accredited.

Even as the school board struggled with these woes, Fort Lauderdale city commissioners had their problems. The city faced the same situation in regard to trying to borrow money under the election law requirements. Its needs were as pressing and more numerous than those of the school board. Traffic in the winter tourist season was bumper-to-bumper and highly exasperating. Many streets badly needed to be repaved and more traffic lights were an urgent necessity. The cost of these improvements would be staggering. And now the State Board of Health put its foot down. The city, it ruled, simply could not continue to build houses with septic tanks. An over-all sanitary sewer system was imperative. "The city," said Dr. W. C. Hatchett, Broward County health director, "is floating on top of a vast cesspool." The existing sewer system extended only through downtown and several principal streets. Almost all new residential areas were without. The cost of providing sanitary sewers was staggering, but the health director warned, "an epidemic would be even more costly." Realizing the impossibility of an immediate compliance, the health board consented to a system under which each proposed site was tested for use of septic tanks. Where usable, grudging approval was given.

City problems did not end there. The water plant, so proudly opened in 1926, worked to its utmost capacity and at times far beyond. Suppose, fearful officials asked, salt water infiltrates the city water system? A new filter plant, new standpipes, and new pumping stations must be built. To make matters even worse, well fields were pumping within feet and even within inches of salt water. Residents began to realize that "bigger" did not necessarily mean "better." Many sighed for the pleasant, sleepy village of yesterday. In retrospect, early-day problems were insignificant.

* * *

Still the new residents came. Victor Nurmi had completed development of the "finger island" section on the north side of East Las Olas Boulevard in Fort Lauderdale and the last traces of abandoned boom-time developments were almost gone. Still remaining as a grim reminder of 1926 was Morang's old "jackknife" bridge at South East 15th Street. The two sides of the span, in raised position, jutted from the open waters of Stranahan River, making an effective, if expensive, channel marker and serving also as a monument to the failure of the early boom. Wooden piling, installed to support the approaches, gradually rotted away. The bridge was a half-mile north of Port Everglades and visible to any entering the port. There was growing talk of the need for a southside crossing to the beach.

During the war the fishing charter fleet had been all but out of operation for a time; then it had run on a partial scale on bottled gas. Now, however, limitations were off and the river front saw its gayest days. It was a "dance of death"; an era was drawing to a close.

The "war of the outriggers" reached a new height, and the city finally persuaded the War Department to put bridge openings on schedules under which boats went through in groups rather than singly. But, since the openings had to be scheduled at peak traffic hours, the congestion on Federal Highway was a distressing source of irritation. Long waits backed up cars for blocks, even miles.

This was the stituation when the Coast Guard announced that its Base Six, south of the municipal casino, was to be transferred. Shortly thereafter the property was declared surplus and offered for sale. And thus was laid the groundwork for another mighty Fort Lauderdale hassle.

Port Everglades. Brook Memorial Causeway (*right center*)

Another Boom

Chapter 21
1946–1950's

The city commission, following World War II, faced problems so complex and difficult as to be completely confusing. Once again the city needed an updated plan to coordinate future development. The old Schermerhorn city plan, adopted in 1926, had served until the city, in 1946, employed George E. Simons, Jr., of Jacksonville, as city planner.

Simons' work was finished in early 1947. The new chart for future progress cost the city ten thousand dollars. It was overwhelmingly approved March 18, 1947, in a special election, and formally adopted by the city commission October 28, 1948. The plan included many specially drawn charts and maps. It must be remembered that the plan envisaged a future city of seventy thousand population, a figure now long since exceeded. Most recommendations were closely followed. It was a master plan for street widening and development, new bridges and other traffic improvements, including acquisition of downtown parking lots.

Simons foresaw unavoidable difficulties that the downtown area must encounter. James Ingraham, who laid out the city in 1895, had remarked ruefully in 1915 in court testimony that he had been unable to foresee the coming of the automobile. Simons, in comments made thirty-three years later, showed much the same dubious attitude about the needs of the central city. Complete remodeling of the downtown section was not financially practical. Other modifications, such as underpasses at the Florida East Coast railway crossings and a traffic cloverleaf at the intersection of East Las Olas and Atlantic Boulevard, were found to be too costly. The bulky program outlined past growth and laid plans for the future. Its charts, graphs, and maps showed trends in population that were to prove invaluable to future planners.

The Broward County Health Department, meanwhile, made disturbing reports on contamination of waterways due to the lack of sanitary sewers. Midwinter traffic jams were such that howls of protest came even from neighboring cities. Lack of sufficient bridges over New River was frustrating to motorists. The East Las Olas bridge across the Intracoastal Waterway was entirely inadequate. Further confusion arose on the great traffic debate issues when the suggested bridge plans were attacked by adherents of vehicular tunnels. The subject immediately became controversial.

* * *

The annual Aquatic Forum had long been a fixture of the Christmas season, but it now bore fruit in a new phenomenon. Collegians who attended had returned to their schools and spread the word of the wonders of Fort Lauderdale. College students were given spring vacation at a time when long and dreary northern winters still had muddy tail ends of cold to go through. They listened to their fellows on the swimming teams and started "Fort Lauderdale plans" for the spring recess. At the start they came to Fort Lauderdale in driblets, then by scores, and soon by hundreds. The city was glad to see them, although pranks were sometimes annoying. They came in March and April, the most beautiful months of the year, and just as the winter tourist season was beginning to taper off. As their numbers grew, they began to pose a problem for the city.

* * *

There was still another difficulty. Fort Lauderdale's suburbs had grown to the extent that homes outside the city almost equaled the number within the limits. The problem was whether or not to annex. Homestead exemption entered into the situation. Tax revenue from a subdivision of small homes was insignificant, but garbage collection and police and fire protection and other costly services would be required. The city commission "sat tight." "We've more than we can take care of now," was the feeling.

Business areas in the suburbs were few in the beginning. That they would come eventually was undoubted, but annexation was then financially a losing proposition. Plantation, four miles west, had a golf course and had become bustling and fast-growing, and was soon to be incorporated. Wilton Manors to the north already had a business section and had formed its own incorporated town for the purpose of avoiding annexation to Fort Lauderdale, thus hoping to escape taxation for city benefits. North of Wilton Manors was Oakland Park, also incorporated. On the south, Port Everglades, half in Hollywood, blocked expansion in that direction. Meantime Fort Lauderdale was adding to its beaches and parks, all free to residents of near-by communities.

Another vital issue was the acquisition of Holiday Park by the city. The move, beginning in 1937, to acquire the park had been sparked by G. H. Martin, local attorney. The city owned a number of lots in the huge area by reason of tax reversion. Many others had been picked up by private citizens on tax deeds at extremely low cost. Martin foresaw that soon the city would be entirely built up and that unless something was done there would be no sizable park in the entire municipality.

The city commission members of 1939, including Mayor Lewis E. Moore, W. J. Eastman, T. B. Manuel, Mrs. Ed. Pynchon, and Charlie Pease, together with City Manager J. H. Philpott, were in complete agreement that a larger park was essential. Stranahan Park, adequate in earlier days, was only one square block in size. Housing the Woman's Club and tourist entertainment facilities, including a covered game area and shuffleboard courts, left no room for further expansion. Southside Park was a little larger, but it housed the tennis courts, a softball diamond, and Southside School.

After the enactment of the Murphy Act in 1937, Martin, a member of the Parks Board, went to Tallahassee, where he helped obtain several hundred lots. By dint of persuasion, threats, wheedling, and finally outright condemnation proceedings in 1946, the city finally acquired title to its long-coveted park—86.2 acres in all. A contest to select a suitable name for the new park was sponsored by the Parks Board, and on March 21, 1947, the board chose the name "Holiday Park."

The ink was hardly dry on the deeds when the school board was making a deal to locate a new high school in the park, provided their

With Mayor Lewis E. Moore (*left*), City Attorney Julian E. Ross presents farewell gift to Commander French of the great Naval Air Station in behalf of the Chamber of Commerce and other city officials

new bond issue was successful. The move caused bitter contention. Acquisition of the park touched off another community campaign. World War II had left many scars, but also many memories that residents wanted to preserve. Some sort of memorial was planned, and after much discussion it was decided that nothing would better serve the community and the memories of those who had sacrificed in the war than a suitable auditorium.

Accordingly, following J. W. McLaughlin's survey Porter Reynolds—who had come to the city early in 1939 as parks and recreation director—designed the plans for the new park. This design was accepted by the city on November 10, 1947. A fund-raising campaign was subsequently launched for an auditorium to be built in Holiday Park. The undertaking was large, but spirits were high and cooperation was complete and wholehearted. Civic groups held entertainments for the benefit of the fund. Plans for the new structure called for a Memorial Chapel at the entrance and for an impressive, landscaped entranceway through the park.

* * *

The library, established by the Woman's Club almost with the founding of the city, had grown beyond the capacity of its quarters in the

Entrance to Fort Lauderdale's new City Hall (CITY PUBLICITY DEPARTMENT PHOTO)

Woman's Club building and had been taken over by the city in 1925, when it was moved into the city hall.

The city hall, though greatly expanded in 1925, soon became too small also and the library was moved to a building on South East First Avenue which the city purchased from Ada C. Kendricks in 1933. After the war the library was again moved; this time to South East River Drive in a building which the city purchased on July 1, 1947, for thirty-five thousand dollars. For many years it had served as the Christian Science church, and early in 1948 the library was moved into it. The church had constructed an imposing building on South Federal Highway. A library site was provided for in Holiday Park, but the city was faced with many other needed new projects.

With building materials now available, new churches were the order of the day. Roman Catholics built the magnificent Saint Anthony's Church and school on North East 2d Street. They sold the old church to the Lutherans, who had it moved by its original builder, John Olsson, to a location on North East 3d Avenue. Elaborate new structures were also built in the Colee Hammock section by First Presbyterian and All Saints Episcopal churches. The Baptists built a beautiful new edifice on East Broward Boulevard.

The city and county remained in dire financial straits. The mushroom-

FIRST LUTHERAN CHURCH

FIRST BAPTIST CHURCH

FIRST METHODIST CHURCH

THE CHURCH OF GOD

SPIRITUALIST TEMPLE OF TRUTH
WOMAN'S BLDG

SEVENTH DAY ADVENTIST

SECOND BAPTIST

CHURCH OF CHRIST

TRINITY LUTHERAN

CATHOLIC CHURCH

PRESBYTERIAN CHURCH

PARK TEMPLE METHODIST CHURCH

CHRISTIAN CHURCH

CHURCH OF THE NAZARENE

ALL SAINTS EPISCOPAL

PROGRESSO METHODIST

CONGREGATION
EMANUEL

FIRST CHURCH OF CHRIST SCIENTIST

THE SALVATION ARMY

CHURCH OF JESUS CHRIST OF LATTER DAY SAINTS

(AUSTIN SMITH)

ing population demanded new facilities, but the tax rolls reflected only collections from the year already past. There was no provision for capital investments for the future, and the negative result of the school bond election left commissioners with no illusions as to what would happen if they sought a general obligation bond issue.

There was one hope for needed roads and bridges. The state returned a certain portion of gasoline tax money to the counties where it was collected. This amount was not sufficient in itself to provide much relief, but it would give service on bonds which could then be handled as a revenue issue without the necessity of a vote of the freeholders. One of the first projects to be undertaken on this plan was a new Andrews Avenue bridge. The existing span was thirty years old and in danger of being condemned. It had been built on masked wooden piling and the wood, below the masking concrete, was dangerously fragile. The new bridge, designed by Veteran County Engineer H. C. Davis,

Pioneer county engineer, H. C. Davis (GIFT, BOB DAVIS)

was named in his honor. But the bridge was a long time a-building. The contract was awarded to Powell Brothers Construction Company, a local firm which enjoyed a high reputation throughout Florida and the Caribbean. Plans called for all concrete and steel foundations and also for a seal mat on the river floor itself. The pressure of time compelled Powell to build a temporary bridge at South West 1st Avenue, which consisted of a pontoon, or barge, that could be swung aside to allow the passage of boats. It worked, but because of changing tides was far from ideal for high-speed traffic or heavily laden trucks. The Andrews Avenue Bridge was dedicated in October, 1949.

Other bridge reconstruction also moved ahead. All the old, low-level turnstile-type swinging bridges in the county over the Intracoastal Waterway were replaced by high-level bascule lift spans. These included those at Deerfield, Pompano Beach, Oakland Park, East Las Olas, Dania, and Hallandale. Fort Lauderdale, however, still had bridge problems. All recent planning had included additional crossings of New River at South West 12th Street and at South East 3d Avenue. The 1947 master plan had called for such a structure at 3d Avenue and the first study was ordered in January of 1953 by Mayor Lewis Moore. The *Fort Lauderdale News* considered the 3d Avenue project so important that in 1955 it offered to underwrite a bond issue, without legal or sales cost, for its construction. A survey by Radar Engineering Company of Miami left open the question of a high-level bridge at $750,000 or a low-level span to cost an estimated $500,000. A citizens' committee, with Peter Foglia as chairman, met to consider the possibility of obtaining rights-of-way. Most of these parcels, it was found, would be donated where no damage to existing structures was involved. The city agreed to provide the remainder.

Fort Lauderdale needed many other improvements. The 1947 flooding of streets by tropical rainfall had created an emergency that justified a referendum to authorize an emergency tax of ten per cent on utilities. The tax had never been repealed and now the city decided to use this occasion to support a bond issue of $5,000,000 to $6,500,000 to be used for city improvements. (In March, 1958, Powell Brothers' low bid of $845,982 was accepted and work on the 3d Avenue span began August 15 of that year. The total cost of the bridge, including lighting, paving, rights-of-way, and construction, was more than $1,500,000. The bridge was opened to traffic in late 1960.)

The *Fort Lauderdale Daily News* had plodded along since it was purchased by Gore in 1929 with a maximum circulation of less than six thousand. It dominated the local advertising field but had, hitherto, been ranked as "another country daily." New circulation figures zoomed, along with advertising, and new presses and a vastly increased staff became essential to the increased operation. Gore owned a building, a bowling alley prior to the war, on South East 1st Avenue. He remodeled it into a completely modern air-conditioned newspaper plant. He later acquired the neighboring Oliver mansion (the one used in 1924 by the fake "wire tappers") and tore it down for use as a parking lot. The Reed Bryan mansion, across the street to the west, was similarly razed for the same purpose.

The big Naval Air Station on South Federal Highway between Fort Lauderdale and Dania, the former Merle L. Fogg Field, was declared surplus by the Navy. At first it declined to sell the property but offered it for lease with the county given first preference—at one dollar per year. The lease stipulated that the county must maintain the base and that it could not operate it for profit. The county commission accepted. The air strip itself was in excellent condition, but the forty-odd temporary, war-use buildings were in various stages of disrepair. Of principal immediate interest to the county were the barracks area which contained eighty-eight small, livable apartments and the bachelor and junior

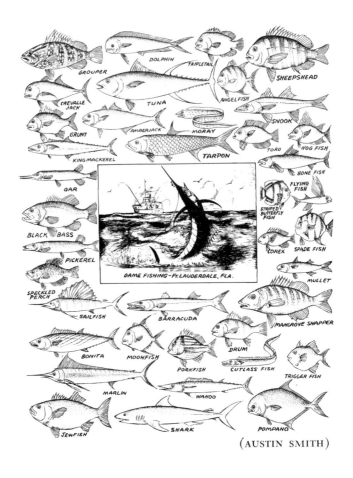

(AUSTIN SMITH)

Below: Barge load of lumber from Great Lakes comes up New River as another building boom begins

Principals in the great Coral Ridge development. (*Left to right*): James S. Hunt, Arthur T. Galt from Chicago, who sold the land, and Stephen A. Calder

officer quarters. Housing was a major headache, particularly housing within the financial reach of young veterans and their families who moved into the county in droves. The living areas in the base were put into repair and offered for rent at prices within the reach of the vets. A waiting list promptly formed.

The county first appointed an assistant engineer, Fred Flanders, to manage the airport, but Flanders was too busy at the court house and recommended Lee E. Wagener, who has been in this post ever since. Among other pressing needs filled by the airport facilities were classrooms for the school system. The Navy had built a large administration building and cafeteria. The school board leased these from the county for the cost of maintenance and repair, and educated hundreds of Broward County children there. The base served a further need by offering space for light manufacturing of several types, largely electronics. Although private craft used the airfield and hangar space and an air cargo line operated from it, the field did not at first attract any scheduled airlines.

* * *

251

FORT LAUDERDALE

Port Everglades' wartime port manager had been Finley Parker, its former manager, R. T. (Dusty) Spangler, having been attracted to managership of the Miami Port Authority. When Parker died in early 1947 Spangler was induced to return. The port returned to peacetime shipping without its former car ferry business. Dan Taylor, head of the ferry service, was induced to move the operation to the Port of Palm Beach. The petroleum business, however, had vastly increased and many new storage tanks were built. Spangler realized the potentialities of cruise ships which annually sailed on Caribbean trips and directed his efforts to attract them to the local port.

* * *

Fort Lauderdale was spreading out of its limits. Melrose Park, a mile-square subdivision west of the city, and lying between it and Plantation, was opened and soon others followed as population continued to mush-room. Among new developers were James S. Hunt and Stephen A. Calder. Hunt had returned after the war and had become friendly with local real-estate broker Calder. The two formed a partnership and managed to purchase from Arthur T. Galt, a former associate of Hugh T. Birch, a block of land between Middle River and the Intracoastal Water-way. They called the new subdivision Coral Ridge. There was still another development about this time that was destined to have a lasting effect on the city. Clyde Beatty was persuaded to sell the land where his old circus and zoo had been to a group represented by Thurman B. (Bud) Starr and Arthur W. Dixon. The new owners developed the area into Gateway Shopping Center and Fort Lauderdale's downtown business center had its first real rival.

From that time forward almost every extensive home development in the surrounding areas included its own shopping center. This kept much retail business that might have gone downtown close to the homes. The shopping centers provided ample free parking space for customers. This had not been contemplated as needed by the original developers of the city who made virtually no provision whatever for this phenomenon of the automobile age. Planning and zoning ordinances subsequently enacted included parking as a dominant part and required all business establishments to provide for parking.

Three years of growth that followed World War II had spurted the city's population to a hitherto unprecedented thirty-six thousand. This very growth brought on the problems that harrassed city officials at every step. Streets, bridges, off-street parking, police modernization, and an adequate answer to increasing demand by health authorities that sewers replace septic tanks were badly needed. Geographically Fort Lauderdale had little growing room. The town of Lauderdale-by-the-Sea, north on the beach, also incorporated. This was Fort Lauderdale as it neared the end of the decade. Prosperity had returned, but with it had come the great problem of "growing pains." Virtually everything was needed. The Board of Health was thundering for sanitary sewers, recognized as an expensive "must"; autoists clamored for better traffic conditions; schools demanded more classroom space. The water plant was rapidly becoming inadequate; electric power was short on cool mornings; long waits were required for installation of telephones.

* * *

Houses, meantime, were being built by the thousands. As Fort Lauderdale crowded over its available landscape it became evident that there was one wholly desirable piece of land ready for development in the immediate surroundings. This was the Arthur T. Galt tract, a portion of which reached almost as far south as Sunrise Boulevard. This was high, delightfully located land and there were at the beginning approximately 4,350 acres extending northward well beyond Oakland Park and mostly east of Federal Highway. Potential developers began wooing Galt, who made it known that, though willing to sell—at a price—he was going to see to it that when it was sold this time it would be developed and that this would be done in a suitable manner.

Into contention for the property stepped Coral Ridge Properties, controlled, as indicated earlier, by James S. Hunt and Stephen A. Calder. Hunt was a suave and able supersalesman, debonair in manner and a dapper dresser; he had a pronounced flair for the spectacular. His operations were on a grand, but sound scale. Calder was a salty, self-styled "cracker boy," who grew up in Fort Lauderdale and spent all his adult life working in real estate. He, like Hunt, had once been an automobile agent. Hunt and Calder were both willing to gamble for any stakes if they thought they were right, and both had unbounded confidence in the future of Fort Lauderdale. Calder had, for years, eyed the high ridge pine land which stretched along north Broward County between Middle River and the Intracoastal Waterway as an ideal site for development. Galt had sold the land during the "boom" to the Floranada developers for eight million dollars. He had been paid one million dollars down, but the balance was defaulted when the big bubble burst and he got the land back.

Completion of the Sunrise Boulevard Causeway made this property easily accessible from the south, but almost simultaneously with the availability of Sunrise Causeway had come the start of World War II. During the war the huge tract became a political football. It was contiguous to the city limits of both Oakland Park and Fort Lauderdale and comprised an area of highly taxable land. Its owner, Arthur T. Galt, had a reputation for prompt, cash tax payment. Oakland Park annexed the land into its city limits by an act of the 1945 legislature, an action that was promptly contested by Galt in court. He sued, asking the court by what right the town could annex and tax his land while rendering it no services of any kind in return. Oakland Park's fathers retorted that the city had no beach and that every Florida town needed a beach. Galt won the suit. In 1947 the state legislature passed a local bill annexing the land to Fort Lauderdale, but this time Governor Millard Caldwell was persuaded by Galt's attorneys to veto the bill, an almost unprecedented action in the case of a local bill.

While this was going on, Hunt and Calder started buying small parcels of land in the south portion of the Galt holdings and developing their subdivision, Coral Ridge. In these activities they had a keen rival in the so-called Cincinnati Syndicate, composed of E. Raymond Moss, William E. Edgemon, and Carroll Muccia. The latter group got the land along the Intracoastal Waterway known as Lauderdale Beach Extension, just north of Hugh Taylor Birch State Park. They were also able to purchase Silver Shores, the western half of Lauderdale-by-the-Sea. Both properties were valuable and both were beautifully developed, but Hunt and Calder were still the favored purchasers.

Finally, in 1953, Hunt and his chief assistant, Joe Taravella, went to Chicago and arranged with Galt for the purchase of the remaining twenty-four hundred acres. The price was an unprecedented $19,280,-000. Shortly after the purchase a declaration was made by Hunt and Calder that they would put their new development into the city of Fort Lauderdale, despite the fact that this would materially increase its tax load. It was a momentous decision for the city's good. A plan was worked out with the city commission whereby the land was to be divided into thirty-five parcels ranging in size from ten acres to a hundred and three acres. The lands were "vacant, unoccupied, unpopulated, unindustrialized, undeveloped" and not in need of municipal benefits. The plan was agreed upon by the owners and the city of Fort Lauderdale. It was also agreed that these lands were different and distinct in character, and that such annexation would assure the continued orderly and high class development of the city of Fort Lauderdale and its environs.

This program of integrating small contiguous parcels of land rather than a mass annexation was a new procedure to incorporate properties into the city limits. As each parcel was integrated it became subject to all city benefits and privileges and was subject to the jurisdiction and all obligations of the city. The first parcels to be integrated into the city were the eight along the ocean, where the Galt Ocean Mile is now located, extending north almost to the old Floranada Road. Hunt pointed out that Fort Lauderdale and its people provided the kind of background that made the development possible and said he wanted to cooperate fully with the city. He proceeded to develop the new purchase on the highest plane, built a golf course, and made other improvements which led to the construction of beautiful and costly homes and to important expansions of business facilities in the area.

The Galt Ocean Mile has developed into one of the finest hotel and apartment areas in the world. Oakland Park Boulevard is developing as a model for all future business streets. The area developed by Hunt and Calder now pays the city almost one-third of the city taxes and the Coral Ridge Development Corporation, headed by them, is the largest taxpayer, other than the public utility companies, in the city. This expansion of business and beautiful homes adds immeasurably to the city's prestige.

In the meantime, other developers were active. The father and son team that formed the Gill Construction Company was busy in the construction of low-cost homes under Veteran and Federal Housing Authority financing. The firm started in the north section, moved to the northeast, then to the southeast, where it continued the process of finger-islanding until this entire area to 14th Street was filled and drained. Thereafter the firm moved westward, building more than five thousand homes in all. Equally significant was the huge development of Jack Marqusee and Associates—mile-square Melrose Park, which was west of the city and outside the limits. Large developments on the outskirts of the city were also completed by Gus F. Nichols, Harold Brolliar Construction Company, and others, and still the county-wide demands for homes continued.

All these homes kept pushing up population and, of course, added to the city's traffic problem. Income from gasoline taxes, however, was also increasing. Under state law a portion of these taxes must be returned to the county in which it was collected. This amount grew to

First tunnel constructed in Florida

proportions that made further revenue bond issues—for road and bridge construction only—once more feasible. Each of the bridges built by the county in 1916 was to be replaced, and two new ones—at Oakland Park Beach Boulevard and at Sheridan Street, Hollywood—were included.

Before the bridge program was even announced a controversy raged in Fort Lauderdale. As early as 1940, the city commission took cognizance of the possibility of a tunnel rather than a new bridge on Federal Highway at New River. With three important new crossings in prospect, advocates of tunnels became vocal. It was strongly felt that these tunnels would be an ideal answer to automobile and boat traffic conflicts at the Federal Highway under New River; on East Las Olas at the Intracoastal Waterway; and at South East 15th or 17th Street, as well as at the Intracoastal Waterway, thus eliminating annoying waits while drawbridges were opened and closed. The tunnel advocates were powerful. In 1948 the firm of Palmer and Baker, Mobile, was employed at a fee of twenty thousand dollars to make preliminary plans. Mayor Reed Bryan, son of the early pioneer of that name, Commissioners Joseph G. Mackey and Tom Austin, and City Attorney Thomas O. Berryhill flew to Mobile with City Engineer E. L. Patterson and City Manager

Carlton Roberts to inspect the Bankhead tunnel. The traffic consulting engineering firm of Colpitts and Coverdale was employed by the city to make a projection of future traffic.

Meantime, the Florida State Road Department had become interested in the tunnel proposal. The state had yet to build its first vehicular tunnel. The firm of Parsons, Brinckerhoff, Hall and MacDonald was engaged by the department, and recommended a tunnel at Federal Highway but a bridge at Las Olas. A bridge was also recommended at South East 17th Street. By 1951 the road department had approved the Federal Highway tunnel at a proposed cost of $4,044,000. The action halted. Controversy over the tunnel had reached fever pitch by 1955. The *Fort Lauderdale News* opposed it editorially. Adherents were so vociferous that the city commission called a referendum. The tunnel won—7,000 votes to 6,443. The Florida State Road Department again approved the tunnel, this time with the cost pegged at $4,500,000. The city was required to provide the right-of-way.

(The city began the process of getting rights-of-way in 1957, and the firm of Singstad and Bailey was authorized to prepare plans. The right-of-way, estimated to cost $400,000, actually cost $1,100,000. The tunnel construction contract went to the low bidder, Thorington Construction Company, of Providence, Rhode Island, at $6,494,432. Work started on October 13, 1958, and the tunnel was opened December 9, 1960.)

The South East 17th Street crossing was named Brook Memorial Causeway, in honor of Commodore A. H. Brook. The Brook Memorial, at its completion, was the newest, most modern, and most impressive structure built in southeast Florida. This span over Stranahan River at its juncture with Port Everglades is truly high-level, with a minimum clearance of thirty-three feet under the central span at high tide. The view from its crest is spectacular. On the south is Port Everglades with its heavy industry and seagoing ships at dockside. To the north lie Stranahan River, Lake Sylvia, and many of the city's finest island residential districts, with Pier 66, luxurious yacht basin-motel development, in the foreground. The structure cost just less than $2,000,000 and measures approximately one thousand feet in length, including a bridge over Mercedes River, which runs east to Stranahan. It was paid for by the Florida State Road Department, with the city furnishing the right-of-way.

(TOM NEAL PHOTO)

Coast Guard Base in 1948—site of present Bahia Mar (*see rear endleaves*)

Bahia Mar

Postwar progress in Fort Lauderdale had been so rapid, and spread on so many fronts, that it was breath-taking—it seemed that anything might happen and, sure enough, it did! Coast Guard Base Six was finally declared surplus and nearly a half-mile of prime ocean frontage, extending through to the bay, and right in the heart of Fort Lauderdale's Las Olas beach was up for grabs, with the city the favored buyer. This was "the big one"; and the citizens determined at once not to let it get away. Possible uses for the property were almost unlimited. Its desirability was outstandingly clear to all. The offer to sell brought on another crisis, for the city, as usual, had no ready cash. Once again community pride was to be called upon. Once again the citizens were to come through.

Bahia Mar: 1948–1955

The story of what was to become Bahia Mar is part fairy tale, part nightmare. The property was originally occupied by the second of the Indian War forts built in 1839. This property again had been put into the public domain with the establishment of the House of Refuge in 1875, and was later converted into a Coast Guard station and, during national prohibition, into Coast Guard Base Six. Construction of Port Everglades and the filling in of the inlet beside the base rendered it obsolete. Its future usefulness was strictly limited. As a civic project it was to become a milestone.

Fort Lauderdale's great municipal yachting center, Bahia Mar, when completed in late 1949, was a national showcase, the first yachting complex built. Furthermore it was without equal, far advanced over any other yacht basin. It pioneered features hitherto unavailable. Its builders evolved and introduced ideas which have since become standard patterns for marinas. In size alone it created a vast image. Application of precast concrete in piers, conceived by its designer, J. H. Philpott, was an innovation. It would accommodate four hundred fifty boats whose lengths averaged 40 feet. Actually, with the average length up to 46.7 feet, it handles three hundred sixty. Bahia Mar offered twenty-eight services and conveniences so integrated and self-sustaining that the transient boatman could live in comfort indefinitely. In completeness and attractiveness to yachtsmen, it stood alone. It was to bring more recognition and publicity, more desirable new business, potential investors, and new citizens than any other single man-made attraction in the history of the city. Robert Osborne Cox, of the Marine Industries Association of Broward County, said that "Bahia Mar was a great stimulus to all shipyards. It helped make Fort Lauderdale 'The Yachting Capital of the World.'" More boating news and publicity was to originate from Fort Lauderdale than from any other city in the United States, and yachting income was to grow to sixty-five million dollars annually.

Until Bahia Mar, yachtsmen, desirable as visitors and usually well financed, were frequently forced to tie up in boat yards and other less desirable sections of places visited, and were largely without access to town, supplies, and needed services. In contrast, Bahia Mar was just off the beach, on the Inland Waterway—"greatest winter yacht highway in the world"—and in the heart of the city's finest residential and hotel area. Slipside telephones were to be installed later. From the beginning Bahia Mar offered slipside utilities—water and electricity. There were a control tower, ship's chandler, marine hardware, post office, catering and baby-sitter service, a restaurant, car parking, and other stores and services. Local sightseeing craft, marine taxis, and a large fleet of big game deep-sea charter guide boats were moored in the yacht basin's eastern section, and one of the nation's finest ocean bathing beaches was just beyond.

Ironically and unfortunately no other development—not even excluding the fight over ownership of the New River water front which split the town asunder in its very young days—was to cause more bitter argument, more varied and extended litigation, and more controversy than that which raged over Bahia Mar for most of its first twelve or fourteen years. The lawsuits were over money, contracts, controls, and performance. But while the acrimony and the disputations continued, yachtsmen fell in love with Bahia Mar. Manager Sam Shelsky said that an average of thirteen hundred yachts per year were attracted. He estimated, conservatively, that two per cent of these marine visitors annually made capital investments and/or bought or built water-front homes in Fort Lauderdale. Huge Playa Del Rey in Los Angeles was more or less conceived at Bahia Mar. Los Angeles commissioners and harbor directors came to Fort Lauderdale, and Mr. Philpott was invited to the West Coast for consultation.

Bahia Mar was recognized as "the Outstanding Achievement in Water-front Development Programs in the United States" in a plaque presented by the National Association of Engine and Boat Manufacturers at the New York Boat Show. Bahia Mar had indeed set an entirely new pattern. Prior to its construction, Lloyd's of London made a study of potential patronage. At that time—the late forties—there were 2,440,000 pleasure craft in use in the United States, according to Shelsky. The explosion in pleasure craft was just beginning. Facilities such as Bahia Mar were needed to excite the minds of prospects for boats. Shelsky estimated that at least forty cities on the East and West coasts and in the Great Lakes areas sought information from, or visited, Bahia Mar, prior to developing their own facilities. Panama City in Florida was one. Ralph Peo, chairman of the board of Houdaille Industries, bought the multimillion dollar R. H. Wright Company after becoming acquainted with the city from Bahia Mar. His action took place in the midst of the litigation. R. Green Annan, a Bahia Mar visitor, made large apartment house investments. Carl Wirgas, another Bahia Mar yachtsman, built the Lauderdale Biltmore at the Beach. K. S. (Boots) Adams, retired Phillips Petroleum president, had a boat at Bahia, and his company later built Pier 66 and all its yacht basin hotels and recreation areas—and the list goes on and on.

Bahia Mar: 1948-1955

In a discussion of Fort Lauderdale of the 1940's, Mr. Adams said that impressions were gained which happily resulted in plans for Phillips to become an important corporate citizen of Fort Lauderdale particularly and Florida generally. His recollection is that the Bahia Mar Yacht Center was the symbol of a beautiful, unique community—a community with great potential from several viewpoints. This gave birth to his "hunch," later confirmed by various inquiries and surveys, that really first-class installations would be good for the company and Fort Lauderdale. Bahia Mar Yachting Center epitomized hospitality in the grand manner, as well as the ingenious and imaginative lengths to which a progressive Fort Lauderdale was capable of going in catering to yachtsmen.

Present-day Bahia Mar was the site in 1839 of the Second Seminole Indian War fort from which Fort Lauderdale got its name; the location, in 1875, of one of the five United States Houses of Refuge built to succor shipwrecked sailors on the Florida coast; and in more modern times, the home of Coast Guard Base Six. The area had, for more than a hundred twenty-five years, witnessed exciting, colorful events.

The following facts are from the story of Bahia Mar compiled by former city clerk, Florence C. Hardy:

On August 2, 1875, the site was reserved from the public domain for life-saving purposes. The Fort Lauderdale House of Refuge with Washington Jenkins as first keeper, was completed September 4, 1876. A half century later, in February, 1926, the houseboat "Moccasin," headquarters from Coast Guard Base Six, was towed from Miami and docked at a new wharf on the west bank of what is now Bahia Mar. Coast Guard Base Six was established in Fort Lauderdale on February 15, 1926, and on March 10, 1926, the transfer of the House of Refuge to the jurisdiction of Base Six was accomplished.

The September, 1926, hurricane blew the "Moccasin" from its mooring, across New River Sound and onto the shore at Idlewyld, where it remained a derelict for several months, and then mysteriously burned.

The Coast Guard was active in the federal effort to prevent illicit liquor from reaching American shores during national prohibition. In 1929 at Base Six, eighty seized rumrunning boats were burned after their engines had been removed.

This was the land the city had considered purchasing since 1927. In that year the city proposed that in exchange for the Coast Guard property a site be obtained and the base moved adjacent to Port Everglades. Although the exchange was looked upon favorably by the Coast Guard, it did not think the government would give up this property unless the city was willing to build a suitable base at Port Everglades. The Treasury Department quoted the city the price of $1,000,000 for Base Six.

This Fort Lauderdale beach property was to be sold to the public. Again in 1940 another attempt was made to acquire the property. A committee composed of W. J. Eastman, T. B. Manuel, H. J. Newsham, and Genevieve Pynchon, commissioners; Lewis E. Moore, mayor; J. H. Philpott, city manager; and H. L. McCann and August Burghard attempted to work out the details. Before plans could be finalized World War II began. The base was used throughout the war. The Coast Guard stated on April 29, 1944, that it did not know of any way the property could be transferred unless the city would provide facilities of equal value at the new Miami Beach site.

At war's end the property was again about to be offered for public sale. The city secured an amendment to the 1938 Bill allowing it a six-month option to purchase at a price to be determined by the Coast Guard. Fort Lauderdale was notified on October 29, 1946, that it had a six-month option and that the price of the property was $1,000,000. A storm of protest arose locally when it became known what the government was asking. No taxes had ever been collected by the city although it had furnished police, fire, and other services, and housing facilities during the war. Citizens could not understand why the government asked more for the property from the city than it could get from individuals who would use it for speculation. (The city proposed public use of the land for beaches, parks, parking areas, boat docks, etc.) J. Alvin Regester and Frank J. Anderson appraised the property at $504,775.

The government wanted $1,000,000, but thanks to the cooperation of then United States Senator Claude Pepper with former City Attorney George W. English, and after months of negotiation, the price was finally set at $600,000. On October 6, 1947, the city was informed that the transaction must be consummated with the full purchase price not later than October 29, 1947. A severe hurricane and flood intervened. It appeared impossible to raise the money. However, several days before it was due, a small group of businessmen raised $627,000. One hundred twenty-four individuals, companies, and organizations participated by subscribing for bonds ranging from $1,000 to $100,000. Just minutes before the option expired, $600,000 was turned over to the Coast Guard, and the remaining $27,000 was held to pay interest on the subscribed bonds until the bond issue for the purchase and development could be validated.

Architect Robert E. Hansen who spearheaded the drive to raise the $600,000 recalls the event:

As was then the custom we were at the "Pot Luck" table at Brown's

George W. English, former City Attorney and outstanding civic and business leader

restaurant. Jim [H. Frazier] Sheffer remarked he had heard that Governor Robert H. Gore would put up a substantial part of the Coast Guard purchase price if other citizens would raise the rest.

The upshot was we called on Governor Gore and he confirmed that he and his companies would put up to $250,000. Then we really went to work. It was a team effort. Commissioner Reed Bryan and a good many others pitched in. Within 10 days the money was turned over to the city. J. D. Camp and Ben Johnson of the Broward National Bank provided repository services.

Citizens were later refunded their money, plus 4% interest. This was a remarkable demonstration of civic pride and initiative—harking back to the time when the town pitched in to finance the Broward Hotel.

About February, 1947, the city accepted a proposal from E. Detweiler and Associates, consultants, and Allen and Company, fiscal agents, to proceed with plans and financing for development of the base. The property acquired had about thirty-two and a half acres with an ocean frontage of about 2,590 feet with a depth ranging from 400 to 650 feet. About sixty per cent of it could be developed without filling. It was bounded on the east by the Atlantic Ocean; on the west by the Intracoastal Waterway; on the south by a then-new area known as Harbor Beach; and on the north it extended to within a few feet of the city-owned casino. The south boundary was at the location of the original New River Inlet, closed earlier by accretion. A good portion of the low land was mangrove swamps. Seabreeze Boulevard, fifty feet wide, crossed the land, curved towards the beach, ran parallel to the ocean, and then curved westward to the Harbor Beach entrance.

Adoption of the entire $6,500,000 project to purchase and improve the former Coast Guard Base as a war memorial project was approved in April, 1947, by the War Memorial Committee, upon motion by R. H. Gore, publisher of the *Daily News*. The Memorial Committee had earlier raised more than $100,000 towards the Memorial Auditorium. It agreed to join with the city commissioners to gain title to the base and develop it as one of the most beautiful cultural and recreational areas in the nation.

Hunley Abbott, John T. Dietz, R. H. Gore, John D. Ritchey, and Arthur H. Ogle were appointed by the city on November 6, 1947, to study the proposed development. At first it was decided to divide the ocean frontage at the base into eight large parcels which could be sold for resort development. Bids were to be received March 22, 1948, but were rejected due to an injunction filed against the city by Harold C. Holden, former mayor, joined by Frank Seaman and W. O. Hundley, automobile dealers.

Meantime original investors were anxious to have their money returned. In one case, under date of August 2, 1948, the city was notified that if something were not done, suit would be instituted. Through his attorney, R. R. Saunders, R. H. Gore pointed out that he had provided the city with $250,000 to help buy the base and that the city had taken no steps toward returning the money. He said that it was his understanding that a portion of the land would be sold, or other steps taken, to pay back the original investment. Later a private enterprise, the Bahia Mar Corporation, presented a proposal which would pay back the investors, build a yachting facility, and operate for twenty years while paying the city an annual rental of six per cent gross revenue.

By this time the city had decided it wanted to keep public title to the entire tract. On September 22, 1948, a lease was given by the city to Universal Construction Company (backed by this Bahia Mar Corporation). Just previously, on the night of September 21, 1948, a violent hurricane began and continued through the next day, when a special meeting had been called to finalize the agreement submitted by Universal Construction Company eight days earlier. The entire commission, Tom Austin, Joe E. Mackey, Joe P. Moe, H. J. Newsham, and Mayor-Commissioner Reed A. Bryan, City Attorney T. O. Berry-hill, and City Deputy-Auditor-Clerk Florence C. Hardy, attended despite the storm. Thus, the dealings with Universal Construction Company not only started on the thirteenth, but they were born in a storm, and had a stormy, stormy life that ended disastrously for Universal.

The annual rent for the property was to be $160,000. The city authorized issuance of $2,500,000 in revenue bonds to finance the project and repay the $600,000, plus $27,000 interest, subscribed for the purchase of the land. "Bahia Mar," a name submitted by Mrs. Gilbert (Elaine) Sayward, was selected and on February 15, 1949, the traditional ground-breaking ceremony was held. The big yacht basin was under way. An investigation and review of the Bahia Mar contract, lease, and building plans was launched the following May by the special Coast Guard advisory board headed by Carl A. Hiaasen, attorney; Walter A. McElfresh, engineer; and M. R. McTigue, George E. Simons, Jr., and Dwight A. Krause, businessmen.

By December, 1949, an island was created, three miles of concrete docks were built, and all buildings, including the shopping center, were completed. Docking spaces for four hundred boats were provided. On December 1, 1949, Bahia Mar was officially open. After two seasons as a private corporation, Bahia Mar Corporation defaulted. The first year's rent of $160,000 was paid (December 1, 1949, to December 1, 1950). The Supreme Court had fixed the date of completion as December 1, 1949. The next due rent was not paid. Every effort was made to secure the payment. A suit charging diversions and misapplication of revenues and other illegal actions was filed by Charles M. White, Moe Katz, R. H. Gore, the North American Company, Hunley Abbott, and O. R. Burkart. On May 1, 1951, the commission cancelled the Bahia Mar lease.

Charles E. Knight, beach hotel owner, was named chairman of an advisory board to probe the financial structure of Bahia Mar Corporation. Robert M. Haskins, insurance broker, was board secretary, and other members were A. H. Moorman, Dwight A. Krause, and L. C. Judd. D. D. Freeman was appointed on September 20, 1951, as trustee in the Bahia Mar Corporation bankruptcy. Bahia Mar Caterers were evicted December 1, 1952. Suit was filed February 12, 1952, against the city by Universal Construction Company for $372,000 for extra work. Suits and countersuits and court proceedings lasted until the end of 1955, when the city gained full possession of Bahia Mar.

FORT LAUDERDALE

An important election was held April 21, 1953, on Ordinance No. C-918 to maintain Bahia Mar Beach as a public beach forever. The vote was: for, 4,309; against, 603. The city continued to operate Bahia Mar. Its fame and popularity as a yachting center were known. Fort Lauderdale was established as one of the world's most marine-conscious cities. The Bahia Mar ocean front and beach were the city's forever.

Planning opening of World War II Naval Air Station. N. B. Cheaney (*second from right*), Governor Robert H. Gore (*right*). Julian E. Ross and D. D. Freeman, two other civilians

The Great Clean-up

Although Fort Lauderdale grew from 1948 on as it had never grown before and prospered mightily in many ways, some business leaders worried. The source of their worry this time was the reputation that Broward County carried with respect to wide-open illegal gambling. The big Miami daily newspapers made continual references to the "independent principality of Broward County" and to the widespread gambling activities which remained immune to the law. Miami and Miami Beach had gambling also, but they had occasional big crackdowns in which many of the leading clubs were closed. In Broward the roulette wheels spun merrily on. The most notable occasion was in the winter season of 1945-46 when "hot money" from the North rained on the county's gaming tables. Dade County was in the throes of one of its periodic spells of righteousness and the nearby Broward places prospered beyond even the dreams of the gamblers.

Chapter 23
1948–1955

Artist's sketch of typical plush Broward gambling room during post-World War II period—no photographs were permitted

Although carefully skirting the laws on libel, the newspapers, including the *Fort Lauderdale News*, made it plain that illegal operations could not be carried out on such a grand scale and with such utter lack of restraint unless the governing offices were corrupt and permitted it by agreement. The cause for concern of the town's business leaders was: Did they, and did our new residents, want to live in such a county? Secondly, would big investors, now becoming interested in Fort Lauderdale, risk their money in a county obviously controlled by dishonest officials?

During the long depression, gambling interests had carefully preserved a "Robin Hood" reputation. They made it appear that they took money only from rich tourists and gave away large portions of it to worth-while charities and needy people. And they did contribute generously to many charities. They likewise contributed to political campaign funds and favored politically powerful persons by finding sinecure jobs for their relatives and in-laws.

In response to direct questioning from reporters as to why he did not close up these gambling places, Broward County Sheriff Walter R. Clark replied that he would do so, forthwith, if any competent person came in to make an affidavit that there was gambling. He stated it as his belief that if this were not done then the people were getting what they wanted. Any reporter was free to enter gambling places and make bets on anything he chose, even though his identity was known to the operators of the club. Clark and his lieutenants, in most cases, kept in close touch with public opinion, but the winter of 1947-48 saw a development in this respect that they either overlooked or underrated. This was a rising tide of indignation among the people, many of them new residents, against conditions. Broward County had become notorious in the nation and in a way that many of its residents hotly resented.

On February 12, 1948, the first telling blow since 1940 was struck. Assistant State Attorney Dwight L. Rogers, Jr., went into circuit court and asked for an injunction against the operation of three notorious gambling houses. These included the fabulous Colonial Inn, owned by Jake Lansky; the Lopez Restaurant, owned by Jerry Lopez; and the Club Greenacres, owned by Frank A. Stone. The action was in chancery, a civil suit, carrying no criminal charges. Rogers listed ten Fort Lauderdale citizens who were willing to testify on behalf of the injunction. These were: Frank O. Brass, Ralph A. Horton, N. N. Case, August Burghard, Fred Cabot, A. Gordon Shand, James D. Camp, Alwen Neuharth, the Reverend John H. Hanger, and Russell McCaughan. The group was composed of high officials in both Fort Lauderdale banks, leading attorneys, the postmaster, and prominent businessmen.

The blow struck home. The "Club," as the Colonial Inn was called, would have to close. The floor show, which counted Joe E. Lewis, Carmen Miranda, and Ray Bolger among its stars, had been engaged for a period extending four days beyond the injunction dead line. The club ran without benefit of gambling for those four nights and then closed as a gambling establishment for all time. The others folded also. This action ended the most obvious gambling, but had no effect on smaller houses which continued to operate as usual, and on the same wide-open policy.

269

Assistant State Attorney Dwight L. Rogers (*seated*) was largely responsible for ending wide-open gambling in Broward County. Phil O'Connell, West Palm Beach (*right*), was also instrumental. Grady Burton from Wauchula (*left*) (CONGRESSMAN PAUL ROGERS COLLECTION)

By 1948, however, horse betting in Fort Lauderdale had been forced to a strictly "sneak" basis. Arrests of bookmakers were frequent and fines were heavy. The temper of the people had been demonstrated. In Hollywood, Lee A. Wentworth filed for an injunction against Jesse G. Wellons' Rainbow Tavern and Albert Petersen's Valhalla, both elaborate downtown establishments.

South Broward was considerably less inclined to make firm efforts to stamp out the gambling. For one thing operators were more securely entrenched and had far more employees. Moreover, being closer to Dade County where periodic raids were in progress, south Broward was considered a better location. In Hallandale, the southernmost Broward city, the various "spots" made weekly contributions to a public playground being built.

But by now gamblers were "running scared." The big, wide-open horse books voluntarily shut off their horse-betting sheets during the Gulfstream season. They all had reason to be nervous. The United States Senate appointed a committee, headed by Senator Estes Kefauver, to investigate criminal activities in the nation and on July 13, 14, and 15 of 1950, hearings were held in the federal court rooms in Miami. Among

The Great Clean-up: 1948–1955

Left: Kossie Goodbread, Fort Lauderdale's first town marshal

Below: D. O. Oliver, W. O. "Deacon" Berryhill, and Tom M. Bryan

the witnesses called upon to testify was Walter R. Clark, sheriff of Broward County.

Accompanied by C. L. Chancey, attorney, Clark's testimony before this committee was a classic of injured innocence.

The Chairman: Sheriff, you are the sheriff of Broward County? *Mr. Clark:* Yes, sir. *The Chairman:* How old are you? *Mr. Clark:* 46. *The Chairman:* When were you elected sheriff of Broward County?

Mr. Clark: I took office in January of 1933. *The Chairman:* You have served almost constantly since that time? *Mr. Clark:* Yes. *The Chairman:* Except during the length of time when you were removed by Governor Holland? *Mr. Clark:* I was suspended, not removed. *The Chairman:* When was that? *Mr. Clark:* I don't remember what year it was. *The Chairman:* It was in about 1944, some time in there? *Mr. Clark:* It was some time in 1944.

The Chairman: Now, Sheriff Clark, let us get right down to the point of our problem here. Up in Broward, in the south end of Broward County, you had operating during the season at various times the Club Greenacres, Colonial Inn, The Club Boheme, and The Farm, and I believed you testified that there were four or five operating in Broward County and have been for quite a number of years, is that right? *Mr. Clark:* Four or five clubs, yes; but not gambling places to my knowledge. They are clubs. *The Chairman:* You have never known that there was gambling in those places? *Mr. Clark:* Rumors, but no actual evidence of it. . . .

The Chairman: Do you know Jake Lansky? *Mr. Clark:* Yes. . . . *The Chairman:* How long have you known Jake Lansky? *Mr. Clark:* He has been living in Hollywood there 12 or 15 years.

The Chairman: Did Jake Lansky and the various operators of these places contribute to your campaign for sheriff? *Mr. Clark:* I couldn't say whether they did or not. *The Chairman:* And you know that he contributed a substantial amount to your campaign for sheriff? *Mr. Clark:* I don't know what he contributed. *The Chairman:* Anyway, he did contribute? *Mr. Clark:* He said he would do what he could and he hired some workers.

On September 12, 1950, informations were filed with the grand jury charging Walter R. Clark, Robert L. Clark, his chief deputy and brother, and Gordon Williams, an associate, with illegal possession of slot machines and, in a separate charge, with conducting a lottery. And on the same day, Frank Shireman, Samuel L. Bratt, Claud Litteral, Meyer Lansky, Jack Lansky, George Sadlo, W. H. Bischoff, Vincent Alo, Percy Vaughn, Louis Oliver, Paul Alexander, H. L. Vaughn, and Louis Matson were charged with operation of gambling houses. Alo, whose nickname was "Jimmy Blue Eyes," was reputed to be a relative of Kingpin Gambler Frank Costello, and Meyer Lansky was reputedly "high" in the New York mob. Most of the others were local men who had "pieces" of various operations. The violations alleged took place at the Greenacres, west of Hallandale, The Club Boheme, on Hallandale Beach, and the It Club, just outside of Fort Lauderdale. This time the law hit the head men, and this time it was no case in chancery. These were criminal counts and the witnesses included among others the accountants for the accused, duly subpoenaed to appear. Many smaller operations had been omitted, but these were the big ones. The trials were set in Broward's newly formed Criminal Court of Record, established on June 1, 1949.

The fact that John Hopkins, a *Daily News* reporter, was getting married on Sunday morning, September 16, 1950, had nothing to do with gambling. Hopkins was popular among his fellow reporters and all were invited to the wedding, and came. One thing the cameramen and reporters would rather have done than attend the wedding would have been to photograph and talk to the big names of the local gambling underworld, most of whom were now under indictment. But on the morning of the wedding the attorney for the gamblers called the judge, W. T. Kennedy, and asked him if he could be in court on Sunday morning. The judge could.

Appearing before him that morning were Frank Shireman, Samuel L. Bratt, Claud Litteral, Meyer Lansky, George Sadlo, W. H. Bischoff, Jack Lansky, and Vincent Alo, all of whom pleaded "guilty" on arraignment and were fined a thousand dollars on each count of operating a gambling house. They paid fines totaling sixteen thousand dollars and left quickly. Later the others, all comparably smaller fry, showed up and each paid a thousand dollar fine.

Shortly thereafter six more, this time all operators of smaller establishments in the Hollywood area, were indicted for operating gambling houses. They, likewise, pleaded guilty and paid their fines. Included were Glenn H. Wood, Raymond Stakely, Holly Stanger, Harry M. Gamble, Thaddeus Richardson, and Ralph Blackburn. The latter, charged only with bookmaking, escaped with a five hundred dollar fine.

Governor Fuller Warren removed Walter Clark from his post as sheriff when the results of the Kefauver investigation became known. Warren then appointed Amos Hall of Hollywood. Hall clamped the lid on gambling as tightly as he could, but bookmaking persisted on a wide scale in backrooms and through handbooks. The new sheriff declared that the "Service," the means by which books got full racing information including lines of probable odds, running descriptions, and pay-off prices, was the "life blood" of the entire illegal industry. "If this can be stopped," he declared, "we can lick them."

The information had to come from the tracks, and the tracks were as bitter against the horse books as was the law. They set track police to keep sharp watch for any persons suspected of sending out betting information. Deputies and state agents checked buildings overlooking the odds boards from which bookmakers with powerful glasses could read information.

Meantime slot machines continued to play a merry tune in the backrooms of small bars and taverns in outlying sections. The big show came up that summer, the trial of the Clarks and Williams for possession of slot machines. To get his testimony into the records the prosecutor, Otis Farrington, granted James Johnson, a top Clark employee, immunity. The trial brought to the stand a parade of witnesses who admitted having had slot machines in their places of business, but not one of them knew, so they said, who owned the machines or with whom they shared the profits. They only knew "Jay" (James Johnson).

Put on the stand, Johnson said he worked for the Broward Music Company, but he didn't know who the owners were. He turned over the money to the bookkeeper. The bookkeeper testified he put it in the bank or in a drawer, but he didn't know who took it out or to whom it belonged. Throughout the trial the defense attorney stressed the legal ruling that guilt must be proved "beyond a shadow of a doubt." Neither the Clarks nor Gordon Williams took the stand. Prosecutor Farrington remarked that he thought that several of the witnesses were guilty of perjury but that proving it might be as difficult as getting testimony against the Clarks. In the end the defendants were found "not guilty." Charges against them of conducting a lottery were nol-prossed.

But the law was taking its toll of gambling. Jesse G. and Merton Wellons were indicted on eleven counts each of operating slot machines in the Hollywood area. They were never tried, but slot machines began to disappear. Sheriff Hall, with full cooperation from Fort Lauderdale Police Chief Roland Kelley, started "bookmaking" arrests regularly and got convictions. Courts were handing down ever increasing punishment, and finally made the price of conviction a mandatory jail sentence.

The state, meantime, was cracking down on the great "service" octopus. That gambling would ever be stamped out completely was highly dubious, but Broward County and Fort Lauderdale were fast becoming "clean" as far as law enforcement was concerned. Walter Clark was a sick man during the latter days of his trial. He was hopelessly afflicted with leukemia and died shortly thereafter. His funeral was magnificent. Lined up, saluting the casket containing the body of the former sheriff as it was carried from the First Presbyterian Church after the funeral service, were police officers from Broward municipalities. The Reverend Edward P. Downey and the Reverend Clarence C. Stauffer led the procession.

So ended the amazing career of Walter R. Clark, who had started out as a butcher's helper and who became one of the most powerful figures in the state. His friends, and there were hosts of them, always insisted that he considered himself an honest man. He was convinced in his heart that his constituents wanted gambling and that it benefited his county and his community. Clark was famed, also, as being extremely soft-hearted and an easy touch for any one with a hard luck story. Most of his profits were either given away outright or "loaned" to needy friends who generally forgot to pay him back and were seldom, if ever, taxed with this omission. He was gentle and kindly in most of his deal-ings, though he lacked neither strength nor courage. As an enforcer of the law he was conceded to be efficient even by his enemies; and no violence ever erupted from any of the gambling activities carried on in the county. He took an interest in many civic projects, donated wil-lingly of time and money. He used his state-wide influence generously in all matters concerning the public welfare. He was widely respected. He was a product of an era that was born of the depression and his attitude had never greatly changed. His passing is still deeply mourned. With him went the "good old days" of open gambling.

Whether or not the end of gambling had anything to do with it, the city was now back in the good graces of northern capital. Money for Florida ventures was no longer any empty dream. The credit that had been "destroyed forever" when the city defaulted on its bonds was now restored. Florida had been rediscovered by bankers, as well as by the home-hungry ex-G.I.'s, so many of whom had trained here and remem-bered with lasting appreciation the hospitality of the people and the famed Service Center.

Fort Lauderdale's problems multiplied in the transition from a charm-ing small city to a metropolis. But now there were more people, many with high degrees of ability, who loved the community as devoutly as had the sturdy pioneers who carved it from forbidding swamplands.

In the great postwar boom the multiplicity of needs could no longer be met by simple and direct community action. Sweeping changes in government had to be made. No longer could each city official be per-sonally responsible or give a personal accounting to each and every citi-zen for his actions. The day when a stranger in town excited curiosity gave way to the day when a chance meeting with a fellow resident who was an old acquaintance or friend became the occasion for a happy reunion. Developments that once would have stimulated the greatest interest became commonplace. Neighborhoods within the city became scattered, separate entities and often worked for highly localized benefits rather than for city-wide improvements.

To say that any but the decade that followed World War II was most important in the city's history would be to deny that place to the era of its greatest growth. But to deny that the physical assets that made this possible were due to staunch-hearted predecessors would be to deny the pioneer his due. This is not to say that the problems of today are not most real and urgent. Continued demands for vision and good judgment will always lie heavily upon the city's leaders.

To the historian, modern history is often difficult and complex, although equally as interesting. Personalities are lost as significant, new events are brought forth on a daily production line, and famous people chase each other across the daily scene in an endless parade.

As the decade closed, it became increasingly clear that the "great city" envisioned by the pioneers was nearing realization; but even as it reached for the stars the heart of town, "old downtown" that had supported the hope, apparently died a-borning. The central section that had spawned the great new ideas and had always paid the lion's share of the taxes was now outmoded. New ideas of modernity made it obsolete, old-fashioned, and unattractive. There were now exciting new places.

The fishing boats were gone from the midcity docks and they took with them much of their quaint charm. The great smelly monsters of the deep no longer hung from the downtown fish racks and the colorful saloons along the water front were gradually shuttered. Their liquor licenses sold, they moved to more remunerative locations.

Television helped destroy the glamorous illusions of a "Saturday night in town." Even the Sunset movie house that had aroused such pride in 1923 was shuttered and then razed for a parking lot. The Queen became a store, the Warnor, press room for the *News*.

The Sweet Building, the proud edifice in which even a small office had only shortly before been a badge of prestige, was suddenly ghostlike and nearly empty. The town was still there, but the people had gone.

Those who had so resolutely faced the challenges of the past are again threatened with disaster for "their" town—old downtown Fort Lauderdale. Many of these are still alive and active. Most are still unafraid.

Appendix

"Founder Citizens"
City Councils & Commissions
City Managers
Fort Lauderdale Memorial Auditorium Project

To All Whom These Presents Shall Come: Know Ye

The persons whose names appear hereon were residents of Fort Lauderdale, Florida, on its incorporation, March 27, 1911, and are to be forever honored as "founder citizens"

DATED March 27, 1961

FORT LAUDERDALE · BROWARD COUNTY FLORIDA · SEAL · MARCH 27 1911

CITY COUNCILS AND COMMISSIONS

City of Fort Lauderdale Incorporated March 27, 1911

1st Council

E. T. King, *President*
W. H. Marshall, *Mayor*
W. O. Berryhill
Tom M. Bryan
W. H. Covington
W. C. Kyle
>J. L. Billingsley, *1st City Attorney*
>F. A. Bryan, *1st City Clerk*
>K. A. Goodbread, *1st City Marshal*

1st Ballot for Election of Mayor—March 25, 1912

W. H. Marshall—Elected
J. G. Ewing
>D. D. Oliver, *City Clerk*
>Chas. Pratt, *1st City Engineer*
>C. E. Newland, *1st Fire Chief*
>(W. C. Kyle resigned; E. C. Parker elected in his place)

April 2, 1913

E. C. Parker, *President*
Geo. G. Mathews, *Mayor*
W. O. Berryhill
B. W. Bollinger
T. M. Bryan
D. G. Staats
>D. D. Oliver, *Clerk* (Replaced by Guy E. Phipps August 5, 1913)
>L. M. Bryan, *Marshal*
>E. S. Randall, *Tax Assessor*
>J. K. Gordon, *Treasurer*
>J. F. Bunn was appointed attorney December 2, 1913

March 31, 1914

B. W. Bollinger, *President*
Dr. C. G. Holland, *Mayor*
F. A. Barrett
F. T. Fisher
E. C. Parker (Died November 17, 1914; vacancy filled by Frank Stranahan)
D. G. Staats
>D. E. Jonson, *Clerk*
>L. M. Bryan, *Marshal*
>E. S. Randall, *Tax Assessor-Collector*

279

Appendix

April 6, 1915

F. T. Fisher, *President*
Dr. C. G. Holland, *Mayor*
F. A. Barrett
F. A. Bryan
Chas. Harper
Frank Stranahan
    H. H. Marshall, *Marshal*
    E. E. Jonson, *Clerk* (Replaced by Geo. W. Hall)

April 4, 1916

C. E. Farrington, *President*
Will J. Reed, *Mayor*
J. G. Farrow
Chas. Harper
J. J. Joyce
Frank Stranahan
    Geo. W. Hall, *City Clerk*
    H. H. Marshall, *Marshal*
    E. S. Randall, *Tax Assessor-Collector*

April 3, 1917

C. E. Farrington, *President*
Will J. Reed, *Mayor*
S. W. Gillian
F. W. Harper (Replaced by Frank Stranahan November 24, 1917)
Chas. Harper (Replaced by W. R. Boyd July 17, 1917)
J. J. Joyce
    Geo. W. Hall, *City Clerk*
    H. H. Marshall, *Marshal*
    E. S. Randall, *Tax Assessor-Collector*

April 2, 1918

Frank Stranahan, *President*
Will J. Reed, *Mayor*
W. R. Boyd
S. J. Clark
C. E. Farrington
S. W. Gillian
    Geo. W. Hall, *City Clerk*
    H. V. Calder, *Tax Assessor-Collector*
    H. H. Marshall, *Marshal*

April 1, 1919

S. J. Clark, *President*
C. E. Farrington, *Mayor*
W. R. Boyd
John G. Miller
Frank Stranahan
Alonzo E. Emans
    Geo. W. Hall, *City Clerk*
    H. V. Calder, *Tax Assessor-Collector*
    H. H. Marshall, *Marshal*

Appendix

March 30, 1920

Frank Stranahan, *President*
C. E. Farrington, *Mayor*
S. J. Clark
Alonzo E. Emans
John G. Miller
W. R. Boyd
    H. V. Calder, *City Clerk*
    Etta E. Calder, *Tax Assessor-Collector*
    D. G. Tenbrook, *Marshal*

April 5, 1921

Frank Stranahan, *President*
Will J. Reed, *Mayor*
W. R. Boyd
S. J. Clark
Alonzo E. Emans
John G. Miller
    H. V. Calder, *City Clerk*
    Etta E. Calder, *Tax Assessor-Collector*
    D. G. Tenbrook, *Marshal*

October 31, 1922

Frank Stranahan, *President*
R. G. Snow, *Mayor*
S. J. Clark
J. H. Fidler
Chas. L. Sheeler
Geo. W. Young
    Jasper Lawson, *City Clerk and Tax Collector*
    J. W. McGee, *Tax Assessor*
    D. G. Tenbrook, *Chief of Police*
    Maxwell Baxter, *City Attorney*

October 30, 1923

E. H. Hart, *President*
R. G. Snow, *Mayor*
R. E. Dye
J. H. Fidler (Resigned; replaced by J. A. Warren September 9, 1924)
Geo. W. Young
Frank Stranahan
    Jasper Lawson, *City Clerk and Tax Collector*
    J. W. McGee, *Tax Assessor*
    Lucian Craig, *Chief of Police*
    Maxwell Baxter, *City Attorney*

November 4, 1924

D. S. Tarbell, *President*
Will J. Reed, *Mayor*
U. S. Cayot
W. S. Holloway
D. Hunter
J. A. Warren
    Jasper Lawson, *City Clerk and Tax Collector*
    J. W. McGee, *Tax Assessor*
    Lucian Craig, *Chief of Police*

Appendix

Under the council form of government, this was the last council to serve, serving until August, 1925.

The Commission-Manager form of government was voted in by the people, and the first commission took office in August, 1925. The commission consisted of five members, with one member as mayor. The mayor was appointed by the other members of the commission and was, with but few exceptions, the man with the highest number of votes gained in the elections.

The city commission became the legislative body. The commission appointed a city manager to carry out its policies in the administration of the city. This form of government has continued from 1925 to the present time, 1966. Commissioners are elected each two years. The first city manager, C. E. Rickard, served until B. J. Horne, a professional city manager, was appointed in September, 1925.

August – 1925

> J. W. TIDBALL, *Mayor*
> T. M. BRYAN (Resigned; replaced by Frank Stranahan May, 1927)
> J. S. HINTON
> C. D. KITTREDGE
> W. C. KYLE

November – 1927

> C. D. KITTREDGE, *Mayor*
> M. A. HORTT
> WILL J. REED
> W. C. KYLE (Resigned; replaced by S. E. Lawrence January, 1928)
> FRANK STRANAHAN (Died July, 1929; replaced by T. E. Hoskins)

November – 1929

> T. E. HOSKINS, *Mayor*
> M. A. HORTT
> J. C. ALLEY (Died March, 1931; replaced by C. C. Adams)
> H. KELSO
> J. W. NEEDHAM

November – 1931

> J. W. NEEDHAM, *Mayor*
> C. C. ADAMS
> M. H. EPSTEIN
> M. A. HORTT
> F. R. OLIVER

November – 1933

> E. A. PYNCHON, *Mayor*–Resigned April 31, 1934
> M. A. HORTT, Commissioner–Elected *mayor*
> JOHN H. FIDLER (Died July, 1935; replaced by Frank J. Norton)
> J. W. NEEDHAM
> J. M. TAUL
> LEWIS E. MOORE (Elected May 22, 1934, to fill Pynchon vacancy as a commissioner)

Appendix

November – 1935

Lewis E. Moore, *Mayor*
Frank Norton
P. V. Pace
Will J. Reed
J. M. Taul

November – 1937

T. B. Manuel, *Mayor*
J. H. Durham
M. A. Hortt
J. W. Needham
Mrs. Genevieve Pynchon

November – 1939

Lewis E. Moore, *Mayor*
W. J. Eastman
T. B. Manuel (Resigned October, 1940; Chas. D. Pease elected to fill vacancy)
Mrs. Genevieve Pynchon
H. J. Newsham

November – 1941

H. L. McCann, *Mayor*—Resigned August 12, 1942
N. B. Cheaney—Elected as mayor
Joseph P. Moe
H. J. Newsham
C. L. Nichols
J. M. Taul

November – 1943

Joe N. Morris, *Mayor*
Joseph P. Moe
H. J. Newsham
George R. Slaton
J. M. Taul

November – 1945

H. C. Holden, *Mayor*
Reed A. Bryan
Lacy D. Croft
W. J. Eastman
J. M. Taul

November – 1947

Reed A. Bryan, *Mayor*
Thomas W. Austin
Joseph C. Mackey
Joseph P. Moe (Died February 29, 1949; W. H. Marshall appointed April 13, 1949, to fill vacancy)
H. J. Newsham

The election date was changed to April by the 1947 legislature after a vote of the people to change the time of elections from October to April, with the commission taking office the first Tuesday in May. The vote was 883 for changing the time of elections and 286 against.

At the same time an election was held to provide for a staggered term for commissioners, leading up to four years. The vote was 795 for the staggered term and 371 against.

May – 1949

F. R. Humphries, *Mayor*	4 years
Reed A. Bryan	Holdover until May, 1951
Joseph C. Mackey	Holdover until May, 1951 (Resigned December 31, 1950; replaced by Lewis E. Moore)
H. J. Newsham	4 years
J. M. Taul	4 years

At the time for the April, 1951, election, the people wanted to hold a special election to change the term of office back to a two-year term. Such an election was held and the vote was 3381 to change back to the two-year term, and 740 to continue the staggered term up to four years.

The election in April, 1951, for commissioners had to be held on the staggered-term provision, as the change back to the two-year term could not become effective until 1953.

May – 1951

Lewis E. Moore, *Mayor*	4 years (Resigned April, 1953; served until July, 1953)
Chas. M. White	4 years
F. R. Humphries	
H. J. Newsham	Holdovers
J. M. Taul	

May – 1953

C. Malcolm Carlisle, *Mayor*	
E. R. Burry	
Florence M. Tustison	
Harry W. Lott	(Elected June, 1953, to replace Lewis E. Moore)
Charles M. White	Holdover

May – 1955

Porter G. Reynolds, *Mayor*	
R. A. Childers	
H. Y. (Doug) Lockhart	(Died November 2, 1956; Niles B. Davidson elected as replacement)
Geo. A. Peterson	(Resigned January 7, 1957; Dr. Curtis D. Benton, Sr., appointed as replacement)
John V. Russell	

CITY MANAGERS UNDER COMMISSION-MANAGER
FORM OF GOVERNMENT

(INAUGURATED AUGUST, 1925)

August 6, 1925	C. E. Rickard		
September 8, 1925	B. J. Horne		$10,000 yr.
November 8, 1927	C. E. Fritz		5,000 yr.
March 31, 1928	C. E. Fritz		350 mo.
July 6, 1928	Glenn E. Turner		325 mo.
	(Served until Oct. 19, 1931. Salary reduced to $250 per mo. Nov. 1929)		
November 4, 1931	A. J. Merrill		200 mo.
March 31, 1932	J. K. Huey		200 mo.
November, 1933-35	R. M. Kerr		200 mo.
November, 1935	R. M. Kerr suspended		
November, 1935-37	A. J. Merrill		200 mo.
November, 1937-39	J. K. Huey	Acting	150 mo.
March 28, 1938	J. K. Huey		150 mo.
November, 1939-41	J. H. Philpott		5,000 yr.
November, 1941-43	A. J. Merrill		75 wk.
September 14, 1942	A. J. Merrill		85 wk.
June 14, 1943	A. J. Merrill		100 wk.
November, 1943-45	A. J. Merrill		100 wk.
November, 1945-47	J. H. Philpott		12,000 yr.
June 28, 1947	Florence C. Hardy	Acting	
November, 1947-48	A. H. Stephens	Acting	7,500 yr.
January, 1948	Carlton M. Roberts	Resigned 4-1-49	7,500 yr.
April 1, 1949	E. L. Patterson	Acting	
		Eng. salary &	1,780 yr.
May 31, 1949	F. D. Rankins		7,500 yr.
September 22, 1950	R. K. Lowry	Acting	7,500 yr.
May, 1951	R. K. Lowry	Acting	
		Resigned 1-1-52	
February, 1952	H. Milton Link		12,000 yr.
		After six months	15,000 yr.
May, 1953	H. Milton Link	Reappointed	15,000 yr.

THE OFFICERS and COMMITTEES CONTRIBUTING THEIR SERVICES TO THE FORT LAUDERDALE MEMORIAL AUDITORIUM PROJECT

OFFICERS

William J. Eastman—President:
Standing

Thomas B. Manuel—Vice President:
Second from left

Howard O. Pierce—Treasurer:
Far left

Logan T. Brown—Secretary:
Right

Campaign Committees
R. H. MAKEMSON, General Chairman

RECORDS AND SYSTEMS
E. Berkey Jones, Chairman

FINANCE DIVISION
Howard O. Pierce—Chairman

ADVANCE GIFTS DIVISION
William A. Hart—Chairman
J. B. Fraser
Dr. Martin L. DeBats

HOTELS
George E. Simons, Jr.—Chairman

RESIDENTIAL
Mrs. Ruth Brennan—Chairman
Mrs. Edwin M. Bell
Mrs. George R. Loehr

Tom B. Manuel, American Legion
A. L. Tibbett, Veterans Foreign Wars
H. D. Leavitt, Lions Club
H. D. Stillman, Kiwanis Club
E. Berkey Jones, Rotary Club
Mrs. Louise Stover, Daughters of
American Revolution

PUBLICITY AND ADVERTISING
August Burghard—Chairman

CLUBS AND ORGANIZATIONS
Craig Benson—Chairman

SPECIAL EVENTS COMMITTEE
W. E. Groene

BUSINESS BRANCHES
Fred Hallstead—Chairman

APARTMENTS
Earl W. Smith—Chairman

MERCHANTS
H. L. McCann—Chairman
A. M. Robbins—Co-Chairman

DIRECTORS OF CORPORATION
Mrs. Ruth Brennan, Business
and Professional Women's Club

Morton T. Ironmonger, Optimist Club
Logan T. Brown,
Chamber of Commerce
D. D. Freeman, Elks Club

SPEAKERS DIVISION
E. R. Heimburger—Chairman

LABOR GROUPS
Anton Naumann

PROJECTS COMMITTEE
Thomas B. Manuel
Nels S. Jacobson

ADVISORY COMMITTEE
R. H. Gore—Chairman
William J. Eastman
Thomas B. Manuel
Howard O. Pierce
Logan T. Brown
George W. English
D. D. Freeman

Wm. Freeman,
Junior Chamber of Commerce

Julius Epstein, B'nai B'rith
Hunley Abbott, At Large
W. J. Eastman, Park Commission
Porter Reynolds, Park Superintendent

MEMORIAL AUDITORIUM ASSOCIATION
CAMPAIGN HEADQUARTERS — MASONIC TEMPLE
FORT LAUDERDALE, FLA.

Selected Bibliography

Grateful acknowledgment is also made to city, county, state, and national authorities for use of material on record in their archives and to Mr. N. B. Cheaney, president, for the free use of material supplied by the Broward County Title Company.

BOOKS

Bassett, John Spencer (ed.): *Correspondence of Andrew Jackson*, Vol. V, 1848.

De Croix, F. W.: *An Historical and Progressive Review of Miami and Fort Lauderdale and Other Sections of Dade County*, Author, 1912.

Forida East Coast Railway: *The Story of a Pioneer*, n.d.

Hanna, Alfred J., and Katherine Abbey: *Lake Okeechobee, Wellspring of the Everglades*, Bobbs Merrill, 1948.

Hortt, M. A.: *Gold Coast Pioneer*, New York, Exposition Press, 1953.

Jesup, General Thomas S.: *Order Book, 1838*, P. K. Yonge Library of History, University of Florida.

Robinson, Dr. Leigh: *Half Century in Retrospect* (History of the Broward Medical Society), Fort Lauderdale, 1962.

Shepard, Birse: *Lore of the Wreckers*, Boston, Beacon Press, 1961.

Smith, Horace: *A Captain Unafraid* (biography of John O'Brian), New York-London, Harper Bros., 1912.

Sprague, John T.: *The Origin, Progress, and Conclusion of the Florida War, 1848*. Floridiana Facsimile and Reprint Series, University of Florida Press, 1964.

Stuart, Hix C.: *The Notorious Ashley Gang*, St. Lucie Printing Co., 1928.

Sunderman, James F. (ed.): *Journey into Wilderness, An Army Surgeon's Account of Life in Camp and Field during the Creek and Seminole Wars, 1836–1838*, by Jacob Rhett Motte, University of Florida Press, 1953.

ARTICLES IN PERIODICALS

Burkhardt, Mrs. Henry J.: "Starch making; a pioneer Florida industry," *Tequesta*, XLI.

Davis, T. Frederick: "The Disston land purchase," *The Florida Historical Quarterly*, XVII, 200.

Hammond, E. A. (ed.): "Dr. Strobel reports on South East Florida, 1836" (Sept., 1829 visit), *Tequesta*, XXI.

Murdoch, Richard K.: "Documents concerning a voyage to the Miami region in 1793," *The Florida Historical Quarterly*, XXXI, 16.

OFFICIAL RECORDS AND DOCUMENTS

Anderson, Robert. Letter to A. Eustis, 1838, National Archives Record Group 94.

Diary of Robert Anderson, 1838, Library of Congress.

Examination File 2002 (Case No. 2596, June 8, 1914). Town of Fort Lauderdale *vs.* Mary Brickell, Supreme Court of Florida, Tallahassee.

Bibliography

House Bill No. 616, 33d Congress (2d Session), January 5, 1855.
House Bill No. 2244, 49th Congress (1st Session), May 24, 1886.
House of Representatives Claims, National Archives Record Group No. 233.
Life Saving Service Correspondence, National Archives, 1875.
Poinsett Papers, Historical Society of Pennsylvania.
Records of Adjutant General's Office, PODT returns; Fort Lauderdale, Feb. 1839 to Jan. 1842.
Records of the Veterans Administration, Pension File No. 12065, National Archives.
Report of Major John C. Pemberton, 1857, National Archives.
Spanish Land Grants in Florida, Confirmed Claim L 15, Dade County, *Deed Record*, Book D.
Territorial Papers, Vol. XXV, 1836.
The Territorial Papers of the United States: letter, Quartermaster to James Gadsden, August 13, 1824; Gadsden to Quartermaster, August 20, 1825.
U. S. Statutes at Large IV, Record Book No. 8, 1823–27. Field Note Division, Department of Agriculture, Tallahassee, Florida.
WYSE, LT. FRANCIS O. Letter to Robert Anderson, 1840, Library of Congress.

MANUSCRIPTS

"Diary of Stephen R. Mallory," MS in the University of North Carolina Library, Southern Historical Collection.
"Lauderdale Papers," MS in the Tennessee State Library, Nashville.
"Minute Book, Fort Lauderdale Board of Trade," MS in the Fort Lauderdale Historical Society (courtesy of Richard Drake).
"Reminiscences of Dr. Thomas S. Kennedy, 1936," MS in the Fort Lauderdale Historical Society.

NEWSPAPERS

Fort Lauderdale News, Wesley W. Stout.
Key West Enquirer, P. K. Yonge Library of Florida History, University of Florida.

MISCELLANEOUS

WHITEHEAD, W. A.: *Lighthouse Letters*, Vol. XI, 1836.

RECORDINGS ON TAPE

(Made expressly for the Fort Lauderdale Historical Society and in its possession)

Tom M. Bryan
Stephen C. Calder
Fred Caudle
Mrs. Charles (Sarah Mathews) Crim
Rev. Martin Davis
George W. English
Samuel Gillian
R. H. Gore
William Hasbrouck
Jodie L. Hollingsworth
Ralph A. Horton
James S. Hunt
Frank Kozla
William Lauderdale*
Mrs. W. H. Marshall
Miss Katherine Rawls (Thompson, Green)
Norman Sommers
Mrs. Frank Stranahan
Mrs. S. S. (D. C. Alexander) Thomas
James B. Vreeland, Jr.
Carl P. Weidling, Sr.
Mr. "X" †

* Great-great-grandson of the Major Lauderdale for whom town was named
† Former bootlegger whose name cannot be revealed

Index

Index

Index